MASTERING FAMILY LAW

CAROLINA ACADEMIC PRESS MASTERING SERIES

Russell Weaver, Series Editor

For other titles, please go to caplaw.com.

Mastering Administrative Law, Second Edition
Linda D. Jellum

Mastering Adoption Law and Policy
Cynthia Hawkins DeBose

Mastering Alternative Dispute Resolution
Kelly M. Feeley, James A. Sheehan

Mastering Appellate Advocacy and Process, Second Edition
Donna C. Looper, George W. Kuney

Mastering Art Law, Second Edition
Herbert Lazerow

Mastering Bankruptcy
George W. Kuney

Mastering Civil Procedure, Fourth Edition
David Charles Hricik

Mastering Constitutional Law, Second Edition
John C. Knechtle, Christopher J. Roederer

Mastering Contract Law
Irma S. Russell, Barbara K. Bucholtz

Mastering Corporate Tax, Second Edition
Gail Levin Richmond, Reginald Mombrun, Felicia Branch

Mastering Corporations and Other Business Entities, Second Edition
Lee Harris

Mastering Criminal Law, Third Edition
Ellen S. Podgor, Cynthia E. Jones, Peter J. Henning, Neil P. Cohen, Sanjay K. Chhablani

Mastering Criminal Procedure, Volume 1: The Investigative Stage, Third Edition
Peter J. Henning, Cynthia E. Jones, Ellen S. Podgor,
Karen McDonald Henning, Sanjay K. Chhablani

Mastering Criminal Procedure, Volume 2: The Adjudicatory Stage, Third Edition
Peter J. Henning, Cynthia E. Jones, Ellen S. Podgor,
Karen McDonald Henning, Sanjay K. Chhablani

Mastering Elder Law, Third Edition
Ralph C. Brashier

Mastering Employment Discrimination Law, Third Edition
Jeffrey M. Hirsch, Joseph A. Seiner, Sandra F. Sperino

Mastering Environmental Law
Joel A. Mintz, Tracy D. Hester

Mastering Evidence
Ronald W. Eades

Mastering Family Law, Second Edition
April Carroll Meldrum

Mastering First Amendment Law
John C. Knechtle

Mastering Income Tax, Second Edition
Gail Levin Richmond, Christopher M. Pietruszkiewicz

Mastering Intellectual Property
George W. Kuney, Donna C. Looper

Mastering International Sales Law
Herbert Lazerow

Mastering Interviewing and Counseling
Kelly M. Feeley, Rebecca C. Morgan

Mastering Labor Law, Second Edition
Anne Marie Lofaso, Joseph E. Slater, Jeffrey M. Hirsch

Mastering Legal Analysis and Communication
David T. Ritchie

Mastering Legal Analysis and Drafting, Second Edition
George W. Kuney, Donna C. Looper

Mastering Legislation, Regulation, and Statutory Interpretation, Third Edition
Linda D. Jellum

Mastering Native American Law, Third Edition
Angelique Wambdi EagleWoman, Stacy L. Leeds

Mastering Negotiable Instruments (UCC Articles 3 and 4) and Other Payment Systems, Second Edition
Michael D. Floyd

Mastering Negotiation
Michael R. Fowler

Mastering Partnership Taxation
Stuart Lazar

Mastering Products Liability, Second Edition
Tim Kaye

Mastering Professional Responsibility, Second Edition
Grace M. Giesel

Mastering Property Law, Second Edition
Darryl C. Wilson

Mastering Sales
Colin P. Marks, Jeremy Kidd

Mastering Secured Transactions: UCC Article 9, Third Edition
Grace M. Giesel

Mastering Tort Law, Third Edition
Russell L. Weaver, Edward C. Martin, Andrew R. Klein, Paul J. Zwier, II, John H. Bauman

Mastering Trademark and Unfair Competition Law, Second Edition
Lars S. Smith, Llewellyn Joseph Gibbons

Mastering Trusts and Estates, Second Edition
Gail Levin Richmond

MASTERING FAMILY LAW

SECOND EDITION

April Carroll Meldrum

PROFESSOR OF LAW

LINCOLN MEMORIAL UNIVERSITY SCHOOL OF LAW

CAROLINA ACADEMIC PRESS

Durham, North Carolina

LIBRARY OF CONGRESS CATALOGING IN PUBLICATION DATA

Names: Meldrum, April Carroll author
Title: Mastering family law / April Carroll Meldrum.
Description: Second edition. | Durham : Carolina Academic Press, 2026. | Series: Mastering series | Includes bibliographical references and index.
Identifiers: LCCN 2025047917 | ISBN 9781531033699 paperback | ISBN 9781531033705 ebook
Subjects: LCSH: Domestic relations—United States
Classification: LCC KF505.Z9 M45 2026
LC record available at https://lccn.loc.gov/2025047917

Carolina Academic Press
700 Kent Street
Durham, NC 27701
(919) 489-7486
www.cap-press.com

Printed in the United States of America

Dedicated *to my Mamaw, who always told me*
I could do anything I set my mind to;
to my parents who have never failed
to offer unwavering support to me;
to my sister, who will always have my back;
to my children, Parker and Lydia, who I adore
and who motivate me to do more and to be my best;
to Charlie, the fella who loves me just as I am; and
to Luke, Case, and Allison, the bonus family
I am honored to claim.

ACM

CONTENTS

TABLE OF CASES

SERIES EDITOR'S FOREWORD

The Carolina Academic Press Mastering Series is designed to provide you with a tool that will enable you to easily and efficiently "master" the substance and content of law school courses. Throughout the series, the focus is on quality writing that makes legal concepts understandable. As a result, the series is designed to be easy to read and is not unduly cluttered with footnotes or cites to secondary sources.

In order to facilitate student mastery of topics, the Mastering Series includes a number of pedagogical features designed to improve learning and retention. At the beginning of each chapter, you will find a "Roadmap" that tells you about the chapter and provides you with a sense of the material that you will cover. A "Checkpoint" at the end of each chapter encourages you to stop and review the key concepts, reiterating what you have learned. Throughout the book, key terms are explained and emphasized. Finally, a "Master Checklist" at the end of each book reinforces what you have learned and helps you identify any areas that need review or further study.

We hope that you will enjoy studying with, and learning from, the Mastering Series.

Russell L. Weaver
PROFESSOR OF LAW &
DISTINGUISHED UNIVERSITY SCHOLAR
UNIVERSITY OF LOUISVILLE,
LOUIS D. BRANDEIS SCHOOL OF LAW

PREFACE

When I started practicing law, a good family law practitioner needed only to familiarize oneself with the state law on divorce grounds, child custody, property division, alimony and child support, with an occasionally researched issue for interstate jurisdiction. With a growing presence of federal statutory and common law playing a role in family law, one can no longer rely on knowing a handful of state laws to ethically and competently represent clients in family law matters.

Historically, many law schools did not require students to take Family Law, but its growing importance has been recognized by practitioners, judges and bar examiners. The NextGen bar exam will include Family Law in its foundational concepts and principles, similar to core subjects. Family Law is highly relevant to modern law practices and impacts many clients.

This book covers all of the major topics that are included in each of the family law books currently in publication. This book is designed as a supplement to help students and practitioners to understand the complicated and complex concepts that relate to legal issues impacting modern families.

April Carroll Meldrum
PROFESSOR OF LAW
LINCOLN MEMORIAL UNIVERSITY SCHOOL OF LAW
APRIL.MELDRUM@LMUNET.EDU

ACKNOWLEDGMENTS

Special thanks to my faculty assistant, Jennifer Richardson, who has helped me every step of the way and to Anna McClure, my hard-working research assistant, who has ensured the law I say exists, actually does.

Recognition to the late Janet Leach Richards, this book's original author. Although I never had the opportunity to meet Professor Richards, I felt like I knew her—most Tennessee family practitioners likely do. She was THE family law guru. Her books offer guidance to practitioners and law students and will always be found on the corner of my desk. Many of the words in this edition of this book come from Professor Richards' original edition. Her accuracy and writing style made my job in updating this book easy.

MASTERING FAMILY LAW

CHAPTER 1

Introduction

ROADMAP

After reading this chapter, you should understand:

- The limited treatment of family law issues in federal court, despite the presence of diversity of citizenship; and
- The major sources of state law, both at the state and federal levels.

A. Scope of Family Law

Federal courts have long avoided deciding family law matters through diversity of citizenship jurisdiction due to a domestic relations exception that limits the federal courts' power to hear certain cases involving family law questions that would typically be decided by state courts. That exception to diversity jurisdiction was announced in an 1858 decision when the Supreme Court proclaimed that it "disclaim[ed] altogether any jurisdiction in the courts of the United States upon the subject of divorce or for the allowance of alimony." *Barber v. Barber*, 62 U.S. 582 (1858). In 1992, the Court clarified that the jurisdictional limitation applied to divorce, alimony and child custody decrees. *Ankenbrandt v. Richards*, 504 U.S. 689 (1992). In a 2004 case, the Court seemed to imply that the limitation on diversity jurisdiction might extend to federal question jurisdiction because family matters are "delicate" and better left to the states except in "rare circumstances" and only when "necessary to answer a federal question that transcends or exists apart from the family law issue." *Elk Grove Unified School District v. Newdow*, 542 U.S. 1 (2004). One such transcendental case—*Obergefell v.*

Hodges—brought an opportunity to the Court to not only decide the constitutional issue of same-sex marriage, but to address whether the domestic relations exception limited the Court's power even in federal question cases. 576 U.S. 644 (2015). Although several federal district courts held the exception did not prevent them from deciding the matter, several other courts reached the opposite conclusion. *Obergefell* did ultimately decide the federal question on the merits, but the Opinion failed to address the applicability of the domestic relations exception to federal questions related to family law matters, apparently leaving intact the *Newdow* decision.

B. Sources of Family Law

There are four sources of family law: Constitutions, Statutes, Regulations and Caselaw. Most common issues that arise are governed by state statutes and caselaw. However, federal statutes, cases and administrative regulations play a greater role in interstate disputes, child welfare, constitutional rights, child support and adoption.

CHAPTER 2

Marriage and Marriage Regulations

ROADMAP

After reading this chapter, you should understand:

- The role of the state in regulating entry into marriage;
- The constitutional limitations on state regulation of marriage;
- The various limitations on the right to marry; and
- The consequences for failure to comply with the state's regulations on marriage.

A. Marriage Defined

Marriage could be defined as a three-party contract, including the two marriage partners and the state, which confers the status, benefits and responsibilities of marriage on the couple. Marriage is a civil right, but only those marriages authorized by a state are considered valid. In order to enter into a valid marriage, the parties (1) must be legally eligible to marry each other, (2) must give mutual consent to marry each other, and (3) must contract to marry as prescribed by the state. States generally require licensing, solemnization and registration, pursuant to state law, to create a valid marriage.

The marriage contract authorized by the state is civil in nature. Some couples choose, however, to combine a religious rite with the civil ceremony or to hold a separate ceremony. States give legal recognition only to those marriages authorized by varying state law. While there is no federal law of marriage, marriages validly entered into in one state are recognized as valid marriages in another state due to the Full Faith and Credit Clause of the U.S. Constitution.

In the late 1990's, a few states, beginning with Louisiana, passed legislation allowing parties to choose between the standard civil marriage and a stricter form of marriage called a *covenant marriage*. Recent legislative movement in a few states could lead to an increase in states that sanction covenant marriages. The covenant marriage regulations differ from state to state, but they are designed to encourage couples to stay married. Typically, covenant marriages require premarital counseling as well as counseling prior to seeking a divorce. Fault grounds for divorce, such as adultery, abuse or abandonment, are usually required. For instance, in Louisiana, couples in a standard marriage may obtain a no-fault divorce, but couples in a covenant marriage have only limited fault-based grounds for divorce, and may do so even then, only after a lengthy two-year waiting period.

Other states have attempted to promote marriage by reducing the fee for a marriage license when the parties attend premarital counseling classes. Churches have also gotten involved by making mandatory premarital counseling programs a prerequisite to a wedding in the church and also by pairing newlywed couples with older couples who serve as mentors.

B. Marriage Regulations

The state has a right to regulate entry into marriage, but that right is not unlimited. In *Loving v. Virginia*, 388 U.S. 1 (1967) the Supreme Court struck down racial restrictions on the right to marry. The Court in *Loving* stated that marriage was a fundamental right entitled to the highest level of constitutional protection. It was debated whether that statement applied to the right to marry generally or was limited to the racial restriction involved. In *Zablocki v. Redhail*, 434 U.S. 374 (1978), the Supreme Court invalidated, on equal protection grounds, a state statute that prohibited persons with unpaid child support from marrying. In *Zablocki,* the Supreme Court held that the right to marry is a right of fundamental importance and set out two levels of constitutional scrutiny for marriage regulations, based on whether the state regulation significantly interferes with the right to marry. Recognizing that states have a legitimate state interest in regulating marriage by requiring marriage licenses, etc., the court held that where the state regulation does not significantly interfere with the right to marry, it is subject to the rational basis test and will be upheld if it is supported by a legitimate state interest and is rationally related to that state interest. If the state regulation does significantly interfere with the right to marry, it must be supported by "sufficiently important" [interpreted as the strict scrutiny level of "compelling"] state interests and must be closely tailored to effectuate only those interests. In *Turner v. Safley*, 482 U.S. 78 (1987), the Supreme Court applied the *Zablocki* standard to find unconstitutional a statute that prohibited prisoner marriages absent permission of the prison superintendent upon a finding of compelling circumstances (usually pregnancy or birth of an illegitimate child).

As will be discussed in greater detail, *infra*, in 2015, the Supreme Court, in settling a hotly contested circuit split, held that the Fourteenth Amendment of the Constitution requires states to issue marriage licenses to same-sex couples, as the right to marry is fundamental. *Obergefell v. Hodges*, 576 U.S. 644 (2015). The Court avoided dictating a specific level of scrutiny applicable to gender-based marriage restrictions and seemingly intended to avoid extending this right to plural marriages by setting forth bases for their decision that seem less applicable to polygamous marriages.

When considering the constitutionality of a marriage regulation, the first issue is whether the regulation significantly interferes with the right to marry. If the answer is no, the regulation is subject to the rational basis test. Under the rational basis test, the state must show (1) that the state has a legitimate state interest to support the regulation; and (2) that the regulation is rationally related to the legitimate state interest identified. If the answer is yes, however, the rigorous scrutiny test of *Zablocki* applies and the state must show (1) that the state has sufficiently important state interests [interpreted as a compelling state interest] justifying the regulation; and (2) that the regulation is closely tailored to effectuate only those sufficiently important state interests.

State regulations are generally characterized as procedural/formal/directory or as substantive/mandatory. These categories will be discussed more fully below.

1. Procedural/Formal/Directory Regulations

The state regulations that fall into this category are those relating to the formalities associated with a valid marriage, such as the requirement to obtain a marriage license from the state and the requirement to participate in a marriage ceremony. Failure to comply with these regulations is generally not seen as a basis for invalidating the marriage. These requirements are often said to be merely regulatory or directory in nature. Violation of these regulations does not typically offend the strong public policy of the state. There may, however, be other consequences for noncompliance, such as charging the responsible official with a misdemeanor, as in the case of a minister who fails to return a marriage license to the state, or a clerk who issues a marriage license in violation of statutory requirements.

a. License

The marriage license requirement is also referred to as the requirement of licensure. The license essentially acts as a legal permit that verifies that the parties are eligible to marry. The state's interest in requiring parties to obtain marriage licenses may include the state's need for record keeping for support purposes, for the orderly administration of estates, for presumptive legitimation of children, to impress on the parties the importance of the undertaking, and to deter bigamous or underage marriages. Certain legal rights and responsibilities are associated with the union, and effective record-keeping is important.

States differ on the significance of the failure to obtain a valid marriage license. However, a majority of states require only substantial compliance with procedural requirements such as a marriage license. Unless the licensing statute specifies that an unlicensed marriage is invalid, public policy favoring valid marriages usually outweighs the defective procedure. *Carabetta v. Carabetta*, 438 A.2d 109 (Conn. 1980).

Many marriage licenses are valid only in the state where issued and only for a limited period of time, usually one to two months.

Some states require that both parties appear in person to apply for the marriage license. The requirement is justified by the prohibition against issuing a license to an underage or incompetent person, and, prior to *Obergefell, supra*, to homosexual couples. Moreover, the state has a legitimate interest in ensuring that both parties mutually consent to be wed, and joint appearances ameliorate that issue. The appearance requirement is usually waived if a party is incarcerated or is disabled to the extent that they cannot come to the clerk's office.

b. Ceremony

The requirement of a marriage ceremony is also referred to as the solemnization requirement. State statutes generally list persons authorized to serve as a marriage officiant. Categories may include clergy and other leaders of various religious groups, judges and county officials, to name a few. Many states have expanded the list of authorized officiants in what appears to be an attempt to curry favor with various local and state officials and their constituents. Statutes are broadly written in order to avoid preferencing one religion over another. There are, however, some mail-order and online services that will ordain anyone as a minister for a fee. Some states have attempted to exclude this category of minister from the approved list of wedding officiants by including some statutory language limiting ministers to those ordained or otherwise designated in conformity with the customs of a particular religion or group and further requiring that the ordination or designation occur through a considered, deliberate, and responsible act. Utah limited internet and mail-ordained ministers, stating "one who so cavalierly becomes a minister might not appreciate the gravity of solemnization a marriage and might not bring to the ceremony the desired level of dignity and integrity. In addition, it is conceivable that the Legislature could rationally be concerned that an individual's decision to use such a minister might be reflective of a cavalier attitude toward the marriage relationship. *Universal Life Church v. Utah*, 189 F. Supp. 2d 1302, 1306 (D. Utah 2002).

Parties usually solemnize the marriage in the same state where the license is obtained. In many cases, however, if a marriage is solemnized in another state, the marriage will be recognized by the state issuing a license, to the same extent that the marriage would be recognized if the solemnization had taken place in the issuing state.

The requirements for the marriage ceremony are often limited to a declaration of an intention to marry one another (or accept each other as spouses) in the presence of an authorized officiant. Witnesses to the ceremony may also be required, along with their signatures on the marriage license. Many states allow proxy marriages, if one party cannot be present for the ceremony. No states allow double proxy marriages. In proxy marriages, someone stands in the place of one of the missing parties. Proxy marriages are rare and are typically used by soldiers or by inmates. Particular scrutiny has been applied to proxy marriages involving aliens who are subject to the Immigration and Nationality Act. *Villa v. United States Attorney General*, 742 Fed. Appx. 682 (3d Cir. 2018). The Uniform Marriage and Divorce Act does recognize proxy marriages.

c. *Other Requirements*

Additional requirements imposed in various states include a waiting period of several days between the application for the license and the ceremony. Some states impose the waiting period only if one of the applicants is under the age of majority. Some states require blood tests for venereal disease and, in the case of women of child-bearing age, a blood test for measles. However, prohibiting marriage due to a medical condition has been deemed violative of the Americans with Disabilities Act. *T.E.P. v. Leavitt*, 840 F. Supp. 110 (D. Utah 1993).

2. Substantive/Mandatory Regulations

Substantive regulations describe who is and is not eligible to marry. These regulations reflect the social values of society and the individual state. These regulations are deemed to be driven by important public policy considerations that are more important than the ministerial regulations discussed above. Due to the importance of these marriage restrictions, purported marriages that do not strictly comply with substantive regulations are usually deemed void *ab initio*, from the beginning, as if they never occurred.

a. Age

There are a number of age-related restrictions on the right to marry. The first is the age at which a party may marry without parental permission or court approval. That age is the age of majority, eighteen in most states.

The second age restriction is the age above which a parent or parents may consent to the minor's marriage. That age is typically a few years below the age of majority, such as age sixteen where the age of majority is eighteen. Historically, some states allowed marriage with parental consent for children as young as twelve, though most states now restrict marriage with parental consent to children who are at least sixteen years old and, in many states, to partners who are no more than two to four years their senior. Some states require the permission of both parents while others require the permission of only one parent.

The third age restriction is the age below which court approval of the marriage of a minor must be obtained. In past decades, courts were authorized in most states to grant a waiver of the age prohibitions on marriage, either because parental consent was not obtained by the parties or because the parties were younger than permitted to marry by statute. While most states have retained the court-authorized waiver process, the authority of most courts has been limited to marriages involving sixteen- or seventeen-year-olds.

The final age restriction is the minimum age below which a minor may not marry. There are currently four states (California, Oklahoma, New Mexico and Mississippi) in which there is no age restriction on the right to marry with either parental or judicial consent. Many critics have sought repeal of these liberal marriage laws and have argued that it is most often girls who are forced to marry much older men or even sold to men for money or to obtain immigration status and are suffering from the lack of restriction.

b. Incest

The incest prohibitions are based in part on strong social taboos, in part on a fear of genetic deformities, and in part on the need to protect children from improper sexual conduct within the family setting. All states have some limitations against incestuous marriages, but the restrictions are not uniform. They fall into two broad categories, those prohibitions based on consanguinity and those prohibitions based on affinity.

Consanguinity refers to blood relationships. Typical prohibitions include parent and child, grandparent and grandchild, brother and sister, aunt and nephew, uncle and niece. Nearly half of the states bar marriages between first cousins.

Affinity refers to relationships created by law, such as relatives through marriage or adoption. Typical prohibitions are similar to those based on consanguinity except that they apply to step-relatives and relatives by adoption rather than blood relatives—parent and stepchild or parent and adopted child, for instance. States differ on whether the prohibition continues after the underlying marriage or adoption ends or is terminated.

Incestuous marriages, acts of incestuous adultery or fornication usually give rise to criminal prosecutions for the crime of incest.

c. Bigamy

Between 1882 and 1978, the Edmunds Anti-Polygamy Act, a federal criminal statute, made it a felony to purport to enter into more than one marriage at a time. The Act primarily targeted polygamous marriages in the Church of Jesus Christ of Latter-day Saints. Since its repeal in 1978, the federal government has left this topic primarily to the states to establish marital restrictions and criminal penalties. No state recognizes polygamy, a practice which permits a party to be married to several persons at a time, or bigamy, the act of being married to two persons at one time. A prior marriage must be terminated before another marriage can be contracted. Bigamy is the act of entering into a second marriage while still lawfully married to another. Bigamy causes the second marriage to be void, and in most instances, can also result in criminal charges for the culpable spouse. In this country, many people have several spouses over their lifetimes, however, they are permitted to have only one spouse at a time.

Although insanity, intoxication, duress or good faith belief that the prior marriage had ended may be appropriate defenses to a criminal charge of bigamy, none of those defenses will render a void bigamous marriage valid.

The issue of bigamy is most often raised as a probate claim within an estate, usually being argued to defeat a claim for inheritance by a purported bigamous spouse.

d. Gender

At the time of this book's first publication, only three states recognized same-sex marriages—Connecticut, New York and Massachusetts. (California had legalized same-sex marriage but voters amended the state Constitution in 2008 to prohibit it.)

Many states made clear their stance against same-sex marriage by enacting Defense of Marriage Acts (DOMAs), also known as baby DOMAs, which provide that only heterosexual marriages are recognized as valid in that state. In addition, some states amended their state constitutions, adding similar provisions. Some of these provisions addressed only the recognition of the marriage, while others prohibit recognition of any rights arising from the marriage, as well.

Congress also weighed in on this issue by enacting its own DOMA that limited the definition of spouse to heterosexual marriages for purposes of determining eligibility for all federal benefits. The Federal DOMA also addressed the Full Faith and Credit Clause, as applied to same-sex marriages, and exempted states from having to give full faith and credit to same-sex marriages legally contracted in sister states. However, in 2013, the U.S. Supreme Court ruled that the Act's limitation of marriage to a "legal union between one man and one woman" deprived same-sex couples who were legally married under state laws of their Fifth Amendment rights to equal protection. *United States v. Windsor*, 570 U.S. 744 (2013). Since the Petitioner in Windsor was legally married in a state that authorized same-sex marriage (New York), the Court did not address whether the right to marry another of the same sex was a protected fundamental right, but its holding, along with the federal government's subsequent extension of other federal rights, privileges and benefits to married same-sex couples, was a prelude to what was to come. In 2015, in response to nationwide upheaval with clerks in many states refusing to issue marriage licenses to same-sex couples, even in defiance of court orders to do so, and other states removing all marriage barriers to same-sex couples, the Supreme Court finally addressed the issue of whether gender-based restrictions on the right to marry violated the U.S. Constitution, and the Court answered affirmatively. *Obergefell v. Hodges*, 576 U.S. 644 (2015). The ruling not only required states to issue marriage licenses to same-sex applicants, but to recognize same-sex marriages that were lawfully licensed and performed out-of-state. And, just as importantly, the ruling compelled states to grant divorces to same-sex couples domiciled in a state that previously refused to do so as such would constitute recognition of the marriage.

e. Capacity

Both parties must be mentally competent at the time of entering into the marriage contract. The test for mental capacity to marry is similar to the capacity tests to enter into a contract, and that is whether the person has the ability to understand the rights and duties of marriage. This restriction is usually deemed necessary to protect vulnerable people, sometimes mentally frail elderly people, from exploitation. If one party lacks mental capacity (*non compos mentis*), the validity of the marriage will be affected. In some states, the validity of the affected marriage depends on whether the *non compos mentis* party has been adjudicated to be incompetent. If there has been an adjudication, generally the marriage is deemed void, but if there has not been an adjudication, the marriage is only voidable. Most states permit a person under the control of a conservator to marry with conservator or judicial permission.

f. Consent

It is not enough for both parties to have capacity to enter into the marriage contract. They must also give their consent voluntarily and without fraud or duress.

Proof of fraud will generally cause a marriage to be voidable. The fraud must go to the essentials of the marriage, such as a party's ability to procreate or engage in sexual relations. Some states allow a more subjective, *ad hoc* determination, but most states strictly limit findings of fraud.

Proof of duress may also demonstrate a lack of consent. Cases finding sufficient evidence of duress are few in number, however, and are generally limited to very extreme circumstances of duress. Although "shotgun weddings" are no longer prevalent in society, such coercion will render a marriage voidable and subject to annulment. Even people who are deemed competent and to have the mental capacity to enter into a marriage could still be deemed to have been fraudulently influenced by the will of another to the extent that their acquiescence to the marriage was not freely done, thereby rendering the marriage voidable. *Nave v. Nave*, 173 S.W.3d 766 (Tenn. App. 2005).

Sham marriages are created without the intent to live together as husband and wife. Sham or limited purpose marriages are attacked as lacking consent, on the ground that the parties' consent to marriage is of such limited purpose that it does not amount to consent to marriage. This allegation arises most often in immigration cases. Another example is when two people participate in a mock ceremony in jest or dare, but in all other ways satisfy the state's marriage requirements. Courts reason that mutual consent with intent to be married for all lawful purposes is necessary to create a valid marriage.

3. Consequences for Noncompliance with Marriage Regulations

The consequences for noncompliance with a state's marriage regulations generally depend on how seriously the noncompliance violates the strong public policy of the state. Depending on the seriousness of the noncompliance, the validity of the marriage may be unaffected, or it may be determined to be either voidable or void. The differences between void and voidable marriages will be explained below.

a. Procedural/Formality Regulations

Some regulations are merely ministerial or directory in nature and do not offend the strong public policy of the state. Noncompliance with such regulations generally does not affect the validity of the marriage, although the official responsible for ensuring compliance may be charged with a misdemeanor. Some states have savings statutes, which expressly provide that marriages are valid, despite noncompliance with certain regulations, as long as other more important requirements are met, such as solemnization. Examples of regulations covered by a savings statute include parental consent requirements, waiting period requirements, and prohibitions against issuing licenses to drunks and non-adjudicated incompetents.

b. Substantive/Mandatory Regulations

Substantive/mandatory regulations are much more important than the procedural regulations or marriage formalities discussed above, in that violation of these substantive regulations generally does violate the strong public policy of the state. These regulations are said to be mandatory and violations will generally result in the marriage being deemed voidable or void, depending on the seriousness of the requirement violated. The differences between voidable and void marriages are reviewed below. The remedies of annulment or divorce are mentioned briefly but will be considered more fully Chapter __. The states are fairly uniform in their treatment of void and voidable marriages, but, as always, there are some states that deviate, to some extent, from the descriptions given below.

i. Voidable Marriage

A voidable marriage is potentially valid. It is valid until a court declares its nullity and usually can only be declared during the lifetime of the marriage, during the infirmity that causes the marriage to be voidable, before death of either party and at the insistence of a party to the marriage. The infirmity that causes a marriage to be voidable is less offensive to the strong public policy of the state than those infirmities that cause a marriage to be deemed void. The infirmities resulting in voidable marriages generally relate to the capacity of one of the parties to enter into the marriage contract freely and knowledgably. The infirmities can arise from either formal or substantive requirements. Typical infirmities include duress, underage marriage, fraud, drunkenness, impotency, mental disability (not adjudicated), pregnancy by another without knowledge of the husband, and mistake, going to the essentials of the marriage.

A voidable marriage is neither valid nor void. It is a little bit of each, but is treated as a valid marriage until it is challenged by one of the parties to the marriage. Often times, it can be challenged only by the party sought to be protected by the requirement that has been violated. For instance, only the underage party can challenge a marriage that is voidable due to age restrictions. Voidable marriages cannot be challenged by third parties, unless the third party has been appointed to act on behalf of the infirm party to the marriage. Challenges to voidable marriages must be brought during the marriage and cannot be raised after the death of one of the parties.

If the infirmity that causes the marriage to be voidable is removed at some point during the marriage, the affected party may be deemed to have ratified the marriage by continuing to stay in the marriage. For example, if an underaged party marries and stays in the marriage for a reasonable period of time after attaining the age of majority, that party will be deemed to have ratified the marriage. Following ratification, the marriage is deemed valid in all respects and annulment is no longer available. Divorce is the only option for ending the marriage thereafter.

If a marriage is found to be voidable, the plaintiff can generally seek either a divorce or an annulment. The infirmities which result in a marriage being voidable are usually included in grounds for divorce in those states that still have fault grounds. A divorce decree dissolves a marriage at the time of the divorce, but an annulment nullifies the marriage, declaring that it never legally existed. The other remedies for annulment are generally the same as those for divorce, where the marriage is found to be voidable. Children of the marriage are deemed legitimate in either case.

ii. Void Marriage

The infirmity that causes a marriage to be void is much more offensive to the strong public policy of the state than those infirmities that cause a marriage to be deemed voidable. The infirmities resulting in void marriages generally relate to conduct that is deemed to be strongly offensive to the moral values of the citizens of that state. The infirmities generally involve violations of substantive marriage requirements. Typical infirmities include bigamy, incest, and marriage to someone adjudicated *non compos mentis.*

A void marriage is *void ab initio*. It generally can be challenged by either party to the marriage or by third parties, such as insurance companies and relatives of one of the parties. Challenges to void marriages can be brought at any time.

Nothing can be done to ratify or validate a void marriage. In theory, it requires no declaration of invalidity, it just is. In practice, however, judicial intervention should be sought.

If a marriage is found to be void, the plaintiff can, but does not have to, seek either a divorce or an annulment. It may be a good idea to do so, however, especially if the grounds giving rise to the claim could be challenged. The financial remedies for a void marriage may differ from those available when the marriage is merely voidable. The rationale is that the marriage never existed so the legal consequences of marriage never attached. Some states do not recognize the property acquired as marital. Some states do not allow an award of alimony. Like most other areas of family law, states differ in their approach to these issues. Children of void marriages are, however, deemed legitimate.

C. Common Law Marriage

In a common law marriage, the parties do not comply with the formal requirements of a license and ceremony, but the marriage is nevertheless recognized as valid by several states when certain other requirements are met. Common law marriages were recognized in most states in colonial times, when compliance with the formal requirements was difficult, due to scattered populations and a scarcity of officiants. Currently, only eight states and the District of Columbia recognize common law marriages, although many states apply a sunset date to common law marriages that were established before the state abrogated common law marriages. A common law marriage is, in every sense, a valid marriage and can be terminated only by death, divorce, or annulment. A valid common law marriage contracted in one state usually will be recognized, under the Full Faith and Credit Clause, in sister states, including those that do not recognize common law marriages.

The requirements for a common law marriage are not uniform, even in those few states that still recognize them, but generally they include the following: (1) eligibility to marry; (2) present intention to marry; (3) holding out as married; and (4) cohabitation. In order to be eligible to enter into a common law marriage, the parties must be eligible to marry, i.e., able to meet the substantive marriage regulations in the state where the common law marriage is contracted. For instance, if one of the parties is already married, a common law marriage cannot be contracted, even if the other requirements are met. The parties must have a present intention to take each other as husband and wife at the time the common law marriage is contracted. A promise to marry when one of the parties obtains a divorce does not meet the present intent requirement. The holding out requirement is generally interpreted as holding themselves out in their community and among their friends and relatives as being married to each other. Cohabitation generally requires both living together and having sexual relations. Each of these elements may have to be proved by clear and convincing evidence, rather than the ordinary civil standard of preponderance of the evidence.

D. Recognition of Foreign Marriages

The first step in determining whether a state will recognize, as valid, a marriage that took place outside that state is to look to the place where the marriage took place. States are much more likely to recognize marriages that are contracted in a sister state than they are to recognize marriages that are contracted in a foreign country. Each of these scenarios is discussed below.

1. Marriages Contracted in a Sister State

The Full Faith and Credit Clause applies to marriages that are contracted in a sister state. States have long recognized a public policy exception to the Full Faith and Credit Clause, which permits states to refuse to recognize a marriage that is deemed valid in a sister state, if that marriage violates the strong public policy of the forum state. Historically, the public policy exception was applied primarily in the incest context, to refuse to recognize marriages validly contracted in one state, but in violation of the incest provisions of the forum state. States also refused to give full faith and credit to marriages when residents of the state got married in a sister state in order to evade the marriage regulations of their home state. Some states also passed marriage evasion statutes which expressly state that any marriage contracted in a sister state by residents of the forum state, that would be void if contracted in the forum state, will not be given full faith and credit. The marriage evasion statute may also contain a reciprocal provision that any marriage contracted in the contracting state by nonresidents for the purpose of evading the laws of their state of residence will be deemed void in the contracting state, as well.

2. Marriages Contracted in a Foreign Country

The Full Faith and Credit Clause does not apply to marriages contracted in foreign countries. States have much more flexibility in choosing whether or not to recognize such marriages under the doctrine of comity. Typically, states will recognize marriages contracted in foreign countries if the marriage is valid in the country where contracted and does not violate the strong public policy of the forum state. States may also require that at least one of the parties be a resident of the foreign country.

E. Broken Engagements

1. Breach of the Promise to Marry

An action for breach of the promise to marry is essentially what it sounds like, an action for a broken engagement. At early common law, a man's promise to marry was generally considered a legally binding contract, for breach of which he could be civilly liable if he lacked a sufficient defense. Women, on the other hand, were generally free to change their minds without legal consequences. The underlying theory was that women were more likely to be seduced by a man who had promised marriage. Even if the woman was not actually seduced, her reputation would suffer if the engagement was broken. The woman would suffer loss of stature and public humiliation, and her future prospects for marriage would be greatly diminished. Society's opinion of women who have been "jilted" has changed dramatically over the years, however. Breach of promise to marry was once one of several quasi-contract/quasi-tort actions known as a heartbalm action—meant as a salve to mend the broken hearted. But, since a broken engagement is no longer deemed by society to damage a woman's reputation, breach of promise to marry actions are no longer recognized in most states.

The action is based on breach of the promise, but the damages are based on personal tort principles involving damage to one's reputation and character. The injured party is allowed to recover for pain and suffering associated with the humiliation of the broken engagement, loss of reputation, and actual damages incurred. Damages generally take into account the age and experience of the parties. And, in some cases, limit recovery to actual financial loss, where the defendant is more than 60 years of age at the time of trial. The tort statute of limitations generally applies, which is typically much shorter than the contracts statute of limitations. Typically, the promise to marry must either be in writing or corroborated by one or more disinterested witnesses. The action generally abates upon the death of either party.

Several defenses are available to a breach of promise to marry action. They include proof of an existing marriage of either party at the time of the promise, if known to the plaintiff; previous unchastity of the plaintiff, if unknown to the defendant; fraudulent concealment by a plaintiff of personal or family matters; ill health of the plaintiff that renders marriage improper; and other ordinary breach of contract defenses.

2. Engagement Gifts

Parties often exchange expensive gifts in contemplation of marriage. The most common example, of course, is the diamond engagement ring. If the engagement is broken, the donor may seek a return of the engagement ring or other gift. States fall into two broad categories in their approach to this issue—a fault-based approach or a no-fault approach.

The older, fault-based approach begins by determining the party responsible for the broken engagement. If the responsible party is the donor, the donee is allowed to keep the engagement gift. If the donee is responsible for the broken engagement, however, the engagement gift must be returned to the donor.

The modern trend, consistent with the no-fault approach to divorce grounds, does not consider the fault of either party in resolving the issue. The engagement gift is treated as a conditional gift, conditioned on the marriage taking place. Because the marriage is not taking place, the gift must be returned to the donor. The Restatement (Third) of Property (Wills and Other Donative Transfers) § 6.2, cmt. m adopts the conditional gift approach as well.

F. Uniform Marriage and Divorce Act (UMDA)

The Uniform Marriage and Divorce Act (UMDA), promulgated in 1970 by the National Conference of Commissioners on Uniform State Laws (NCCUSL), has been adopted, at least in part, by only a few states. The age restrictions under the UMDA are as follows: eighteen is the age of majority; sixteen is the age of parental consent (both parents), below sixteen requires court approval and parental approval. The act contains a judicial bypass provision for applicants between sixteen and eighteen who cannot obtain parental approval. The waiting period is three days, and it applies to all parties, absent a court order. The license is effective for six months. Proxy marriages are permitted with the approval of the officiant or by court authorization.

Marriages may be solemnized by a judge of a court of record, a public official whose powers include solemnization of marriages, or in accordance with any mode of solemnization recognized by any religious denomination, Indian Nation, or Native Group. A savings provision validates marriages solemnized by unauthorized officiants if the parties, in good faith, believed the officiant to be qualified.

Prohibited marriages include (1) bigamous marriages; (2) incestuous marriages between an ancestor and a descendent, or a brother and a sister, whether the relationship is by half blood, whole blood, or adoption; and (3) incestuous marriages between an uncle and a niece or between an aunt and a nephew, whether the relationship is by half or whole blood, except for marriages permitted by the established customs of aboriginal cultures. Parties to such prohibited marriages may validate their marriages by continuing to cohabitate after removal of the impediment. Such marriages are valid as of the date of the removal of the impediment.

The UMDA does not take a position on common law marriages. Instead, it offers two alternatives for states to consider. One alternative validates common law marriages and the other states that common law marriages contracted in the state after adoption of the act are invalid, thus saving existing common law marriages and leaving open the possibility of recognizing common law marriages validly contracted in other states.

The UMDA does not have provisions that specifically define or prohibit same-sex marriage. In states that have adopted the UMDA in whole or in part, courts will necessarily construe the applicable statutes to apply equally to heterosexual and same-sex marriage.

CHECKPOINTS

- Marriage is a personal relationship, which confers the status of marriage on the couple, when all of the valid regulations of the state are met.
- In order to enter into a valid marriage, the parties (1) must be legally eligible to marry each other, (2) must give mutual consent to marry each other, and (3) must contract to marry as prescribed by the state.
- Regulations governing entry into state recognized marriages are considered the province of the individual states and vary from state to state.
- Formal regulations generally include the requirement of a license and ceremony.
- Mandatory regulations generally pertain to restrictions regarding age, incest, bigamy, capacity, and consent.
- When considering the constitutionality of a marriage regulation, the first issue is whether the regulation significantly interferes with the right to marry. If the answer is no, the regulation is subject to the rational basis test. If the regulation does significantly interfere with the right to marry, it must be supported by sufficiently important state interests [usually construed as a compelling interest] and must be closely tailored to effectuate only those interests.
- Failure to comply with a state's marriage regulations may have no consequence upon the validity of the marriage itself, if the regulation is determined to be merely directory in nature. If the regulation is determined to be mandatory, however, noncompliance may result in the marriage being voidable or void.
- Voidable marriages are generally considered valid until they are successfully challenged, whereas void marriages are void *ab initio*.
- Common law marriages, if recognized in a state, are valid marriages in every way. They are generally recognized in other states, if valid where contracted and can be terminated only by death, divorce or annulment.
- Valid marriages contracted in one state are generally entitled to recognition in a sister state under the Full Faith and Credit Clause.

- Valid marriages contracted in a foreign country are generally entitled to recognition in a forum state under the doctrine of comity.
- In breach of promise to marry actions, the contracted engagement must be proved, but the damages are based on personal tort principles involving damage to one's reputation and character. The plaintiff may also recover actual damages incurred.
- Under the fault-based approach, engagement gifts are returned if the donee is responsible for the broken engagement, but retained if the donor is the responsible party.
- Under the no-fault approach to engagement gifts, the gift is conditional upon the marriage and must be returned when the engagement is broken.

CHAPTER 3

Marriage Alternatives

ROADMAP

After reading this chapter, you should understand:

- The basic differences between the various alternatives to marriage; and
- How each marriage alternative compares to a valid marriage.

The putative spouse doctrine and marriage by estoppel are equitable doctrines that have long been recognized to avoid the harsh results of an invalid marriage for an innocent spouse. These two doctrines of de facto marriage were created to take care of persons who fail to observe the technical legal requirements for contracting a valid marriage in the same way common law marriages do, but these alternatives are more restrictive. Contractual cohabitation and implied partnership are more recent doctrines that have developed as a means of affording a remedy for parties in long standing heterosexual relationships. Reciprocal beneficiaries and civil unions are the newest marriage alternatives and each was developed as an alternative for same-sex couples before they were permitted to marry.

A. Putative Spouse Doctrine

The putative spouse doctrine was developed to protect the innocent spouse in a putative marriage. A putative marriage is one in which the marriage has been solemnized but is invalid because it fails to meet one or more marriage regulations, but one or both parties believes in good faith that the marriage is valid, although it is legally voidable or void. The doctrine usually requires co-habitation, as well. Some states treat the marriage valid, but others simply afford the putative spouse an equitable remedy, taking into account the possibility that there may be a legal spouse or other putative spouses. In some cases, the putative marriage can be recognized as valid after the impediment has been removed.

Different approaches have been applied to provide a remedy to the putative spouse. One approach is to treat the property accumulated during the putative marriage as quasi-marital property, to the extent that it would be classified as marital or community property if the marriage was valid, and distribute it accordingly. Another approach treats the putative marriage as a partnership, with half of the property belonging to each spouse in the putative marriage. A third approach makes an equitable distribution between the legal and putative spouses, according to the circumstances and the interests of justice.

A putative marriage differs from a legal marriage in that the putative marriage may not be recognized as valid, even after the impediment has been removed. Even in those states that do recognize the validity of the putative marriage, the impediment to the validity of the marriage must be removed first. Removal of the impediment may not be possible as in the case of an existing legal spouse. The putative spouse may receive the same financial remedies available to a legal spouse, but the putative spouse's claims cannot supersede those of a legal spouse, barring an estoppel argument. In some states, once a putative marriage is found to exist, the putative spouse not only has available remedies against their spouse, but to other benefits incidental to marriage, such as the right to inherit, to sue for the wrongful death of their spouse and benefits under the Social Security Act. *Aubrey v. Folsom*, 151 F. Supp. 836 (N.D. Cal. 1957).

B. Marriage by Estoppel

Marriage by estoppel is another doctrine designed to provide a remedy for an innocent spouse, but it does not result in recognition of a valid marriage. Under the doctrine of marriage by estoppel, the culpable spouse is estopped to assert the infirmity of the marriage against the innocent spouse in a divorce or other court proceeding in which the validity of the marriage is an issue. The innocent spouse must have a good faith belief in the validity of the marriage. If both parties know they are not validly married, the doctrine cannot apply. The doctrine has been held not to be applicable to bigamous marriages, because the parties were unable to enter into a valid marriage at the time of their marriage ceremony. The prior subsisting marriage prevents the parties from contracting a valid second marriage and, thus, there can be no marriage by estoppel.

C. Contractual Cohabitation

A few states will recognize and enforce contracts entered into between parties who agree to cohabit without the benefit of marriage, even though they are eligible to marry. Most states, however, refuse to enforce such agreements, holding that the agreements are against public policy because part of the consideration for the contract is sexual conduct between the parties. Even in those states which do recognize contractual cohabitation, no marriage is recognized and no marital rights are enforced. The court simply enforces the contract that the parties made, applying general contract principles.

D. Implied Partnership

If cohabiting parties are jointly involved in a business enterprise that is titled only in one party's name, a state may recognize the doctrine of implied partnership as a way to protect the financial interests of the untitled party. The doctrine is not dependent on the parties cohabiting. It is a straightforward application of general partnership principles. No marriage or marriage relationship is or need be recognized. The doctrine is not based on the subjective intent of the parties, so they do not need to have an agreement to be partners in the enterprise. If an implied partnership is recognized, the court will divide the partnership assets, but cannot address other financial remedies that would be available in a divorce, such as spousal support or division of non-partnership assets, like pensions, for instance.

E. Reciprocal Beneficiaries

Prior to permitting same-sex marriages, Hawaii created reciprocal beneficiaries to give marriage-like benefits to those unable to marry. In order to be reciprocal beneficiaries, a couple need only register. In order to be eligible to register as reciprocal beneficiaries, the couple must be eligible to marry, but not eligible to marry each other. The designation was intended for same-sex couples, but since same-sex marriages are now permitted in Hawaii, same-sex couples no longer qualify for this designation. Other circumstances, although rare, could exist where this doctrine is applicable. For instance, a grandmother could register an adult grandson as a reciprocal beneficiary in order to provide health care benefits for the grandson under the grandmother's health care plan. Reciprocal beneficiaries have some but not all of the state financial benefits of marriage. Reciprocal beneficiaries have hospital visitation rights, the right to make medical decisions for each other, the right to inherit from each other in the absence of a will, rights to sue for the death of each other, and certain other limited rights under Hawaii state law. The relationship can be ended with a simple filing and does not require a divorce or annulment.

F. Civil Unions

Civil unions were first recognized in Vermont, prior to the recognition of same-sex marriages. Civil unions have since been recognized in a number of states and are not uniform from state to state. Generally, the benefits afforded to civil unions are equal to, or at least very similar to state benefits for marriage. Civil unions are usually terminated only upon death, divorce, or a divorce-like process. Civil unions were once limited to same-sex couples and since *Obergefell* was decided, finding that same-sex couples have a fundamental right to marry, many of the marriage alternatives like civil unions that were created as an equitable solution to couples who could not marry have become obsolete.

G. Uniform Marriage and Divorce Act (UMDA)

The Uniform Marriage and Divorce Act adopts only one of the marriage alternatives, the putative spouse doctrine. Most of the other alternatives were not in existence at the time that the UMDA was promulgated, in 1970, by the National Conference of Commissioners on Uniform State Laws (NCCUSL). The UMDA provides that a putative spouse acquires the rights of a spouse, whether the marriage is void or voidable. The rights of the putative spouse may not supersede the rights of a legal spouse or other putative spouses, however. In that event, the court must apportion property, alimony, and child support rights among the claimants as appropriate in the circumstances and in the interest of justice.

CHECKPOINTS

- A putative spouse must have a good faith belief in the validity of the marriage. The doctrine also usually requires cohabitation.
- In some states, the putative marriage is treated as valid if the infirmity is removed, but other states simply afford the putative spouse and equitable remedy.
- The putative spouse's claims may not supersede those of a legal spouse, barring an estoppel argument.
- Marriage by estoppel does not recognize the invalid marriage, but merely prevents the culpable spouse from asserting the truth against the innocent spouse.
- Contractual cohabitation does not recognize a marriage, but only enforces the contract that the parties have made, according to general contract principles. Some states refuse to recognize such contracts, finding them to be against public policy.
- An implied partnership is an application of general partnership law and can be used to divide partnership assets between two unmarried parties who were jointly involved in a business enterprise. The division of property is limited to partnership assets, and other financial remedies associated with divorce, such as spousal support, are not available.

- Reciprocal beneficiaries receive some, but not all, of the state conferred benefits of marriage. Registration is available to any two people who are eligible to marry, but are not eligible to marry each other. Divorce is not necessary to terminate the relationship.
- Civil unions generally confer most or all of the state-conferred benefits of marriage and are mostly obsolete since the Supreme Court's recognition of the right to same-sex marriage. Termination of a civil union generally requires a divorce or divorce-like proceeding.

CHAPTER 4

Marital Rights and Obligations

ROADMAP

After reading this chapter, you should understand:

- The obligation of support in a marriage;
- The basic differences between community property jurisdictions and common law jurisdictions regarding management of property during marriage;
- The extent to which spouses may sue each other or third parties as a result of torts occurring during the marriage;
- The limitations on choosing one's name in a marriage; and
- The circumstances under which one spouse may testify against the other.

Historically, when a couple married, the two were said to become one and that one was the husband. He had the obligation of support, coupled with the right to wife's income and the right to manage the wife's property. Today, the legal disability suffered by a wife, known as the disability of coverture, has been removed. Women are able to own and manage their own property and to sue and be sued in their own name. There are still, however, certain rights afforded to and duties owed by both parties that arise as a result of the marital union.

A. Doctrine of Necessaries

The doctrine of necessaries is a legal doctrine that obligates spouses for the debts accrued by their partners and minor children for essential needs such as food, clothing, shelter and medical care. A third party who provides such things to either spouse or their minor children can seek reimbursement from either spouse or both parties, under the doctrine of necessaries.

Hospitals and other health care providers have attempted to collect outstanding health care debts from the non-patient spouse under the doctrine of necessaries. States split on the outcome of such litigation, depending on how they responded to the need to change the common law obligation of support. In those states where the obligation was extended to both spouses, the non-patient spouse would probably be liable. Some states require the spouses to be cohabitating at the time the debt is incurred, some states place caps on the amount of debt for which the other spouse may have responsibility and some states require evidence as to the reasonableness and medical necessity of the procedures for which charges are sought.

In those states where the obligation was eliminated, the non-patient spouse would probably not be liable. Those states typically require the non-patient spouse to sign an agreement, undertaking some responsibility, before the patient spouse is admitted or treated.

B. Property Management During Marriage

States follow two very different approaches in determining property rights between spouses during marriage and at the time of divorce. Most states follow the common-law approach, which, historically, was based on title ownership to the property. Several states follow the community property approach, which treats most property acquired by the parties during the marriage as owned by the marital community. These concepts will be discussed more fully in the chapter on Property Division.

1. Common Law States

The common law states still follow the title approach in determining property rights during marriage. Typically, the spouse in whose name the property is titled has the right to manage, transfer, and encumber the property without the consent of the other spouse.

It is also possible in common law states for the parties to have joint ownership of property as tenants in common, joint tenants, and, in some states, tenants by the entirety. As tenants in common, each spouse has an equal undivided share in the property, an equal right to possess the property, but no right of survivorship. Joint tenants and tenants by the entirety differ from tenants in common in that they each possess a right of survivorship in the other spouse's share of the property. A tenancy by the entirety differs from a joint tenancy in that it is available only to married couples. In those states recognizing a tenancy by the entirety, one will be presumed when title to property is taken in both spouses' names. A tenancy by the entirety also differs from a joint tenancy in that a tenancy by the entirety generally can be terminated only by dissolution of the marriage or the death of one of the parties.

When one spouse takes separately owned property, titled only in that spouse's name, and adds the other spouse to the title, a strong but rebuttable presumption generally arises that the original owner of the property intended to make a gift of one-half interest to the other spouse. In some states, the jointly owned property will presumptively be classified as marital property upon divorce.

Title to property also governs distribution at death in common law states. Surviving spouses are protected under intestacy statutes, if there is no will, and by doctrines that allow them to dissent from the will and receive a portion of the deceased spouse's estate. The portion of the estate that the surviving spouse receives is called either a forced share, statutory share, or elective share, depending on the state.

2. Community Property States

There are nine states that follow the community property approach. Eight states have traditionally been community property states (Arizona, California, Idaho, Louisiana, Nevada, New Mexico, Texas, and Washington) and the ninth, Wisconsin, is considered a community property state, following its adoption of the Uniform Marital Property Act in 1983.

Title to property is not the controlling factor in determining the right to manage property during the marriage in community property states. Community property states generally treat all property acquired during the marriage as property of the marital community, also referred to as community property, with each spouse owning an undivided half interest. Some states, like Tennessee, are not considered a community property state because the presumption upon divorce is that the property will be "equitably" divided instead of split equally. But, several states, including Tennessee, do apply a rebuttable presumption that property acquired during the marriage, no matter how titled, is marital property. An exception to the foregoing rule arises in the case of property owned prior to marriage, gifts from third parties, and property inherited by a spouse during the marriage. These items will generally be treated as the separate property of that spouse. Parties may also be able to designate property as the separate property of one spouse by entering into a valid contract for that purpose.

A spouse has the sole right to manage and transfer his or her separate property. Community property states differ, however, regarding the management and control of community property. Some states allow each spouse to act independently, while other states require mutual consent. Still other states alternate between the two approaches, depending upon the transaction.

Each spouse, upon death, is generally entitled to dispose of, by will, that spouse's separate property and half of the value of the community property. Community property states do not recognize tenancy by the entirety or elective shares, because each spouse is assured a half interest in the marital estate.

C. Interspousal Tort Liability

Interspousal tort liability has become an increasingly important part of divorce practice for two reasons. The first reason is that a number of states have abolished the doctrine of interspousal immunity. The second reason is that, with the increasing adoption of no-fault principles with regard to divorce grounds, division of marital property, and alimony, the injured spouse often will not be compensated for the fault-based conduct of the other spouse, except through a tort claim. Under the old fault-based system of divorce, when evidence of fault was considered by the court during a divorce proceeding, the injured spouse often received indirect compensation for the tortious conduct of the other spouse through increased property and/or alimony awards.

1. Interspousal Immunity

Historically, spouses were not allowed to sue one another for tort actions resulting in personal injury because of the doctrine of interspousal immunity. The underlying rationale for the doctrine was that litigation between spouses would disturb the harmony of the family and, historically, because the doctrine of coverture treated married spouses as one legal person—namely the husband. In addition, it was thought that spouses might collude together to defraud third parties or insurers. Initial inroads were made by some states that carved out exceptions for intentional torts and motor vehicle torts. Today, a majority of states have abolished the doctrine of interspousal immunity altogether.

2. Marital Torts

In those states where interspousal immunity has been abolished or partially abrogated, attorneys must be aware of the possibility of marital tort claims when counseling clients seeking a divorce. Some states allow the tort claim to be pursued in the same action with the divorce, while other states require that the claims be bifurcated. Importantly, attorneys need to carefully craft divorce settlement agreements to include or exclude tort claims that arose or accrued during the marriage.

Much of the conduct that gave rise to fault-based grounds for divorce also constitutes tortious conduct. Examples include negligence, intentional or negligent infliction of venereal disease, tortious interference with custody, fraud or misrepresentation, or assault, battery, defamation, intentional infliction of emotional distress, and false imprisonment.

D. Claims against Third Parties

1. Loss of Consortium

Consortium is currently defined broadly to include all the benefits, enjoyment, services, companionship, and pleasures arising out of the marital relationship, which one spouse is entitled to receive from the other. Consortium includes sexual relations, but it also includes affection, companionship, and other benefits of the marital relationship. The action is derivative in that the uninjured spouse claims damages for loss of consortium in a personal injury or wrongful death action against a third party, resulting in injury to the other spouse, which prevents the injured spouse from providing consortium to the uninjured spouse. Historically, a loss of consortium claim could be brought only by the husband because only the husband was granted rights of consortium in the marriage. Virtually all states now allow either spouse to claim damages for loss of consortium.

2. Heartbalm Claims

Most states have abolished the common law claims against third parties known as heartbalm claims. The name arose from the fact that these claims seek to compensate for the injury associated with loss of or damage to a personal relationship. These claims include alienation of affection, criminal conversation, and seduction. Breach of the promise to marry, which is discussed in the chapter on Marriage and Marriage Regulation, is also included in the heartbalm claims. The statutes abolishing these common law claims are generally referred to as heartbalm statutes. States that have abolished these actions, however, will generally still enforce judgments obtained in other states.

a. Alienation of Affection

Alienation of affection is a claim brought against a third party, charging that party with alienating the affection of plaintiff's spouse away from the plaintiff. The plaintiff must generally show that the couple had a warm loving relationship prior to the interference of the third party, and that the third party's interference alienated the plaintiff's spouse's affection for the plaintiff, causing injury to the marital relationship. The third party is usually a paramour, but sexual relations are not a requirement for this action. The third-party defendant could even be a meddling in-law or an acquaintance.

b. Criminal Conversation

Criminal conversation is a tort action brought against a third party, who engages in sexual intercourse with the plaintiff's spouse. Historically, criminal conversation was available only to husband as plaintiff, but, of course, is now available to either spouse. Only a handful of states still recognize this tort.

c. Seduction

Seduction is not really a marital tort, but it is included here because it is considered one of the heartbalm actions. Seduction, historically, is a tort claim brought by a father against a third party who seduces the father's unmarried daughter and then abandons her. The tort seeks financial payment for the disruption of the daughter's romantic prospects and the possibility of unmarried pregnancy. Like criminal conversation, this claim also requires a showing of sexual intercourse. In modern times, this tort has been replaced in most states by civil and criminal penalties for rape and without the necessity of an agent, like a father, to bring the claim on the woman's behalf.

E. Marital Surnames

It has long been customary in this country for the wife to assume the husband's surname upon marrying. More recently, some women have chosen to retain their maiden name after marrying, and some couples assume hyphenated surnames. There is no legal requirement that a woman assume the husband's surname, however. In fact, parties may use whatever surname they choose, as long as the name is changed consistent with state law and is not motivated by any fraudulent intent.

Women often request a return to their maiden name, as one of the remedies sought in a complaint for divorce. Again, the name change is not required by law, and frequently women will retain their marital surname if they have minor children of the marriage.

F. Marital Communications Privilege

There are two issues associated with marital communications. The first is whether a spouse may or must take the stand to testify against the other spouse. The second is whether communications between the spouses are privileged and inadmissible. The underlying rationale for each of these privileges, where recognized, is the public policy interest in protecting the marital relationship and its fiduciary nature.

1. Testimonial Privilege

Under the common law, one spouse could not testify against the other. Some states continue to apply the common law rule, at least in criminal cases. Other states no longer recognize the testimonial privilege in either civil or criminal proceedings. Some states have expanded the privilege to include "domestic partners."

The Supreme Court held, in *Trammel v. United States*, 445 U.S. 40 (1980) that, in federal criminal prosecutions, the privilege to refuse to testify adversely belongs to the witness-spouse, and that the witness-spouse cannot be compelled to testify or foreclosed from testifying. Most states quickly followed suit and amended their testimonial privilege laws. But a handful of states still strictly follow the common law and allow the defendant-spouse to prevent spousal testimony. There must be a valid marriage in existence at the time of the trial, in order for this privilege to be recognized.

2. Confidential Communications Privilege

This privilege pertains to confidential communications between spouses and applies in both civil and criminal cases. The confidential communications must take place during a valid marriage. The communications must also be made under circumstances that indicate an expectation of confidentiality, i.e., not in the presence of a third party. The fact that the parties later married will not create a privilege if they were not married at the time of the communication. On the other hand, the fact that the parties are no longer married at the time the testimony is sought to be introduced does not affect the privilege. This privilege belongs to both spouses, making confidential communications between spouses privileged and inadmissible if either spouse objects. The communications privilege does not apply, however, in cases involving child abuse or spousal abuse.

In criminal proceedings, some states apply a test to determine whether the marital communication is privileged. If the communication meets the test, the privilege applies and can be asserted by either spouse, subject to the exception for cases involving spousal abuse or child abuse. A typical test states that a marital confidential communication will be privileged if all four of the following factors are met:

1. The communications originated in a confidence that they will not be disclosed;
2. The element of confidentiality is essential to the full and satisfactory maintenance of the relation between the parties;
3. The relation must be one which, in the opinion of the community, ought to be sedulously fostered; and
4. The injury to the revelation that disclosure of the communications outweighs the benefit gained for the correct disposal of litigation.

The Supreme Court, also in *Trammel*, held that, in federal criminal prosecutions, any communications privately disclosed between spouses in the confidence of the marital relationship are privileged.

G. Uniform Marital Property Act (UMPA)

The Uniform Marital Property Act (UMPA) was promulgated in 1983 and reflects changes in divorce law that occurred during the 1970s and 1980s, including adoption of no-fault divorce legislation and the enactment of equitable distribution statutes in most states. The act adopts a partnership concept of marriage, based on the principle of shared ownership of property during the marriage. Its provisions draw on the community property model. Wisconsin is the only state that has ever enacted the UMPA, and did so just a year after it was first promulgated.

Rights to management and control of property are title-based under the UMPA. Each spouse may manage and control that spouse's separate property, and, in most cases, marital property, as well, if it is titled only in that spouse's name. If the property is titled in both spouses, the spouses must act together in management and control of the jointly titled property. If title is held alternatively, as in a bank account titled "Husband or Wife," either spouse may act alone to manage and control the property. Each spouse is under an obligation of good faith with respect to the other spouse in matters involving property.

CHECKPOINTS

- The common law rule that the husband was responsible for the wife's necessaries has been abolished in some states and expanded to both spouses in others. This doctrine, if applicable, not only allows one spouse to hold the other spouse responsible for necessaries, but also allows third parties who provide necessaries to one spouse or their minor children to collect the reasonable value of those necessaries from the other spouse.
- Each spouse has the right to manage and control his or her own separate property. The right to manage and control marital property in common law states is governed by title ownership. In community property states, community property is subject to joint management and control in some states and equal, independent control in others. Parties are also free to contract regarding these issues in community property states.

- The common law doctrine of interspousal immunity prevented recovery for tort claims between spouses, but most states have now abolished the doctrine, and other states have created exceptions for certain torts.
- If the doctrine of interspousal immunity has been abolished, one spouse may pursue a tort claim against the other spouse, either in the divorce action or in a separate proceeding.
- An uninjured spouse may claim damages for loss of consortium, in a personal injury or wrongful death action against a third party, for injuries to the other spouse that prevent the injured spouse from providing consortium to the uninsured spouse.
- Heartbalm statutes have been passed in most states, abolishing the heartbalm claims including alienation of affection, criminal conversation, seduction, and breach of promise to marry.
- Parties are generally free to assume any surname they choose, both during the marriage and at the time of divorce, if they comply with state requirements for name changes and are not motivated by a fraudulent intent, such as deception of creditors.
- The testimonial privilege has been abolished in some states. The privilege belongs to the witness spouse in most states that have retained the privilege.
- The confidential communications privilege generally belongs to both spouses and may be invoked by either. The communication must be confidential in nature and must take place during the time that the parties are validly married.

CHAPTER 5

Domestic Violence

ROADMAP

After reading this chapter, you should understand:

- The role of the order of protection in preventing domestic violence;
- The federal response to domestic violence;
- The remedies available to a victim of domestic violence; and
- How evidence of domestic violence affects other issues in divorce proceedings.

Historically, a husband was allowed and even expected to discipline both his wife and his children through corporeal punishment. The "rule of thumb" is based on the common law rule that permitted the husband to discipline his wife with a stick, as long as the stick's diameter was not larger than the diameter of the husband's thumb. Today, as a society, we have a better understanding of domestic violence and view it as a crime based on control through fear, intimidation and often violence, even to the point of death.

Prior to the 1980s, society was much more tolerant of domestic violence. It was largely considered inappropriate behavior, but not a crime in the legal sense. States did not aggressively prosecute cases of domestic violence either, generally allowing the victim to decide whether the crime would be prosecuted. Police were often reluctant to make an arrest, opting instead to remove the perpetrator from the home for a cooling off period. In the 1980s, several federal court cases imposed liability on municipalities for failing to respond to reports of domestic violence and for applying special arrest policies in domestic violence cases. States responded by increasing protection for victims of domestic violence.

A. Orders of Protection

Most states responded to the need to increase protection for victims of domestic violence by authorizing orders of protection. Orders of protection may also be called restraining orders, protective orders, or civil protective orders.

1. Types of Protective Orders

There are two primary types of protective orders—an *ex parte* order and a permanent order. As a general rule, the victim of domestic violence can obtain an *ex parte* order of protection upon a showing of immediate and present danger of abuse. Usually, a hearing must be held within a specified period of time following the issuance of an *ex parte* order, upon notice to the defendant. In some states, a hearing will be held only if the defendant requests one. If the defendant fails to appear at the hearing, doesn't request a hearing, or if the court finds adequate statutory grounds at a hearing, a permanent order of protection will be issued. The permanent protective order is effective for a specified period, usually a year or less. It can generally be renewed.

2. Scope of Protective Orders

Some states limit the protective order solely to the issue of domestic violence. Other states allow the protective order to address additional issues such as child support, visitation, and alimony.

The protective order will typically prohibit the respondent from committing or threatening to commit abuse against the petitioner or petitioner's minor children. It may also prohibit the respondent from telephoning, contacting, or otherwise communicating with the petitioner, directly or indirectly. Some states include prohibitions against stalking within the scope of the protective order. Frequently, the order of protection will give the petitioner exclusive possession of the residence, by evicting the respondent. Some state statutes provide for the respondent to be ordered to attend counseling or other programs that address violent behavior and substance abuse problems. Finally, the protective order may order payment of attorney fees and court costs.

3. Eligibility

An order of protection is generally available to any adult or minor who is found to be a victim, as defined by statute. The definition generally includes current or former spouses; parties who live together or have lived together; parties who are dating or have dated or who have or had a sexual relationship; parties related by blood or adoption; parties related or formerly related by marriage; or children of any person falling within the previously listed categories.

4. Enforcement of Protective Orders

Even though the order of protection is civil in nature, violation of the order of protection is a crime. Violations of protective orders are misdemeanors in most states, although many states impose mandatory jail time for a violation. State statutes generally provide for assessment of fines, as well. In addition, the court may hold the defendant in criminal or civil contempt. States generally provide that an arrest may or even must be made, for violation of a protective order, with or without a warrant.

B. Police Response

Some states have mandated a preferred response on the part of police officers to arrest the primary aggressor. Additionally, some states provide that arrest is not an appropriate response for anyone who is not, in the judgment of the police, the primary aggressor. Officers are generally given discretion in determining responsibility and deciding whether to arrest some, all, or none of the parties. The officer is generally required to offer to transport the victim to a place of safety, to assist the victim in obtaining an arrest warrant, to give the victim notice of the legal rights available, and to advise the victim of services available in the community.

C. Insurance Anti-Discrimination Statutes

Some insurance companies have denied coverage of claims by victims of domestic violence, taking the position that the injuries were not accidental, but were voluntarily incurred in cases where a pattern of abuse had developed and the victim of domestic violence remained in the residence with the perpetrator. Some insurance companies also refuse to insure victims of domestic violence, or attempt to charge higher premiums, because of the increased risk associated with providing health care coverage to victims of domestic violence. Most states have enacted statutes prohibiting insurance companies from denying health care coverage to victims of domestic violence, but many states have not addressed the same forms of discrimination in life and disability insurance policies. The federal government has enacted several laws that prohibit insurers from discriminating against domestic violence victims, the most recent of which is the Patient Protection and Affordable Care Act (PPACA) of 2010. 42 U.S.C. §§ 18116 et seq. *See also* 29 U.S.C. § 1182.

D. Federal Laws

1. Violence Against Women Act (VAWA)

In 1994, Congress passed the Violence Against Women Act (VAWA). The Act has been reauthorized four times since its original passage, with the latest reauthorization occurring in 2022. The original VAWA, was the first federal legislation acknowledging domestic violence and sexual assault as crimes and provided federal resources to encourage community-coordinated responses to combating violence against women. One of the Act's, arguably, most impactful provisions is the requirement that states give full faith and credit to valid orders of protection issued in sister states.

Each reauthorization has expanded initiatives and funding necessary to increase the federal response to this problem and to expand its application to LGBTQ+ groups, and others. One particular provision of VAWA provides for immigration relief to certain victims of domestic violence, and thus, given the political and policy considerations related thereto, VAWA is often the subject of much policy debate and may, in the future, be altered to conform to administrative policies on immigration.

2. The Violent Crime Control and Law Enforcement Act

VAWA was part of the Violent Crime Control and Law Enforcement Act. Provisions of the Violent Crime Control and Law Enforcement Act that attempt to address domestic violence concerns make the death penalty applicable for sexual abuse that results in death; gives victims a right to make a statement at federal sentencing hearings; urges states to offer similar rights; prohibits the sale or disposal of a firearm to someone subject to a protection order for stalking or abuse; prohibits the abuser from shipping, receiving, or processing a firearm; and requires that attendance at a first-time domestic violence offender rehabilitation program be made a condition of probation or supervised release for first-time offenders, if geographically available. Other "tough-on-crime" provisions within the Act have been criticized as causing an increase in disparate racial incarcerations and, overall, exponentially increasing the number of people who are either incarcerated or living with arrest records. *Sorichetti v. City of New York*, 482 N.E.2d 70 (N.Y. 1985).

E. Civil Remedies

A victim of domestic violence can sue the perpetrator in state court for the underlying tort claim. The victim does not, however, have a federal right of action against the state, under § 1983, for the state's failure to enforce the order of protection. *Town of Castle Rock, Colo. v. Gonzales*, 545 U.S. 748 (2005). In many states, though, in certain circumstances, law enforcement may be held liable in tort for failure to protect an individual, especially when there is a specific duty created by statute or due to a special relationship.

F. Effect of Domestic Violence in Divorce Actions

Under no-fault grounds for divorce, the wrongful conduct of either spouse is not relevant as grounds for divorce. Some states, however, do still recognize fault-based grounds for divorce. In those states, domestic violence does generally constitute grounds for divorce. The abusive conduct may also be considered by the court in determining alimony in those states where the court has discretion to consider fault. Finally, states increasingly are considering spousal abuse as a factor in determining custody and visitation rights.

G. Marital Rape Exception

Under common law, the husband could not be found guilty of rape of his wife. Three theories explained the exception. The first was that the wife's implied consent to sexual relations, contained in the marriage contract, could not be withdrawn. The second theory was that the husband and wife, in law, were considered one, and that one was the husband. Consequently, the husband could not be guilty of rape of himself. The third theory treated the wife as the husband's property and allowed the husband to treat his property as he wished.

During the 1980s, states began to eliminate the statutory marital rape exception from their criminal laws. At present, all fifty states have criminalized marital rape and sexual assault, although some still do not permit prosecution for marital rape under all circumstances.

CHECKPOINTS

- An order of protection is widely available to a victim of domestic violence. The order may also address additional issues, including spousal support, child support, custody, and visitation.
- Violation of the order of protection may be a crime in itself or the basis for a contempt petition.
- Victims of domestic violence may bring a civil action against the perpetrator, based on the underlying tort claim.
- VAWA requires states to give full faith and credit to valid orders of protection issued in sister states.
- The Violent Crime Control Act prohibits someone who is subject to a protection order for stalking or abuse from possessing a firearm.
- Domestic violence may be a factor in determining alimony, child custody, and visitation in some states. Domestic violence can also constitute grounds for a fault-based divorce.
- Most states have eliminated or restricted the marital rape exception, but a few states have expanded its application to some unmarried couples.

CHAPTER 6

Divorce

ROADMAP

After reading this chapter, you should understand:

- The history of divorce;
- The jurisdictional requirements for a divorce;
- The grounds and defenses to divorce; and
- The alternatives to divorce.

Historically, the church-controlled access to divorce, but later that power was transferred to the state, and exercised first through the legislature and later through the courts. In colonial times, divorce was not available through the court system. A divorce could be obtained only from the state legislature through private divorce laws. Later, private divorce laws were eliminated, and all divorces became judicially obtained by court decree, based on state laws setting forth grounds for divorce.

A. Access to the Court

In *Boddie v. Connecticut*, 401 U.S. 371 (1971), indigents successfully challenged Connecticut's refusal to allow them to file divorce complaints without paying court fees and costs for service of process. The Supreme Court recognized a due process right to access to the courts for dissolution of a marriage and found that an indigent party's interest in obtaining a divorce was sufficiently compelling to require the state to waive its filing fees and costs for service of process. Because courts were the exclusive means to obtaining a divorce, the Supreme Court held that indigents could not be denied an opportunity to be heard "absent a countervailing state interest of overriding significance." The state's interest in preventing frivolous litigation did not meet this test.

Courts must allow parties to file for divorce on a pauper's oath attesting to their inability to pay the filing fees and costs. Courts may make a determination of indigency, however, and may later assess costs in the case if either party is found to have sufficient assets at the conclusion of the proceeding.

B. Jurisdictional Issues

1. Subject Matter Jurisdiction

In order to grant a divorce, the court must have subject matter jurisdiction over the *res* or status of the marriage. *Williams v. North Carolina*, 317 U.S. 287 (1942) (*Williams I*) held that if at least one of the parties is domiciled in the state, that state has a sufficient basis for subject matter jurisdiction to adjudicate the status of the marriage, even if the other party is not subject to the court's jurisdiction. Domicile is different from residency. A person may have multiple residences, but only one domicile at any given time. A person is domiciled in the state where they are physically present (usually residing) with the intention of making it their permanent abode and with no present intent to live permanently elsewhere. In some states, special rules apply to members of the military, who are presumed to be domiciliaries of a state where they have been stationed for a specified period of time, usually three months to a year.

Before no-fault divorces were recognized, parties would sometimes seek a divorce in another state in order to avoid the divorce restrictions in their home state. Oftentimes, only one party would seek the out-of-state divorce, and the stay-at-home spouse would later attempt to challenge the foreign divorce decree in the home state. *Williams v. North Carolina*, 325 U.S. 226 (1945) (*Williams II*) held that in *ex parte* divorces, where only one party is before the court, that court's finding regarding domicile may be challenged when another state is asked to recognize that divorce decree. Divorces where one spouse moves temporarily to another state in order to obtain a divorce are called *migratory divorces*. With the relaxation of the grounds for divorce in all states, migratory divorces have diminished dramatically.

If both parties are before the court granting the divorce, however, domicile may not be challenged in a later proceeding in that court or in another state's court. In *Sherrer v. Sherrer*, 334 U.S. 343 (1948), the Supreme Court held that where both parties participate in the divorce proceeding and acknowledge domicile and jurisdiction, the finding of domicile may not be collaterally attacked.

Williams I held that domicile was sufficient for subject matter jurisdiction, but it did not hold that it was mandatory. Other courts have recognized alternative grounds for subject matter jurisdiction to dissolve the marriage, such as the commission within the state of the fault-based conduct which constitutes grounds for the divorce.

Because domicile is a sufficient basis for subject matter jurisdiction, it is possible for two states to claim jurisdiction to hear the divorce at the same time. Some courts follow the first to file rule, but others take the position that the final decree of divorce entered first in time is the valid decree because it dissolves the status of the marriage. Thus, the other court is deprived of jurisdiction because the *res* no longer exists.

2. Residency Requirements

Many states require that at least one of the parties reside in the state for some period of time prior to filing for divorce, requiring parties to have a meaningful connection to the state before seeking a divorce therein. The constitutionality of Iowa's durational residency requirement was upheld in *Sosna v. Iowa*, 419 U.S. 393 (1974). The state argued, in part, that the residency requirement furthered the state's interest in protecting its divorce decrees from collateral attack (based on the *Williams II* holding). The plaintiff relied on *Boddie* for the constitutional right of access to the court for purposes of obtaining a divorce. The court distinguished *Boddie* because the durational residency requirement merely delayed, rather than totally denied, access to the court and that the nonresident antidiscrimination clause of the Privileges and Immunities Clause was not violated.

Some states require the plaintiff to meet the residency requirement while other states allow the residency requirement to be met by either party. The residency requirement ranges from several months to several years. The requirement is often waived if either of the parties is a domiciliary. In some states, special rules apply to members of the military, who are presumed to be residents of a state where they have been stationed for a specified period of time, usually three months to a year.

It is important, however, to remember that the requirement of domicile and the residency requirement are different requirements. A party might meet a six-month residency requirement if her work causes her to be temporarily living in state X for 6 months, but she will not be able to file for divorce in state X because she is not a domiciliary of state X.

3. Bifurcated Proceedings

The court may have subject matter jurisdiction to grant the divorce, but it may not have jurisdiction to grant the other types of relief sought by the parties, such as division of marital property, spousal support, child custody, visitation and child support. Jurisdictional issues for each of these areas will be discussed in the chapter covering each respective topic, but these topics are mentioned here to point out there are many jurisdictional issues that an attorney must consider when deciding whether to take a case. If a state has jurisdiction to adjudicate some, but not all of the issues incident to the divorce, the proceeding may be bifurcated and resolved in more than one proceeding, sometimes involving more than one state. This type of divorce is also called a divisible divorce. It is usually in the client's best interests, however, to litigate all of the issues in one proceeding, if possible.

4. Full Faith and Credit

Under the Full Faith and Credit Clause of the Constitution, states must recognize valid divorce decrees from sister states. This requirement is subject to the independent domicile determination recognized in *Williams II* and discussed above. As discussed in Chapter 2, DOMA previously allowed states to refuse to grant or to recognize divorces arising out of same-sex marriages. The Respect for Marriage Act (RFMA) largely nullified DOMA.

5. Comity

The Full Faith and Credit Provision applies only to sister states, so it does not require states to recognize divorce decrees from foreign countries. States do so, if at all, under the doctrine of comity, which is subject to a public policy exception. States will generally recognize a valid and final divorce decree from a foreign country, under the doctrine of comity, as long as one of the parties was domiciled there and the decree does not violate the strong public policy of the forum state (the state that is being asked to recognize the foreign decree). Courts have found, however, that comity is not a rule of law, but rather an exercise of respect that is discretionary. *In re Marriage of Butler*, 2024 Wash. App. LEXIS 1358 (July 9, 2024).

C. Venue

The proper venue for a divorce is generally the county in which the defendant resides or the county where the parties lived within the marital state. In cases where the defendant is a nonresident, venue may also lie in the county where the plaintiff resides. Because venue is an objection, which if made at trial can be corrected, many states take the position that the issue of improper venue is waived on appeal if it is not raised at trial. Parties can agree to waive venue in order to move the trial to a mutually convenient location but generally can do so only with the consent of the court that will hear the case.

D. Fault Grounds

Historically, divorce was a remedy that was available only to the innocent spouse who could prove sufficient fault-based conduct of the other spouse to justify the granting of the divorce. In this country, grounds for divorce varied greatly from colony to colony and later from state to state. One or more grounds for divorce generally had to be proved, and in most cases, had to be corroborated by one or more witnesses. Typical grounds for divorce are included in the following list, along with a general definition of each. One should keep in mind, however, that divorce grounds and their definitions vary from state to state. Most professors will direct you to read the statute of a particular state.

Cruel and Inhuman Treatment

This ground, also known as *Cruelty*, and more recently euphemistically titled *Inappropriate Marital Conduct* is the most broadly defined, catchall ground. It has been defined strictly, to include "conduct that renders cohabitation dangerous or unendurable" and more leniently, to include "any series of misconduct which makes cohabitation unacceptable." This ground is often pled as an alternative to irreconcilable differences (a no-fault ground), and if all other fault-based grounds fail, the Court will most commonly find this ground in order to grant the divorce.

Adultery

Adultery is usually defined as voluntary sexual intercourse with someone other than one's spouse and cannot be proven by mere suspicion. It can, however, be proven by circumstantial evidence demonstrating both an *inclination* and a *disposition* to commit adultery, along with the *opportunity* to do so. Some states require that the alleged sexual partner been named in the pleadings, along with specific allegations as to the time and place that the adulterous conduct took place. Post-separation, even post-divorce filing, sexual relations with a non-spouse are considered adultery in many states, even where the divorcing spouses attempt to contract otherwise.

Impotency

The ground of impotency usually requires proof that one of the parties was, at the time of the marriage, and still is, naturally impotent and incapable of procreation. Periods of temporary impotence usually do not qualify, nor does impotency that is curable, unless the affected partner refuses to accept treatment. Sterility, alone, is generally not sufficient. Instead, the impotent spouse generally must be shown to be unable to engage in sexual relations.

Bigamy

Bigamy requires proof that a party has knowingly entered into a second marriage, in violation of a previously existing valid marriage. As a legal technicality, since most states assume a bigamous marriage is void and thus nonexistent, a divorce to dissolve a marriage that never was, is impossible.

Desertion

Desertion is usually defined as the willful or malicious absence of either party without a reasonable cause for a specified period of time—usually one to two years. Some states also recognize constructive desertion, where the mistreatment by one spouse forces the mistreated spouse to leave the home or to separate within the home and stay away from the other spouse.

Abandonment

Abandonment differs from desertion in that it usually requires proof of willful nonsupport. Abandonment sometimes also includes a situation where the mistreated spouse is forced to leave the marital home without just cause and without support.

Conviction of a Crime

Proof that a spouse has been convicted of certain crimes, such as a felony or an infamous crime constitutes a ground for divorce in some states.

Alcohol and Drug Abuse

Alcohol and/or drug abuse generally have to be shown to be habitual, with the habit having developed after marriage. If the complaining spouse knowingly marries someone who is addicted to alcohol or drugs, this ground is generally not available, but the conduct flowing from the alcohol or drug abuse will generally give rise to other grounds, such as cruelty. Some states require the complaining spouse to demonstrate failed attempts to get the addicted spouse to pursue treatment.

Indignities

This ground usually requires proof that the offending spouse has offered such indignities to the injured spouse as to render that spouses condition intolerable, and thereby forcing the injured spouse to withdraw from the marital home or relationship, or both. Examples include false accusations of adultery or persistent verbal abuse.

Pregnancy by Another Man

This ground is generally available to the husband where the wife is pregnant by another man at the time of marriage and the husband enters into the marriage without this knowledge. The husband may be estopped to assert this ground in cases where he also had sexual relations with the wife, prior to the marriage. This estoppel is most likely to be applied when the proof demonstrates that, prior to such premarital sexual relations with the husband, the wife was chaste. This ground, like other grounds, however, may be applicable to same-sex couples.

Legal Separation

Proof that the parties have been legally separated for a period of time, usually one or two years, constitutes grounds for divorce in some states. In some states, only the party obtaining the legal separation can use it as a basis for obtaining a divorce. Other states take the position that, after a certain period of time, it is clear that the marriage is over, and either party should be able to obtain a divorce. A party may be statutorily required to establish fault grounds in order to obtain a legal separation, especially where the other spouse objects.

E. Defenses

Fault-based grounds for divorce developed at common law, along with common law defenses. As some states moved to statutory grounds for divorce, they also enacted statutory defenses, thereafter, eliminating both common law grounds and common law defenses which were not codified. Other states retained some or all of the common law defenses. Again, it is important to review the statutory and common law of the relevant jurisdiction. Under a fault-based divorce regime, the party seeking the divorce must prove that the other party has engaged in fault-based conduct for which no defense is shown. If a defense is established, a divorce may not be granted on that particular ground, although the plaintiff may be able to establish another ground for which there is no defense. The most common defenses will be reviewed below.

Connivance

Connivance requires proof of one's spouse's corrupt consent for the other spouse to engage in wrongful conduct. This defense usually applies only to the wrongful conduct of adultery or other sexual misconduct. The consent may be express or implied.

Condonation

Condonation implies forgiveness, is generally limited to adultery, and requires proof that the injured spouse has voluntarily entered into sexual relations with the offending spouse after learning about the adultery. Some states, however, extend the defense of condonation to other grounds, including desertion, cruelty, and habitual drunkenness. The doctrine of laches may also apply where the party has unreasonably delayed filing for divorce with knowledge of the grounds for divorce.

Recrimination

Recrimination requires proof that the complaining party also engaged in the same fault-based conduct. This defense is usually limited to adultery.

Justifiable Cause

Where the wrongful conduct relied upon is cruelty or abandonment, for instance, it may be a defense for the offending spouse to prove that there was a justifiable cause for the wrongful conduct.

Insanity

Insanity is usually a common law defense that excuses the offending spouse's conduct when it is shown to be the result of insanity.

F. No-Fault Divorce

Societal changes are reflected in the changes in family law. Nowhere is this phenomenon more apparent than in the adoption of no-fault grounds for divorce. The 1960s were a time of great social changes—birth control pills were available; more women were working outside the home; and divorce carried less of a stigma—to name a few. Beginning in California, in the 1960s, the no-fault movement swept the country, with all states eventually enacting some form of no-fault divorce. No-fault is also called *irreconcilable differences* or *irretrievable breakdown* in some states. Some states enacted no-fault as the only ground, eliminating fault grounds, while other states simply added a no-fault ground to the list of fault grounds. Some states chose to add a specified period of separation as a ground, without the requirement of showing fault. Still other states enacted a modified no-fault ground, usually requiring the consent of both parties, evidenced by a separation agreement. The parties are generally required to show that they have lived *separate and apart* for a specified period, usually six months to three years. Living separate and apart usually means living in separate residences and not having sexual relations. The goal was to eliminate some of the acrimony and collusion generated by the requirement of proving fault. Under the fault system, the nastier the conduct, the better the outcome for the victim, in terms of financial issues as well as parenting decisions. On the other hand, parties who were not at war but simply wanted to divorce often had to collude to prove fault grounds, threatening to make a sham of the court process. Although the goal was laudable, the effect of no-fault was a significant increase in the number of divorces.

G. Alternatives to Divorce

When an attorney consults with a divorce client, the attorney should include a discussion of the various alternatives to divorce, in order to ensure that the client's needs are met. These alternatives include annulment, legal separation and separate maintenance.

1. Annulment

A divorce decree dissolves a marriage, but an annulment voids the marriage, as though it never existed. Parties may seek either a divorce or an annulment for both void and voidable marriages (which are discussed in the chapter on Marriage and Marriage Regulations). Void marriages, however, are *void ab initio*, thus, the annulment by the court just confirms that fact. It may be in a client's interest to obtain an annulment, however, when the facts are contested that give rise to the claim that the marriage is void. The voidable marriage, on the other hand, is deemed valid, unless one of the parties obtains a divorce or annulment. An annulment may be sought by a party for religious reasons, as in the case of a Catholic client who wants to remarry in the church.

2. Legal Separation

A party who has grounds for divorce may seek a legal separation (formerly known as a *divorce from bed and board*) instead. Some states allow the court to grant a legal separation without proof of grounds, if neither party objects. Historically, a legal separation was the injured spouse's ultimate revenge because the legal separation prevented the offending spouse from remarrying, but allowed the injured, and often financially dependent, spouse to remain married, but cease marital sexual relations. Many legislatures have found the judicially enforced celibacy without limitation to be unreasonable and have enacted provisions allowing either party to seek a divorce after a period of legal separation, usually one or two years.

When the parties are legally separated, they are still married. If one spouse dies, the other is the surviving spouse for estate purposes. The parties are not free to engage in sexual relations with other parties, yet they are relieved from any obligation to have marital sexual relations. The other obligations of marriage, such as support, remain intact. Parties often include in the court-endorsed Separation Agreement a distribution of marital assets and a proclamation that assets acquired during separation do not become marital assets.

3. Separate Maintenance

At common law, separate maintenance was a remedy for the dependent spouse who was abandoned and needed support. When a spouse files for separate maintenance, it affirms the marriage and simply asks for a support order. Presumably, the offending spouse is free to return to the marriage and marital bed at will. This remedy may be helpful for older clients who do not wish to remarry, but who need support and also need to remain married in order to continue to receive medical benefits from the other spouse's health care policy. Legal separation used to protect health care coverage, but, increasingly, policies are being drafted to exclude legally separated spouses from coverage.

H. Remedies Available

In fault-based divorces, the court may grant the divorce only to the innocent party who proves grounds. If both parties prove grounds, many states permit the court to grant the divorce to the party less at fault or simply to declare the parties divorced. In no-fault divorces, the court usually awards the divorce to the plaintiff or declares the parties to be divorced. Being awarded the divorce may be important for personal or social reasons, but it can also have financial consequences. Some states allow costs and fees to be awarded only to the *prevailing* party.

After the court grants the divorce, annulment, legal separation or separate maintenance, it will usually address a number of other issues, as well. Among the remedies that the parties may request are the following: division of marital or community property, spousal support, child support, allocation of parenting responsibilities, restoration of one's maiden name and an award of costs and attorney fees. These issues will be discussed more fully in subsequent chapters.

I. Presumption of Divorce

The presumption in favor of the validity of the latest marriage is one of the strongest presumptions in the law. If one of the parties was married prior to the current marriage whose validity is before the court, there is a rebuttable presumption that the current marriage is valid, without proof of death or divorce, etc. regarding the first marriage. The law presumes that the parties do the right thing and end the prior marriage before entering into a subsequent marriage.

Some states also regard a marriage as dissolved where one spouse is missing for a period of time, usually five to seven years, as long as the missing spouse is not known to be living. This type of statute, often referred to as an "Enoch Arden" law, allows the remaining spouse to remarry without being charged with bigamy, in the event that the first spouse reappears.

J. Right to Counsel

Courts have not recognized a right to counsel in divorce cases. Oftentimes, only one party will be represented in a divorce. In some cases, both parties are *pro se*. Increasingly, courts are developing forms to help *pro se* litigants navigate the divorce process. An attorney cannot ethically represent both clients in a contested divorce because of the inherent conflict of interests. Some states allow an attorney to represent both parties, more as a scrivener, writing down the agreement that they have made and presenting it to the court, but the attorney is usually required to make sure (1) that the parties give signed informed consents and (2) that there are no conflicts present between the parties. If conflicts arise, the attorney will have to withdraw from the case.

K. Religious Divorces

Court ordered divorces and annulments are civil in nature. Some parties, for religious reasons, also want to obtain a religious divorce or annulment, consistent with the tenets of their religion. These religious issues should be discussed with the client.

In the Jewish faith, for instance, a rabbinical divorce can be obtained only after the husband gives a *get* to the wife. She cannot remarry unless the husband gives her a *get* (a document signed by the rabbi to grant a divorce). This requirement does not apply, however, to members of the reform faith. An attorney representing the wife should ascertain whether she wants to get a *get* from her husband. Some courts will order the husband to comply and hold him in contempt for failure to do so.

In the Catholic faith, remarriage is not allowed, so the existing marriage must be annulled by the church before the parties may marry another in the church. The religious annulment is granted, if at all, by the church and is separate altogether from the civil annulment.

L. Soldiers' and Sailors' Civil Relief Act

The Soldiers' and Sailors' Civil Relief Act requires the courts to stay any divorce or related family matter for military personnel who are prevented from being present and participating in the proceedings due to their military service.

M. Orders of Reconciliation

While the divorce is pending, the parties may decide that they want to try to reconcile. Society has an interest in preserving marriages where possible. In order to support the parties' attempt to reconcile, many courts provide for an order of conciliation. This order essentially puts the divorce on hold and allows the parties to resume the marital relationship without affecting the divorce litigation in any way. If the reconciliation is successful, the divorce can be dismissed. If not, the divorce proceedings may be resumed.

Reconciliations are usually governed by a court-approved agreement that sets forth the duration of the reconciliation and other parameters as agreed upon. Reconciliation agreements have been deemed to be binding contracts for which the reconciliation of the parties is considered sufficient consideration. Most litigation surrounding reconciliations arises from any additional consideration promised, such as alimony or an unequal distribution of assets. If the agreement is silent on its term, the court is left to construe a reasonable period of time in order to deem the agreement "satisfied," with consideration paid so that the additional monies or assets promised do not have to be paid by either spouse. In that circumstance, if the court deems the consideration to have been paid, the contract is fulfilled, and the parties are still free to divorce with all remedies available to them.

N. Uniform Laws

1. Uniform Marriage and Divorce Act (UMDA)

The Uniform Marriage and Divorce Act (UMDA), promulgated in 1970 by the National Conference of Commissioners on Uniform State Laws (NCCUSL), has been enacted, at least in part, by a number of states. The UMDA adopts a no-fault approach to divorce, requiring courts to enter a decree of dissolution upon a finding that the marriage is irretrievably broken and that the parties have lived separately for more than 180 days preceding the commencement of the divorce proceeding. If one of the parties denies, under oath, that the marriage is irretrievably broken, the court must consider all relevant factors and make a finding as to whether the marriage is irretrievably broken. Alternatively, the court may continue the matter; suggest that the parties seek counseling; and, at the request of either party or on its own motion, order a conciliation conference.

If either party requests a decree of legal separation rather than a decree of dissolution, the court must grant the decree of legal separation, unless the other party objects. The act dispenses with all fault grounds for divorce and expressly abolishes previously existing defenses to divorce and legal separation, including, but not limited to, condonation, connivance, collusion, recrimination, insanity, and laches.

2. Uniform Divorce Recognition Act (UDRA)

The Uniform Divorce Recognition Act (UDRA), promulgated in 1947, is a divorce evasion statute. It provides that a divorce, obtained in another jurisdiction, will not be recognized in the forum state if both parties to the marriage were domiciled in the forum state at the time the divorce proceeding was commenced. The act also provides that prima facie evidence of domicile may be found upon proof that a party seeking a divorce in another jurisdiction:

a. Was domiciled in the forum state within 12 months prior to the commencement of the divorce proceeding and resumed residence in the forum state within 18 months after the date of departure; or
b. Maintained a place of residence within the forum state at all times after his departure from the forum state and until his return.

CHECKPOINTS

- Domicile is a sufficient basis for subject matter jurisdiction to grant a divorce.
- A valid final decree of divorce from a sister state is entitled to full faith and credit, but the forum court may make its own determination of domicile if the foreign decree was obtained *ex parte*.
- Domicile requirements and residency requirements are separate determinations. Each must be satisfied.
- Under a fault-based regime, the plaintiff must prove the existence of fault-based grounds in order to be entitled to a divorce. If the defendant establishes a defense to the asserted ground, that ground is no longer a sufficient basis for granting a divorce to the plaintiff. The plaintiff must prove another ground.

- If a marriage is annulled, the marriage is treated as though it never existed.
- If the parties are legally separated, they are still married, but do not have to co-habit or have sexual relations.
- An order for separate maintenance generally affirms the marriage and orders support for the dependent plaintiff spouse.

CHAPTER 7

Jurisdiction to Divide Property and Order Support

ROADMAP

After reading this chapter, you should understand:

- The requirements for jurisdiction to address the financial aspects of divorce;
- The different ways of acquiring personal jurisdiction over the defendant;
- The special provisions applicable to military personnel; and
- The jurisdiction provisions related to interstate support orders.

A. Jurisdiction to Divide Property

Only the state in which real property is located has *in rem* jurisdiction to determine ownership of that property. The state does not have to have personal jurisdiction over the defendant, nor does the defendant have to have other contacts with the state.

Even if the real property is not located in a state, if that state has personal jurisdiction over the parties, it can order the parties to convey title to the property located in another state. That order can be enforced through the court's contempt powers in the issuing state and is also recognized by the state where the property is located in a number of states.

B. Jurisdiction to Order Support

The Due Process Clause of the Fourteenth Amendment limits a state court's jurisdiction to enter judgments affecting the rights or interests of nonresident defendants. *Shaffer v. Heitner*, 433 U.S. 186, 198–200 (1977). The court must have personal jurisdiction over the defendant in order to issue an order that is binding on that party. Personal jurisdiction over the defendant is required whether the court is ordering the defendant obligor to pay support or ruling that the defendant recipient is not entitled to support. Even if the court has jurisdiction to grant a divorce, based on one of the parties being domiciled in the state, that state may not extinguish a party's right to support absent personal jurisdiction over the party. *Vanderbilt v. Vanderbilt*, 354 U.S. 416, 418–19 (1957). Nor may the court modify or terminate a support order entered in another state, without personal jurisdiction over the defendant. *Estin v. Estin*, 334 U.S. 541, 549 (1948). In such cases, the divorce is divisible, with one state granting the divorce and the other state adjudicating support or other financial issues. *Id.* Likewise, if the plaintiff spouse seeks a divorce and support in a state that does not have personal jurisdiction over the obligor defendant, the plaintiff will be limited to obtaining a divorce in that state and will have to seek support in a state that can exercise personal jurisdiction over the defendant spouse. Alternatively, the recipient spouse may initiate a proceeding *quasi in rem* by attaching or sequestering any property owned by the obligor spouse that is located within the jurisdiction.

1. Personal Service

One way to obtain personal jurisdiction over the defendant is through personal service within the state. If the defendant is personally served within the state, no additional contacts with the state need be shown. *Burnham v. Superior Court*, 495 U.S. 604 (1990). This type of service is referred to as "tag jurisdiction" or "transient jurisdiction."

2. Long-Arm Service

Personal jurisdiction over the defendant can also be obtained through substituted service under the state's long-arm statute. In order to be enforceable, the state must satisfy the minimum contacts requirements of *International Shoe Co. v. Washington*, 326 U.S. 310, 316 (1945) (sufficient minimum contacts with the forum state such that the maintenance of the suit does not offend traditional notions of fair play and substantial justice). Sufficient minimum contacts were found to be lacking in *Kulko v. Superior Court*, 416 U.S. 84 (1978), where the court based the long-arm jurisdiction on the fact that the defendant father permitted his child to move to California to live with the mother and purchased the child's plane ticket. The *Kulko* case was distinguished in *In re Parentage of W.J.B.*, because the parent did more than acquiesce to the child living in the state. 68 N.E.3d 977 (Ill. App. 2016).

3. *Quasi in Rem* Jurisdiction

A support proceeding may be initiated in a state without personal jurisdiction over the defendant if the defendant owns property located within the state. The recipient spouse may initiate a proceeding *quasi in rem* by attaching or sequestering any real or personal property owned by the obligor spouse that is located within the jurisdiction. Any judgment will be limited, however, to the property attached. The Supreme Court ruled that such judgments were entitled to full faith and credit in *Harris v. Balk*, 198 U.S. 215 (1905). *Harris* was overruled in *Shaffer v. Heitner*, 433 U.S. 186 (1977), where the Supreme Court held that the mere presence of defendant's property within the state, absent other contacts, would not be sufficient to confer jurisdiction to enter a judgment against the defendant, not even a judgment limited to the property attached. The opinion goes on to state, however, that when claims to the property attached are the source of the underlying controversy between the parties, it would be "unusual" for the state where the property is located not to have jurisdiction. In such cases, the defendant's claim to the property located in the state would normally indicate that he expected to benefit from the state's protection of his interests. Presumably those facts would satisfy the minimum contacts requirement.

The husband relied on the reasoning of *Shaffer* to seek a division of marital property in Georgia. The dissent in *Abernathy v. Abernathy*, 482 S.E.2d 265 (Ga. 1997), argued that minimum contacts were not met when the couple had never lived in Georgia and the husband filed for divorce there, seeking division of the real and personal property that he had acquired in or brought to Georgia. The majority relied on *Shaffer* to find *quasi in rem* jurisdiction, but the dissent argued that because the wife never lived in Georgia and did not participate in her husband's decision to acquire property in Georgia, forcing her to litigate in whatever state her husband happens to relocate violates the traditional notions of fair play and substantial justice required under *International Shoe*.

C. Interstate Support Jurisdiction

1. Uniform Interstate Family Support Act (UIFSA)

The Uniform Interstate Family Support Act (UIFSA) was promulgated in 1992 and amended in 1996, 2001 and 2008, and by 2016, adopted by all states. The Act requires personal jurisdiction over the defendant obligor in order to enter, enforce, or modify a support order. Personal jurisdiction can be obtained through personal service within the state or through substituted service under the state's long-arm statute. UIFSA provides that a court may exercise long-arm jurisdiction in the following circumstances:

1. The defendant resided with the child in this state;
2. The defendant resided in this state and provided prenatal expenses or support for the child;
3. The child resides in this state as a result of the acts or directives of the defendant;
4. The defendant engaged in sexual intercourse in this State and the child may have been conceived by that act of intercourse;
5. The defendant asserted parentage in this state's putative father registry; or
6. There is any other basis consistent with the constitutions of this state and the U.S. for the exercise of personal jurisdiction.

The Act specifies that jurisdiction to modify a previously entered support order differs from initial jurisdiction. Continuing enforcement jurisdiction requirements are set forth in the Act and were expanded in the 2008 amendment to ensure parties' ability to enforce support orders against defendants who might relocate out of the issuing state or even to a foreign country, in compliance with the 2000 Hague Convention.

2. Full Faith and Credit for Child Support Orders Act of 1994 (FFCCSOA)

The Full Faith and Credit for Child Support Orders Act of 1994 (FFCCSOA), amended in 2014, requires states to give full faith and credit to child support orders of sister states, provided that the issuing state had personal jurisdiction over the defendant. States are also prohibited from modifying child support orders from other states with continuing exclusive jurisdiction. The provisions of FFCCSOA are consistent with the provisions of UIFSA and compliant with the 2000 Hague Convention.

D. Continuing Jurisdiction

Many states provide, by statute or case law, for continuing jurisdiction over the parties for purposes of modifying support orders. Continuing jurisdiction applies even when the party moves from the state, provided that the court originally had personal jurisdiction over the party.

E. Uniformed Services Former Spouses Protection Act (USFSPA)

The Uniformed Services Former Spouses Protection Act (USFSPA) applies to military pensions. USFSPA allows some former spouses of military members to receive a share of the member's retirement pay, military medical benefits, commissary and exchange benefits, as determined by a state court within a divorce decree. The Act was supplemented by the 2017 National Defense Authorization Act (NDAA). Specifically, the NDAA amended the USFSPA to limit the amount of "disposable pay" that is eligible for division in a divorce proceeding. The USFSPA provides that a court may exercise jurisdiction over a military pension only when:

1. The forum state is the domicile of the service person; or
2. The service person consents to the exercise of jurisdiction; or
3. The service person resides in the forum state for reasons other than military assignment to that state.

CHECKPOINTS

- Only the state where the real property is located has *in rem* jurisdiction to determine ownership of that property.

- If the court has personal jurisdiction over the parties, it can order them to transfer title to property located in another state and enforce its order through the court's contempt powers.
- The court must have personal jurisdiction over the defendant in order to issue an order to pay child or spousal support.
- Personal jurisdiction over the defendant may be obtained through personal service within the state or through long-arm service.
- In order for long-arm service to be constitutional, it must meet the minimum contacts test of *International Shoe* (sufficient minimum contacts with the forum state such that the maintenance of the suit does not offend traditional notions of fair play and substantial justice).
- A support proceeding may be initiated by attaching the property of the obligor spouse that is located within the state. The judgment will be limited, however, to the property attached.
- Once the court has jurisdiction over the parties to determine support issues, the court usually has continuing jurisdiction for purposes of modification.

CHAPTER 8

Property Division

ROADMAP

After reading this chapter, you should understand:

- The basic differences between community property jurisdictions and common law jurisdictions;
- The three steps that courts follow in order to divide marital property;
- The difference between separate and marital property; and
- The doctrines of tracing, commingling, and transmutation.

The first step to property division is classifying property of the married parties as either marital or separate property—the latter, of course, is not subject to division by the court in a divorce proceeding. Sounds simple enough, but classification is often the subject of debate. Historically, states followed two very different approaches in dividing marital property and classifying property as marital or separate. Most states followed the common law, which divided property according to title ownership. Property jointly titled would be subject to division as marital property, and property titled in only one spouse's name would be deemed separate and allocated to that spouse, not subject to any equitable or statutory division. Nine states, however, known as community property states, viewed all property acquired through marital labor, title notwithstanding, as belonging to the marital community, to be shared by the spouses at the time of divorce. These states effectively treat the marriage as a partnership resulting in a division of all assets acquired by the "partners" during the term of the "partnership."

In those marriages where most of the property was titled in the name of the monied spouse (breadwinner), the dependent spouse fared much better in the community property states. The dependent spouse in a common law state who was not named on the title to property, even property that was acquired during the marriage with marital labor, had no claim to any share of that property upon divorce, unless the dependent spouse could establish a constructive trust. Today, however, the two systems are more similar, at least in regard to property division at the time of divorce, as will be explained below. The community property states are Arizona, California, Idaho, Louisiana, Nevada, New Mexico, Texas, Washington, and Wisconsin.

A. The Common Law System

In the common law states, the monied spouse usually held the title to most of the marital assets and was awarded those assets at the time of divorce. The title doctrine followed by the common law states resulted in great inequities, eventually leading all of the common law states to adopt the doctrine of "equitable distribution." Equitable distribution allows the court to divide the marital property equitably, without regard to title, taking into account several statutory factors. In some states, the property is divided equally, but again it is divided without regard to title ownership.

The adoption of equitable distribution by the common law states resulted in greater similarity between the common law states and the community property states regarding division of marital property, but not in other regards. The doctrine of equitable distribution applies only in the context of divorce or legal separation. The doctrine of equitable distribution does not give the untitled spouse any ownership interest in the other spouse's property during the marriage or upon death.

B. The Community Property System

Community property law also recognizes both separate and community (marital property). The major difference between this system and the common law system is that both spouses are deemed to have equal, undivided ownership interests in all of the property that is community property. Upon divorce, the property of the marital community is divided equally between the spouses, or in some cases, "equitably."

Currently, only three community property states require equal division of marital property (California, Louisiana, and New Mexico). The other six community property states (Arizona, Idaho, Nevada, Texas, Wisconsin, and Washington) allow the court some discretion to make an equitable distribution of the community property.

Community property law affects spousal property rights during the marriage, at divorce, and upon death. Recall, however, that the doctrine of equitable distribution (adopted in common law states and discussed above) is not applicable during the marriage or upon death.

C. Three-Step Analysis for Dividing Property at Divorce

Most courts follow a three-step approach in dividing marital property. The first step is to classify the property. The second step is to value the property, and the third step is to divide or distribute the property. Each of these steps will be considered below.

1. Classification

a. Community Property States

i. Dual Property States

Community property states will determine whether the property is communal or separate, without regard to title ownership. Community property is generally defined as any property acquired during the marriage or acquired through marital labor, although some exceptions are commonly recognized for gifts and inherited or bequeathed property. Property acquired prior to marriage is generally not considered community property but is the separate property of the title holder. The burden of proof is usually on the party claiming that property should be classified as separate.

ii. All Property States

One community property state, Washington, does not distinguish between community and separate property. The Washington statute allows the divorce court to make an equitable division of all property owned by the parties.

b. Common Law States

i. Dual Property States

Most common law states classify the parties' property as either separate or marital, allowing the court to make an equitable division of only the property that is classified as marital. A number of states recognize a presumption that property acquired during the marriage is marital, placing the burden on the party claiming otherwise. Property classified as separate is usually not subject to equitable distribution. Exceptions are generally recognized for gifts and inherited or bequeathed property, even when received during the marriage. Separate property also generally includes any property owned prior to the marriage, along with the income from and appreciation in value of that separate property.

ii. All Property States

There are a few *hotchpot* or *all property* states that divide all of the property owned by the parties at the time of divorce, without regard to title, but also without regard to whether the property was acquired during the marriage or owned by one spouse prior to the marriage.

c. Conflicts of Law Issues

Whose law should apply if a couple lives in a community property state throughout the marriage, but one spouse purchases property located in a common law state and takes title only in that spouse's name? The general rule is that the law of the matrimonial domicile at the time of acquisition determines both the ownership of the property acquired by either spouse, as well as its classification as separate or community/marital property.

d. Special Classification Issues

i. Tracing

Most states apply the doctrine of tracing when classifying marital property. Tracing allows the court to "trace" a piece of property back to its source, for purposes of classification. For instance, if one spouse inherited $10,000 during the marriage, which would ordinarily be classified as separate property, and later spent the $10,000 to purchase a motorcycle, under the doctrine of tracing, the motorcycle could be traced back to the inheritance and would also be classified as separate property.

ii. Commingling

Sometimes it is not possible to trace the separate property, especially if it has been commingled with marital property, such as depositing separate funds and marital funds into the same bank account. If marital property and separate property become inextricably commingled, such that the court cannot separate out the property claimed to be separate, all of the commingled property will be classified as marital property and subject to equitable distribution by the court.

iii. Transmutation

The classification of property can change based upon the intention of the parties or, in some cases, the application of statutory factors. The first type of transmutation can be called *intentional transmutation, transmutation by conduct* or just *transmutation*. Transmutation resulting from the application of statutory factors is called *statutory transmutation.*

Intentional transmutation can cause a change in the classification of property in three different ways: (1) from marital property to separate property; (2) from separate property to marital property; or (3) from the separate property of one spouse to the separate property of the other spouse. Intentional transmutation is based on the intention of the parties, but that intention may be presumed from their actions. For instance, if one spouse owns a home prior to the marriage, it will generally be classified as separate property, but if the spouse subsequently retitles that home in both parties' names, the home will be presumed to be marital property. Adding the other spouse's name on the title to property generally creates a strong presumption of gift, transmuting the property from separate to marital property. The presumption is rebuttable, however. If one spouse takes money from a joint savings account to purchase a birthday gift for the other spouse, the money would generally be classified as marital property, but the gift would probably be classified as the separate property of the birthday spouse, through the application of the doctrines of transmutation and tracing. If the money used in the previous example came from an inheritance received by the first spouse, the transmutation would reclassify the property from the separate property of the donor spouse to the separate property of the donee spouse. It should also be noted that a few states have not recognized transmutation by conduct, even when the title to the property is changed. Other states require written proof of intent to make a gift.

Statutory transmutation generally works only to transmute separate property into marital property. It depends on the presence of statutory factors rather than the intention of the parties. For example, a statute might provide that the income from and appreciation of separate property will be classified as marital property if the court finds that both spouses substantially contributed to the preservation and appreciation of the property. The contributions may be direct or indirect, including one spouse's contributions as homemaker, wage earner, parent or family financial manager. If one spouse owned undeveloped land at the time of the marriage, but then used marital funds to build a house on the property during the marriage, while the other spouse worked and contributed to the marriage in other ways, the court might find that the requirements for statutory transmutation are met, irrespective of the intention of the parties with regard to ownership rights in the property. In the example given, the doctrine of statutory transmutation applies only to the income from and appreciation in value of the separate property. The separate property itself would remain the separate property of the titled spouse and would not be subject to equitable distribution in dual property states.

iv. Income from and Appreciation of Separate Property

The classification of income received during the marriage from separate property varies greatly among states. Some states treat all of the income as the separate property of the titled spouse. Other states treat all of the income received during the marriage as marital property. In still other states, the income classification is dependent upon whether the income is derived from spousal effort. If the income is derived from the personal effort of a spouse, the property will be classified as marital. Passive income, on the other hand, will be classified as the separate property of the titled spouse.

There are also three different approaches to the classification of appreciation of separate property during marriage. Some states classify the appreciation as separate property, and permit reimbursement to the other spouse, if marital funds or the other spouse's labor contributed to the appreciation. Other states classify the appreciation as marital, based on the theory that everything received during the marriage, including the appreciation of separate property, is marital. The third approach distinguishes between active and passive appreciation. Active appreciation generated by marital funds or labor is classified as marital and passive appreciation, and that generated by market forces or other nonmarital factors is classified as separate property. This approach may result in apportioning the appreciation. Some states allocate the appreciation pro rata, based on the percentages of active and passive appreciation, while other states subject the appreciation to a right of reimbursement.

2. Valuation

States also differ as to when marital property should be valued but generally seek to have the property valued close to the time that the court will make its decision regarding distribution of the marital property. Some states have statutory provisions which designate the date or dates selected for the valuation of assets, while other states have given the courts discretion to select an appropriate date. The range of valuation dates include the following: the date of separation, date of commencement of the pending divorce action, date of trial, date of divorce, date of distribution, date within the court's discretion, and date as near as reasonably possible to the final divorce hearing.

3. Division

a. Community Property States

Three of the community property states, California, Louisiana, and New Mexico still require equal division of community property upon divorce. The remaining six community property states, however, have enacted equitable distribution statutes, which allow the court to make an equitable distribution of the community property, much like the common law states.

In eight of the community property states, the court will divide only the property that is classified as community (marital) property. Washington stands alone as the only community property state that has enacted an all-property approach, permitting the court to make an equitable division of all property, whether classified as separate property or community property.

b. Common Law States

Among the common law states, the doctrine of equitable distribution is sometimes interpreted to require an equal division of marital property, absent a reason for deviation. In other states, a rebuttable presumption of equal division is recognized. The third approach makes clear that the court is required to apply the statutory factors to divide the marital property equitably, though not necessarily equally. A number of states require the court to divide marital property before considering the issue of spousal support. The rationale is that the award of marital property should be considered in determining the spouse's need for spousal support. Frequently, one of the statutory factors in determining spousal support is the amount of marital property awarded to the dependent spouse.

Trial courts are usually required to consider certain statutory factors in making an equitable distribution of the marital property. The exceptions, of course, are the several common law states that mandate an equal division of the marital property. The statutory factors vary from state to state, but Tennessee's statute is illustrative.

In making an equitable distribution of marital property, the court shall consider all relevant factors including:

1. The duration of the marriage;
2. The age, physical and mental health, vocational skills, employability, earning capacity, estate, financial liabilities and financial needs of each of the parties;
3. The tangible or intangible contribution by one (1) party to the education, training or increased earning power of the other party;
4. The relative ability of each party for future acquisitions of capital assets and income;

5A. The contribution of each party to the acquisition, preservation, appreciation, depreciation or dissipation of the marital or separate property, including the contribution of a party to the marriage as homemaker, wage earner or parent, with the contribution of a party as homemaker or wage earner to be given the same weight if each party has fulfilled its role;

5B. For purposes of this subdivision (c)(5), dissipation of assets means wasteful expenditures which reduce the marital property available for equitable distributions and which are made for a purpose contrary to the marriage either before or after a complaint for divorce or legal separation has been filed;

6. The value of the separate property of each party;
7. The estate of each party at the time of the marriage;
8. The economic circumstances of each party at the time the division of property is to become effective;
9. The tax consequences to each party, costs associated with the reasonably foreseeable sale of the asset, and other reasonably foreseeable expenses associated with the asset;
10. In determining the value of an interest in a closely held business or similar asset, all relevant evidence, including valuation methods typically used with regard to such assets without regard to whether the sale of the asset is reasonably foreseeable. Depending on the characteristics of the asset, such considerations could include, but would not be limited to, a lack of marketability discount, a discount for lack of control, and a control premium, if any should be relevant and supported by the evidence;

11. The amount of social security benefits available to each spouse;
12. Such other factors as are necessary to consider the equities between the parties; and
13. The total amount of attorney fees and expenses paid by each party in connection with the proceedings; whether the attorney fees and expenses were paid from marital property, separate property, or funds borrowed by a party; and the reasonableness, under the factors set forth in Rule 1.5 of the Tennessee Rules of Professional Conduct, and necessity of the attorney fees and expenses paid by each party ....

TENN. CODE ANN. § 36-4-121(c) (2022).

In a separate statutory provision, the court is directed to make the equitable distribution of marital property without regard to *marital fault*. Most states do not consider marital fault when dividing marital property, although there are states that do allow marital fault to be considered and others that leave the matter to the court's discretion. *Dissipation of assets* or *economic misconduct* is generally a permissible consideration, even in those strict no-fault states that do not permit consideration of marital fault/misconduct as a factor in making an equitable distribution of marital property. For example, the court would not be permitted to consider one spouse's adulterous conduct as a factor in making an equitable distribution of the marital property, but it could consider proof of that spouse's dissipation of the parties' joint savings account to fund the adulterous conduct.

D. Special Property Issues

1. Pension and Retirement Benefits

a. Classification

Oftentimes, pensions represent one of the most valuable, if not the most valuable asset to be divided upon divorce. Pensions are considered marital property, in most states, to the extent that they were earned with marital labor. In some states both *vested* and *unvested* pensions are considered marital property, along with all other fringe benefit rights relating to employment that accrue during the marriage. In other states, only vested benefits are classified as marital property. Oftentimes, new employees are subject to a vesting period of several years, during which the pension benefits they accrue are contingent upon their remaining employed. Generally speaking, if they quit or are fired during the vesting period, they lose any pension benefits that might have accrued during employment. If they make it through the vesting period without quitting or being fired, the pension is said to vest and, thereafter, the employees have a right to those benefits earned during the vesting period, as well as any other pension benefits that accrue during employment, even if they later quit or are fired. The employee will not be able to collect those benefits, however, until the pension *matures*. Most plans do not mature until the employee reaches a certain age, work a specified number of years, or some combination of the two. If the employee dies before the pension matures, most plans make some provision for payment of a portion of the benefit to a beneficiary designated by the employee.

A spouse may have worked for the same company both prior to and during the marriage, in which case only part of the pension benefits will have been earned with marital labor. In dual property states, the court must determine which portion of the pension was earned with premarital labor (classified as separate property) and which part was earned with marital labor (classified as marital property). Many states use the *coverture fraction* to determine the portion of the pension that will be considered marital property. The coverture fraction is obtained by dividing the number of years of employment during the marriage by the total years of employment. For instance, if a spouse has a pension worth $120,000 at the time of divorce and that spouse worked for the same company for five years, prior to his ten-year marriage, the calculation would look like this: 10/15 = 2/3; 2/3 x $120,000 = $80,000. Two-thirds of the spouse's pension was earned with marital labor, so that portion will be classified as marital property. If the court divides the pension equally, each spouse will receive half of the $80,000. In addition, the nonemployee spouse will receive the portion of the pension that represents nonmarital labor as separate property, in this case $40,000. The employee spouse will receive a total of $80,000 ($40,000 as separate property and $40,000 as marital property). The nonemployee spouse will receive $40,000 as marital property.

Valuation issues can arise with certain pensions. Pensions generally fall into two categories—*defined contribution plans* and *defined benefit plans*. Defined contribution plans have individual accounts for each employee which contain contributions made by the employee, the employer, or both. Defined benefit plans do not have individual accounts for employees but rather have a pool of money from which benefits are drawn when a pension matures. Upon retirement, the amount of the payment is calculated using a formula which factors in variables such as age, years of service, and prior salary figures.

Pensions also present distribution problems in that the actual value of the pension, and, in the case of unvested pension, the certainty of the pension, may be unknown at the time of the divorce. In such cases, the court may award percentages to each spouse, (66.67 % and 33.33% in the example above) to be applied when the amount is determined, or contingent on the vesting of the pension, where it is unvested at the time of divorce. Another alternative is to reserve jurisdiction until the contingency is resolved. A third option is to reduce the amount to present value and make an award based on that estimated value.

Federal pensions raise an additional issue because of the Supremacy Clause. Current law allows state courts to classify as marital/community property certain annuities associated with railroad retirement benefits and military retirement benefits. Veterans' disability payments are not subject to distribution by the divorce court, pursuant to the USFSPA (see Jurisdiction to Divide Property and Order Support Chapter), although the income may be considered by the court for determination of the veteran's support obligation or need. This restriction applies even when the serviceperson waives military pension pay in order to receive increased veteran's disability payments.

b. QDRO's

It would certainly benefit the nonemployee spouse if the portion of the pension that is awarded as marital property could be paid directly to that spouse, rather than going through the employee spouse. A direct payment system would also preserve judicial resources by eliminating possible contempt hearing for nonpayment of pension disbursements. Most pension plans are governed by federal law (ERISA) which initially prohibited alienability of the pension benefits in order to protect employees' pensions from claims of creditors. No exception was included for domestic obligations. As a result of the 1984 Retirement Equity Act, 29 U.S.C. § 1001, ERISA was amended to allow direct payments by the plan administrator of the pension plan directly to the nonemployee spouse (alternate payee) if those payments are ordered by the court in a form that meets the statutory requirements. The order from the court is a domestic relations order. After it is checked by the plan administrator and found to meet the federal statutory requirements, it becomes a qualified domestic relations order (QDRO).

It is possible, in most cases, for the court to order that pension payments be paid directly to the nonemployee spouse through the use of Qualified Domestic Relations Orders (QDRO's). They are not applicable, however, (because ERISA is not applicable) to government and church plans. The federal government provides QDRO-like forms for some federal pension plans, such as those for the military, and some states have enacted statutory provisions that allow direct payments under state pension plans. In the absence of QDRO like legislation, the alienability restrictions of most state plans will prevent the court from ordering direct payments to the nonemployee spouse. If there are other assets of equal value, such as home equity or savings, they can be awarded to the nonemployee spouse in substitution for that spouse's share of the pension.

2. Professional Practices and Closely Held Businesses

If one of the spouses has a professional practice or an ownership interest in a closely held business, the court will have to determine whether the goodwill associated with that professional practice or closely held business is marital property, and if so, how it should be valued. Many states classify the goodwill as marital/community property, because the goodwill developed during the marriage has value that one spouse will continue to reap following the divorce. The other spouse, having contributed directly or indirectly to the development of that enterprise, should be entitled to claim a share of the value of that goodwill. Some states take the position that goodwill is not property at all, or that it is the separate property of the spouse upon whose reputation that goodwill is based. Finally, a few states take the position that the classification depends upon whether the goodwill has a market value. If the goodwill does have a market value, it will be classified as marital property. Alternatively, if the goodwill does not have a recognized market value, it will not be classified as marital property. For example, if it can be shown that a dentist is able to sell his sole practice to another dentist and is able to include a value for goodwill in the price, then the court will classify the goodwill as marital property. If goodwill is not typically valued, as in the case of the sale of a sole practitioner's legal practice, then the court will not classify the goodwill as marital property. The difference is that patients will often continue going to the same dental location after the practice is sold, so buyers are willing to pay a price for the goodwill of the practice. That situation is much less likely to occur in the case of an experienced sole practitioner who sells the office space to a new lawyer. The lawyer's goodwill is personal to the attorney and is based on that individual's reputation, which is not transferable.

If the court classifies the goodwill as marital property, it will generally have a great deal of discretion in determining how to value the intangible for purposes of making an equitable distribution of marital/community property.

States are in agreement that the net assets of any business associated with the professional practice or closely held business will be considered marital property, such as the accounts receivable, furniture, etc. in the medical or law office of the spouse.

3. Degrees, Licenses, and Career Enhancement

Most states do not consider professional credentials, such as a medical license or license to practice law, to be marital property, even if the credential is earned during the marriage, and even if the non-degree spouse contributes to the ability of the other spouse to earn the degree or license, etc. Even though the professional credential is not, itself, classified as marital/community property, the contributions of the non-degree spouse to the increased earning capacity of the other spouse may be considered by the court in making an equitable distribution of the other property, at least in those states that do not mandate an equal division of marital property.

4. Personal Injury and Workers' Compensation Awards

Personal injury, worker's compensation, and other similar awards generally include compensation for some or all of the following damages: past and future medical expenses, past and future pain and suffering, and past and future lost wages. Oftentimes, the awards are lump sum amounts and do not designate specific amounts for the various elements of damage.

Older decisions routinely classified the award as separate property of the injured spouse. More recent decisions have tended to apply one of two approaches, referred to as the mechanistic and analytic approaches. The mechanistic approach classifies all of the award as marital/community or separate by applying the definitions of marital/community and separate property. In all-property states, the award is classified as marital/community property. In dual property states, the award is classified as marital/community property if the spouse was injured during the marriage. If the injury occurred before or after the marriage, the award is classified as separate property of the injured spouse.

Under the analytic approach, the court classifies the award according to the asset that the award was intended to replace. For instance, those amounts that represent compensation for loss of marital assets, such as wages and medical expenses incurred during the marriage, will be classified as marital/community property. Separate property, on the other hand, includes pain and suffering awards, victim of crime compensation awards, future medical expenses, and future lost wages, or, in the case of injuries arising before marriage, wages lost, and medical expenses incurred prior to the marriage.

5. Insurance Policies and Proceeds

There are basically two types of life insurance policies, whole life policies and term life policies. Whole life policies can accrue a cash surrender value and can be used as collateral. Term life policies, on the other hand, only cover the risk of death during the term of the policy, and do not accrue a cash surrender value. Courts generally classify whole life policies as marital/community property, to the extent that premiums were paid with marital/community funds. Term life policies, however, having no cash surrender value are not considered marital property even though the premiums may have been paid with marital funds. Term life policies may be automatically renewable. In cases where both spouses have medical conditions which make them essentially uninsurable (except at very high premium rates) and where only one spouse has a renewal term life policy, an argument can be made that the other spouse should be awarded additional marital property to compensate for the increased costs of obtaining term life insurance equal to that of the insured spouse.

If one of the spouses is disabled at the time of the divorce and the disability policy premiums were paid with marital funds, many states will look at the asset that the insurance proceeds are intended to replace and classify the proceeds accordingly.

In order to ensure payment of property division and support obligations, the court may order the obligor spouse to obtain term life insurance, naming the other spouse as the beneficiary, and to maintain the insurance until the debt is paid.

6. Deferred Compensation

When one of the parties has expended marital labor but has not been compensated for that labor at the time of the divorce, the court may confront both allocation and valuation issues. The allocation issue arises when the party will also have to expend post-divorce labor in order to earn the compensation at issue. For instance, if one of the divorcing parties is a plaintiff's personal injury lawyer who has won a contingent fee case at trial, which is on appeal at the time of the divorce, the attorney's contingent fee, when collected, will represent both marital and post-divorce labor. Because the fee is contingent, it also presents valuation issues. The Court does not know at the time of the divorce, what the value of the contingent fee will be. It may be zero if the case is lost on appeal. In such cases, the court will hear expert testimony concerning the number of marital labor hours already expended on the case at the time of the divorce, as well as evidence concerning the expected number of post-divorce hours anticipated for the appeal. The court can then assign percentages of the recovery, if any, to each spouse, or the court can reserve jurisdiction to decide the matter, once the amount of the actual fee is determined.

E. Debt Allocation

Debts must also be classified and, to the extent that they are classified as marital, will be subject to equitable distribution by the court. Some states consider marital debt as only those debts that are traceable to the acquisition of marital property. In other states, all debt incurred during the marriage is classified as marital debt to be equitably distributed by the court. In making an equitable distribution of the marital debts, the court will consider four factors: (1) the debt's purpose; (2) which party incurred the debt; (3) which party benefited from the debt; and (4) which party is better able to pay the debt.

F. Legal Separation

If the parties are not ready to end the marriage permanently, but do not wish to continue living together, they may ask for a legal separation. Under an order of legal separation, the parties are still married, but live separately. The parties may later decide to reconcile, to get divorced, or to remain legally separated indefinitely. (See further discussion of legal separation in the chapter on Divorce.)

When the parties obtain a legal separation, the court can either divide the marital property at the time of the decree of legal separation or at the time of the divorce. If the marital property is divided at the time of the legal separation, any after acquired property by either spouse is classified as separate property of that spouse, even though the parties are still legally married. The property is generally valued as closely as possible to the date of the entry of the order finally dividing the marital property or the order of legal separation.

G. Uniform Laws

There are several uniform acts that have influenced the way that states approach various property division issues, each with the goal of providing more uniformity among the states.

1. Uniform Marriage and Divorce Act (UMDA)

The Uniform Marriage and Divorce Act (UMDA), promulgated in 1970 by the National Conference of Commissioners on Uniform State Laws (NCCUSL), has been adopted, at least in part, by a number of states. As originally formulated, it adopted a dual property approach to classification of marital property. In 1973, an all property approach to the classification of property was added.

2. Uniform Marital Property Act (UMPA)

The Uniform Marital Property Act (UMPA) was promulgated in 1983 by the National Conference of Commissioners on Uniform State Laws (NCCUSL) and reflects changes in divorce law that occurred during the 1970s and 1980s, including adoption of no-fault divorce legislation and the enactment of equitable distribution statutes in most states. The act adopts a partnership concept of marriage, based on the principle of shared ownership of property during the marriage. Its provisions draw on the community property model. Wisconsin is the only state that has enacted the UMPA, with some modifications.

3. American Law Institute Principles of the Law of Family Dissolution (ALI Principles)

The American Law Institute's Principles of the Law of Family Dissolution: Analysis and Recommendations (ALI Principles), was promulgated in 2000. Its provisions on the division of marital property are generally consistent with current law in most states, except that the ALI Principles leans in favor of the community property states by adopting a strong presumption of equal division of marital property and rejecting the discretionary factors currently used by most states to distribute marital property. The ALI Principles also endorse the principle of recharacterizing separate assets to marital assets over the course of a marriage of long duration.

CHECKPOINTS

- States generally follow one of two systems for dividing property upon divorce: the common law system or the community law system.
- The community law system affects spousal property rights during the marriage, at the time of divorce, and upon death.
- The doctrine of equitable distribution, used in common law states, applies only in relation to distribution of marital property at the time of divorce. It has no application during the marriage or upon death of one of the spouses.
- Courts follow a three-step approach in dividing property: classification, valuation, and distribution.
- When dividing marital property, states are either dual property states, which distribute only marital property, or all property states which distribute all property, whether marital or separate.
- When classifying property, the court will generally consider the doctrines of tracing, commingling, and transmutation.
- Property is generally valued close to the time that the court will make its decision regarding distribution of the marital property.
- Marital property may be divided equally or equitably.
- Debts must also be classified, valued, and distributed at the time of divorce.
- In some states, property can be divided at the time that the parties are legally separated. In those cases, after acquired property is usually considered the separate property of the individual spouse.

CHAPTER 9

Spousal Support

ROADMAP

After reading this chapter, you should understand:

- The history of alimony;
- The basis for awarding alimony;
- The different types of alimony;
- The basis for modifying and terminating alimony; and
- The means of enforcing alimony.

Historically, alimony was available only to the innocent wife (who was not found to be guilty of any of the fault grounds for divorce) and ordered against a husband who was found to be guilty of at least one of the fault grounds for divorce, legal separation, etc. Divorce itself was a remedy that was available only to the innocent spouse. There were generally only two types of alimony available—alimony *in solido* and alimony *in futuro*. Alimony *in solido*, also called lump sum alimony, was a set amount of alimony known at the time of the divorce and usually payable in a lump sum, typically an award of part of the marital property. Alimony *in futuro*, also called permanent or periodic alimony, was awarded in the form of periodic payments indefinitely, usually until death or remarriage of the recipient.

Alimony was not available to the husband, even if he was the innocent spouse, because at common law only the husband had a duty of support. Following a successful equal protection challenge in the Supreme Court, in *Orr v. Orr*, 440 U.S. 268 (1979), all of the states began to recognize the right of either spouse to seek alimony. Thereafter, a number of state=s changed the nomenclature from alimony to more gender-neutral terms such as spousal support or maintenance. Also, around that time, perhaps even in partial response to the new possibility that men could become the recipients of alimony, a burgeoning preference trended for ending all spousal obligations at divorce.

Women are still more likely than men to receive alimony because they are more likely to be the financially dependent spouse in most relationships. There are many reasons for this situation, including, but not limited to: (1) the fact that women often assume more of the caretaking responsibilities in a marriage; (2) the fact that women earn less than men; and (3) the fact that men are more likely to marry someone with less income earning capacity than are women.

A. Rationale for Support

There are a number of rationales that states have articulated as the basis for alimony, including the recipient's need, the recipient's contributions to the marriage, compensation for breach of the marital contract, restitution, economic detriment and compensation for loss. Moreover, public policy considerations of many states favor support of a party by a former spouse in lieu of public support in the event the disadvantaged spouse might become reliant upon public assistance.

B. Support Standards and Factors

States have varying standards for determining whether alimony is warranted, based on the underlying rationale for such award, reviewed above. Once the standard is met, the court will consider a number of factors to determine the type and amount of alimony to award. Historically, the standard was the innocence of the wife and the fault of the husband. The factors the court considered when that standard was met included, primarily, the recipient's need and the obligor's ability to pay. The amount could be increased or decreased by the egregiousness of the fault involved. As the no-fault movement spread across the country, allowing parties to seek divorces without regard to fault, many states also eliminated consideration of fault in the determination of alimony. Eliminating fault as a basis for alimony caused states to search for new alimony standards. A number of states stayed with a showing of need. Need was not clearly defined. It could be need in the sense of being on welfare, or need in the sense of being unable to maintain the marital standard of living, or need in the sense of suffering economic detriment relative to the other spouse. Some states began to recognize other standards for affording relief such as the need to reimburse a spouse for financial contributions to the other spouse.

In determining whether alimony is appropriate and in determining the type of alimony and the amount, the court must consider a number of factors. These factors are typically statutory and generally include a catchall provision that allows the court a great deal of discretion. The following list of factors is illustrative:

1. The relative earning capacity, obligations, needs, and financial resources of each party, including income from pension, profit sharing or retirement plans and all other sources;
2. The relative education and training of each party, the ability and opportunity of each party to secure such education and training, and the necessity of a party to secure further education and training to improve such party's earnings capacity to a reasonable level;
3. The duration of the marriage;
4. The age and mental condition of each party;
5. The physical condition of each party, including, but not limited to, physical disability or incapacity due to a chronic debilitating disease;
6. The extent to which it would be undesirable for a party to seek employment outside the home, because such party will be custodian of a minor child of the marriage;
7. The separate assets of each party, both real and personal, tangible and intangible;
8. The provisions made with regard to the marital property;
9. The standard of living of the parties established during the marriage;
10. The extent to which each party has made such tangible and intangible contributions to the marriage as monetary and homemaker contributions, and tangible and intangible contributions by a party to the education, training or increased earning power of the other party;
11. The relative fault of the parties, in cases where the court, in its discretion, deems it appropriate to do so; and
12. Such other factors, including the tax consequences to each party, as are necessary to consider the equities between the parties.

Courts traditionally focus primarily on the recipient's need and the obligor's ability to pay as the most important factors, coupled with the length of the marriage. Increasingly, states are less likely to allow the court to consider fault and more likely to state a preference for alimony designed to maximize the recipient's earning capacity. Although some litigants have argued that alimony awards violate the Fourteenth Amendment, so long as awards do not discriminate based upon gender, the courts have found that states have a legitimate interest in ensuring the financial security of a spouse who needs assistance.

The length of the marriage is a very important factor in most states. Increasingly, courts are unlikely to order alimony *in futuro* (permanent) except in long term marriages, generally in the range of twenty years or more. And, even then, many states have either a statutory or common law rebuttable presumption against *in futuro* awards, encouraging instead alimony that facilitates the temporary transition or educational rehabilitation of the payee—both of which are short in duration. In marriages of short spans, typically seven years or less, it is very unlikely that courts will award support at all. Instead, the courts focus on returning the parties, as much as possible, to their premarital positions.

C. Types of Alimony

If the court determines that alimony is appropriate, it must decide what type of alimony to award, the amount of the award, and the duration of the award. States recognize several different types of alimony, including: *in solido*, *in futuro*, rehabilitative, transitional, and reimbursement. Each of these types of alimony will be explained below.

In addition to these five types of alimony, the court may also award alimony pendent lite or nominal alimony. Alimony pendente lite means "alimony pending the litigation." The court may, in its discretion, at any time prior to the final divorce hearing, order the payment of alimony for the support of the other spouse and to enable the recipient to prosecute or defend the divorce. Pendente lite alimony may also be ordered to pay the expenses of job training and education of the recipient spouse while the divorce is pending.

Nominal alimony is essentially a "placeholder," in that it allows the court to retain jurisdiction to increase the amount of alimony in the future, should circumstances justify doing so. Nominal alimony, of perhaps a dollar, might be ordered at the time of the divorce if the recipient spouse is facing some medical condition that may or may not result in permanent disability in the near future. The recipient spouse is not disabled at the time of the divorce, so alimony may not be warranted. On the other hand, if the court enters a final decree of divorce without awarding alimony, the court will lack jurisdiction to reopen the case to consider alimony if the spouse does become disabled thereafter.

By awarding nominal alimony of one dollar per month until death or remarriage, the court retains jurisdiction to modify the alimony award if the recipient spouse later becomes disabled. Naturally, such an award would be strongly opposed by the obligor spouse.

1. Alimony *In Solido*

Alimony *in solido*, also known as lump-sum alimony, is a type of support, the total amount of which is ascertainable when awarded, but which is not designated as transitional alimony. It can usually be paid in installments, as long as the amount to be paid is determinable at the time of the decree. The purpose of alimony *in solido* is to provide financial support to a spouse, but attorney fees may also be awarded as alimony *in solido*, where appropriate, generally when the recipient spouse does not have sufficient assets to pay for attorney fees, but the obligor spouse does.

Alimony *in solido* is usually not modifiable, except by agreement of the parties. It usually does not terminate upon the death or remarriage of the recipient or obligor. It is very much like a distribution of marital property in those respects. If there are sufficient assets to make an award of alimony *in solido*, it has the advantage of allowing the parties to make a clean break and go their separate ways, thus saving future acrimony between the parties and future use of judicial resources. For the obligor, the advantage is that the total amount to be paid is known and can't be increased if the recipient's needs increase. The disadvantage is that the amount can't be decreased if the obligor's ability to pay decreases and the payments are usually not tax deductible because they do not automatically terminate upon the death of the recipient. The reverse is true for the recipient.

An example of alimony *in solido* would be a decree ordering the monied spouse to transfer to the recipient spouse the following: Blackacre rental property, all of the stock in ABC company, and $500,000 in cash. Courts commonly will use alimony *in solido* as a way for the payor-spouse to reimburse the payee-spouse for attorney's fees.

2. Alimony *In Futuro*

Alimony *in futuro* is also known as permanent, periodic, or long-term alimony. This type of alimony is paid for an indefinite period, usually until the death or remarriage of the recipient. Many states have limited the availability of alimony *in futuro*, indicating a preference for other types of alimony and restricting the court's ability to award alimony *in futuro*. In order to award alimony *in futuro*, the court may be required to find that there is relative economic disadvantage and that rehabilitation is not feasible, for instance.

Alimony *in futuro* is generally modifiable upon a showing of a substantial and material change in circumstances. It usually terminates automatically upon the death or remarriage of the recipient. It is, therefore, deductible by the obligor and includible in the income of the recipient. It may be modifiable if the recipient cohabits with another adult without the benefit of remarriage. Alimony *in futuro* usually terminates upon the death of the obligor, as well, unless otherwise specifically stated.

An example of alimony *in futuro* would be a decree ordering the monied spouse to pay to the recipient spouse $2,000 per month until the recipient dies or remarries.

3. Rehabilitative Alimony

Many states now recognize a preference for rehabilitative alimony. Rehabilitative alimony is usually designed to maximize or at least increase one's earning capacity, usually by furthering one's education or training. To be rehabilitated means different things, much like the old definitions of need. It may mean to be able to meet one's basic needs or to avoid being a public charge or it may be tied to the marital standard of living or to the other spouse's standard of living. An example of the latter definition might state that to be rehabilitated means to achieve, with reasonable effort, an earning capacity that will permit the economically disadvantaged spouse's standard of living after the divorce to be reasonably comparable to the standard of living enjoyed during the marriage, or to the post-divorce standard of living expected to be available to the other spouse, considering the relevant statutory factors and the equities between the parties.

Rehabilitative alimony is usually modifiable upon a showing of a substantial and material change in circumstances. In order to extend it beyond the term in the divorce decree, or to increase the amount, the state may place a burden on the recipient to prove that all reasonable efforts at rehabilitation have been made and have been unsuccessful. If a dependent spouse does not satisfactorily strive for self sufficiency, the Court may withdraw part or all of the support allocated to finance rehabilitation. On the other hand, if the dependent spouse is not able to become rehabilitated, despite reasonable efforts to do so, the court may modify the rehabilitative award and order *in futuro* support.

Rehabilitative alimony usually terminates upon the death of the recipient. Rehabilitative alimony usually terminates upon the death of the obligor, as well, unless otherwise specifically stated.

An example of rehabilitative alimony would be a decree ordering the monied spouse to pay to the recipient spouse $1500 per month and to pay the cost of tuition, books, and fees at the state university for the next three years, in order for the recipient spouse to complete his or her undergraduate degree.

4. Transitional Alimony

Transitional alimony is one of the newer forms of alimony which is recognized in some states. It is designed to assist parties in reaching an agreement about alimony because it is generally not modifiable, thus making it more palatable to the obligor. Transitional alimony is an amount paid for a determinate period of time. Transitional alimony is appropriate when the court finds that rehabilitation is not necessary, but the economically disadvantaged spouse needs assistance to adjust to the economic circumstances of divorce.

Unlike rehabilitative alimony and alimony *in futuro*, transitional alimony is generally not modifiable, unless the parties agree, or the court so orders, or the "live-in lover" rule applies (discussed below under cohabitation).

Transitional alimony usually terminates upon the death of the recipient. It also terminates upon the death of the payor, as well, unless otherwise specifically stated. The court may provide additional conditions such as termination upon remarriage of the recipient.

An example of transitional alimony would be a decree ordering the monied spouse to pay to the recipient spouse $2000 per month for two years, while the recipient rebuilds his or her business as a realtor, where that spouse had not been an active realtor during the last years of the marriage.

5. Reimbursement Alimony

Reimbursement alimony, where recognized, may be appropriate in cases where one spouse works to put the other spouse through school and the parties divorce before the supporting spouse gets to enjoy the financial fruits of the investment in the degree-earning spouse. Reimbursement alimony might also be appropriate, where one spouse makes a large investment in another spouse's business and the parties are divorced shortly thereafter. In each case, the reimbursement alimony seeks to reimburse the financially contributing spouse in circumstances where it is appropriate to do so, considering the equities between the parties.

An example of reimbursement alimony would be a decree ordering the monied spouse to pay to the recipient spouse $80,000, payable in installments of $2000 per month, to reimburse the recipient spouse for his or her investment of separate funds into the monied spouse's business.

D. Modification

1. Standard for Modification

As noted above, some types of alimony are modifiable, and others are not. If the alimony is modifiable, the court will retain jurisdiction over the matter and will rule on future petitions for modification by either party. A petition to modify alimony must be filed prior to the termination of the award of alimony by any of the contingencies upon which the award is based, because the court's jurisdiction to modify terminates when the alimony obligation ceases to exist. For instance, if the alimony award is for ten years or until death or remarriage of the recipient, a petition to modify that is filed after the ten-year period is too late, even if the recipient is still alive and unmarried, because the expiration of the ten-year period terminates the alimony obligation and the court's jurisdiction to modify.

Alimony modifications generally involve a two-step process. The first step is a determination of whether the threshold standard of showing a substantial and material change of circumstances has been met. If so, the next step is for the court to determine, usually by applying certain statutory factors, whether a modification should be granted.

In construing the term *substantial and material change of circumstance*, courts have generally held that changed circumstances are *material* only when they arise after the divorce and were not within the contemplation of the parties at the time of the divorce. In order to be *substantial*, the change must significantly affect either the obligor's ability to pay or the recipient's need for support. The recipient may petition when the obligor's ability to pay increases or the recipient's needs increase. An increase in the obligor's income, standing alone, is generally not a sufficient basis for a modification. The obligor may petition for a decrease if the obligor's ability to pay decreases or the recipient's needs decrease.

Courts have a great deal of discretion in determining whether a substantial and material change of circumstances exists. Generally speaking, the following facts have not been found to constitute a substantial and material change of circumstances:

1. The obligor's increased expenses, absent proof of the obligor's inability to pay the ordered support;
2. An increase in either party's income, standing alone;
3. Recipient's reentry into the workforce;
4. Income produced from the proceeds of the sale of property awarded to a spouse in the division of marital property;
5. Obligor's willful underemployment;
6. Voluntary assumption of new financial obligations;
7. Remarriage, alone, when the alimony is rehabilitative;
8. Cohabitation, alone, when the alimony is rehabilitative;
9. Change in Income Tax laws;
10. Recipient's increased residential time with the parties' children; and
11. Recipient's receipt of Social Security Benefits.

2. Nonmodification Stipulations

One particular factor that makes obligors less willing to pay any type of alimony is that in most cases, there is a potential for later modification. In order to entice obligors to voluntarily pay alimony as part of a settlement, many parties will include a nonmodification clause within their settlement agreement. Many courts have grappled with the public policy considerations regarding enforcement of such clauses, particularly in cases involving a significant increase in the need of the payee spouse. Most courts though, like the Uniform Marriage and Divorce Act (UMDA) approach, have found that such agreements are enforceable under contract principles and that policy factors like fostering settlements, predictability and judicial economy weigh in favor of enforcement.

3. Factors

If the court finds that the threshold standard of a substantial and material change in circumstances has been demonstrated, the court will next determine whether under all the circumstances, a modification is appropriate, and, if so, what it should be. In doing so, the court will generally apply the same statutory factors that it uses to determine an initial award of alimony.

4. Retirement

States disagree on whether the obligor's retirement justifies an alimony modification. Some states take the position that retirement is always foreseeable, so it cannot be a basis upon which to seek a modification. Other states take the opposite view. Some states have fashioned a hybrid test, based on the reasonableness of the decision to retire, rather than its foreseeability at the time of the divorce. When the obligor's retirement is objectively reasonable, it does constitute a substantial and material change in circumstances—irrespective of whether the retirement was foreseeable or voluntary—so as to permit consideration of the alimony modification petition. The modification is not automatic, however. The trial court must examine the totality of the circumstances surrounding the retirement to ensure that it is objectively reasonable. The burden of establishing that the retirement is objectively reasonable is on the party seeking modification of the award, but a retirement cannot be deemed objectively reasonable if it is primarily motivated by a desire to defeat the support award or to reduce the alimony paid to the former spouse.

E. Termination

1. Death

Because alimony is intended to provide for the actual support of the recipient, it typically terminates upon the death of the recipient. Not all forms of alimony automatically terminate upon death, as indicated above. The most notable exception is alimony *in solido*, but the parties are also free to structure the payments as they see fit and can even agree that the payments will not end upon death.

2. Remarriage

Most forms of alimony terminate upon remarriage, because, at common law, the new spouse would assume the obligation of support. Notable exceptions are alimony *in solido* and rehabilitative alimony, in many states. In some states, the recipient is obligated to notify the obligor immediately upon remarrying. Failure to do so may allow the obligor to recover all amounts paid to the recipient after the recipient's remarriage.

3. Cohabitation (Live-in-Lover Rule)

Alimony *in futuro* is also subject to modification or termination based on what has become known as the "live-in lover" rule. If the alimony recipient lives with an adult third person, a rebuttable presumption arises that the third person is contributing to the support of the recipient, or that the recipient is contributing to the support of a third party. In either case, it is presumed that the recipient does not need the amount of alimony previously awarded. The presumption was originally designed to address the situation of a "live-in lover," but has been extended, in some states, to other adults living with the recipient, including adult children.

The "live-in-lover" provision does not automatically terminate the alimony obligation. It merely gives rise to a presumption that alimony, in the amount previously ordered, is no longer needed, and shifts the burden of proof to the recipient to show a continuing need. If the recipient can demonstrate current need, many states will allow a reduction in alimony rather than termination, or perhaps even a finding that the current amount of alimony is still appropriate.

4. Annulment

Because the alimony obligation originally arose out of the common law duty of the husband to support the wife, some states take the position that alimony cannot be awarded if the marriage is annulled, rather than dissolved by divorce. The rationale is that an annulment is a declaration that the marriage never legally existed, thus, the obligation of support never arose and, therefore, cannot be continued by the court.

F. Reinstatement

Annulment can also cause reinstatement of a prior alimony obligation. If the court orders the obligor to pay alimony upon the dissolution of marriage #1, and the recipient remarries, the alimony obligation automatically terminates in most cases. If, however, marriage #2 is later annulled, the original alimony obligation may be reinstated. Some states allow reinstatement, while others do not. Some states rest the reinstatement on the basis for the annulment. If the underlying marriage (marriage #2) was void, it is void *ab initio*, and the annulment reinstates the original alimony obligation. If the underlying marriage (marriage #2) is only voidable, it is deemed valid until it is annulled, so the original alimony obligation is not reinstated.

G. Insurance

1. Life Insurance

Alimony is typically ordered as monthly payments of a specified sum, except for alimony *in solido*, which might involve the transfer of property, or rehabilitative alimony, which might include an order to pay tuition or other fees in addition to a monthly support amount. In order to secure payment of the alimony obligation in the event of the obligor's death, the court may order the obligor to obtain a life insurance policy for the same term and aggregated amount as the alimony award, and to designate the recipient as the beneficiary of that policy. The policy generally must be maintained until the alimony obligation is terminated. An alternative to life insurance is a lien on assets owned by the obligor. This option usually is implemented when the obligor's health renders insurance costs prohibitive.

2. Health Care Insurance

The obligation to pay for health care expenses generally falls under the doctrine of necessaries and, as a result, many states include health care insurance as a support obligation. The court can generally order one spouse to pay the health insurance premiums for the other spouse if the court deems it appropriate under the circumstances. Since former spouses can no longer be covered under the other spouse's insurance plan, for disadvantaged spouses who cannot afford health insurance premiums, particularly if their former spouse likewise cannot, legal separations, as discussed in Chapter 6, are a good alternative.

H. Tax Consequences

Spousal support awards ordered before December 31, 2018, were tax deductible to the payor and taxable income to the payees. Recognizing that the tax brackets of payors in most circumstances is higher than that of payees, the 2017 Tax Cuts and Jobs Act eliminated the deduction for payors and the claimed income for payees. This change eliminated the incentive to payors to pay higher support payments due to the tax deduction they would receive.

I. Enforcement

There are a number of ways to secure enforcement of the alimony obligation. The court can require the obligor to post a bond to secure payment; sequester rents and profits from the obligor's real estate and personal estate, if any; and impose a lien on the obligor's real and personal property. Alimony obligations may also be enforced by executing on the obligor's property or garnishing the obligor's wages. A restraining order can be used to restrain the obligor from transferring or disposing of property.

The enforcement tool used most often is a petition to have the obligor held in civil contempt of the court's order to pay alimony. If the obligor is shown to have the ability to pay, the court may order the obligor to jail, indefinitely, until the alimony is paid. The obligor is said to "hold the keys to the jail."

Alimony, like maintenance, support and property settlements incurred during a divorce proceeding are generally protected against discharge in bankruptcy.

J. Uniform Laws

1. Uniform Marriage and Divorce Act (UMDA)

The Uniform Marriage and Divorce Act, promulgated in 1970 by the National Conference of Commissioners on Uniform State Laws (NCCUSL) reflected the no-fault reform movement that began in California in 1969. The UMDA eliminated marital fault as a factor in determining spousal support. Instead, it focused on the recipient's financial need and the need to care for children of the marriage. The UMDA explicitly conditions spousal support upon a finding that the recipient spouse lacks sufficient property to provide for his or her reasonable needs and is unable to support himself or herself, through appropriate employment or is the custodian of a child under circumstances that make it appropriate for the recipient not to be required to work outside the home.

2. American Law Institute Principles of the Law of Family Dissolution (ALI Principles)

The American Law Institute's Principles of the Law of Family Dissolution: Analysis and Recommendations (ALI Principles), was promulgated in 2000. Instead of using need as the basis for awarding support, the ALI Principles bases alimony on the duration of the marriage and the recipient's loss. The loss can be evidenced by (1) loss of earning capacity from years spent as the primary caretaker of children or other family members or (2) by loss of the marital standard of living.

Alternatively, alimony for loss not based on the duration of the marriage is deemed appropriate in two instances: (1) where the recipient has suffered a loss from not receiving a fair return on his or her investment in the other spouse's earning capacity, and (2) where there is an unfairly disproportionate disparity between spouses in their ability to recover their premarital living standard after a marriage of short duration.

CHECKPOINTS

- Alimony is available to either spouse, based on the criteria established by each state.
- The rationale for alimony used to be fault based; many states have now moved to a no-fault approach.
- Current rationales include need, rehabilitation, marital standard of living, and reimbursement.
- The court usually has a great deal of discretion in determining whether and what type of alimony to award, as well as in setting the amount and duration of the award.
- States recognize different types of alimony. The various types differ regarding grounds for termination and modification.

- Payor spouses no longer receive tax deductions for alimony payments, nor do payees pay income taxes on alimony payments.
- The most important considerations in awarding traditional alimony are generally the recipient's need or loss, the obligor's ability to pay, and the length of the marriage.
- An order for rehabilitative alimony generally focuses on the extent to which the recipient can increase his or her earning capacity through additional training or education, and the extent to which the obligor has the ability to pay for such training or education.

CHAPTER 10

Child Custody Jurisdiction and Enforcement

ROADMAP

After reading this chapter, you should understand:

- The basic differences between the UCCJA and the UCCJEA;
- The basic provisions of the PKPA and what it accomplishes;
- The difference between jurisdiction to make an initial child custody determination and jurisdiction to modify another state's decree; and
- The enforcement provisions included in the UCCJEA.

Once a court determines custody at the time of divorce, it retains jurisdiction to modify custody during the child's minority. Because the child custody order remains modifiable, the Supreme Court, in *New York ex rel. Halvey v. Halvey*, 330 U.S. 610 (1947), held that the Full Faith and Credit Clause does not prevent states from modifying custody orders of sister states. In 1953, the Supreme Court, in a plurality opinion, in *May v. Anderson*, 345 U.S. 528 (1953) also held that the full Faith and Credit Clause did not require a State to recognize a custody decree entered in a sister state that lacked *in personam* jurisdiction over the custodial parent. This decision has been criticized, and most states have followed the interpretation given in the concurring opinion by Justice Frankfurter, that although the full Faith and Credit Clause does not require recognition of the custody determination of a sister state lacking *in personam* jurisdiction over the custodial parent, neither does it preclude recognition in such a case. Based on that interpretation, the vast majority of states turned to the child's domicile as the basis for child custody jurisdiction, rather than personal jurisdiction over the parents. This jurisdictional approach led to numerous cases of forum shopping and parental kidnapping in which each parent would seek, and often obtain, a favorable custodial determination in different states.

Two uniform state laws were promulgated, and one federal law was enacted to address the growing problem of multiple child custody orders and conflicting claims of child custody jurisdiction. The first effort at reform was the Uniform Child Custody Jurisdiction Act (UCCJA), promulgated in 1968, by the National Conference of Commissioners on Uniform State Laws (NCCUSL). The UCCJA was not a panacea, though, for a couple of reasons. One reason was that some states were not moving to adopt the UCCJA and some adopting states had enacted non-uniform provisions. Another reason was that jurisdictional conflicts persisted, even among sister states that had adopted uniform versions of the UCCJA. In 1980, Congress enacted the Parental Kidnapping Prevention Act (PKPA), motivated in part by the goal of preventing the few non-UCCJA states from becoming havens for parental kidnappers and in part by the need to address the competing jurisdictional claims that continued to arise between states that had passed the UCCJA. The PKPA prioritized jurisdictional grounds, but conflicts continued. Part of the problem was that some states failed to apply the PKPA, while other states simply misapplied the PKPA. In addition, the PKPA did not address the priority issue as to emergency-based jurisdiction. In 1997, NCCUSL proposed an amended version of the UCCJA—the Uniform Child Custody Jurisdiction and Enforcement Act (UCCJEA)—that attempted to address the remaining jurisdictional conflicts and to add enforcement provisions that had not previously been addressed in either the UCCJA or the PKPA. By 2010, all but one state had adopted the UCCJEA.

A. Purpose and Scope

1. The Uniform Child Custody Jurisdiction Act (UCCJA)

The scope provisions of the UCCJA apply to custody proceedings, which are defined as proceedings in which a custody determination is one of several issues, such as an action for divorce or separation, and includes child neglect and dependency proceedings. The UCCJA did not specifically address coverage of adoption, guardianship proceedings, or tribal court proceedings. Massachusetts is the only state that continues to follow the UCCJA.

2. The Uniform Child Custody Jurisdiction and Enforcement Act (UCCJEA)

The UCCJEA also applies to child custody proceedings and child custody determinations, but the terms are defined more clearly to bring greater uniformity in application than had been the case under the UCCJA. Child custody proceedings are very broadly defined to include proceedings such as divorce, separation, neglect, abuse, dependency, guardianship, paternity, termination of parental rights, and protection from domestic violence, in which the child custody issue may appear. Child custody determinations are broadly defined to include orders for legal custody, physical custody, or visitation. The definition applies to permanent, temporary, initial, and modification orders.

Expressly excluded from the UCCJEA provisions are child support proceedings, juvenile delinquency proceedings, emancipation proceedings, UCCJEA enforcement provisions, Indian Child Welfare Act (ICWA) proceedings, and adoption proceedings.

Even though Indian Child Welfare Act (ICWA) proceedings (applicable to adoptions and foster placement of Indian children) are excluded from the UCCJEA provisions, states are given the option to extend the UCCJEA to Indian Tribes. Doing so requires the state to treat Indian Tribes as sister states for purposes of applying the provisions of the UCCJEA.

3. The Parental Kidnapping Prevention Act (PKPA)

The PKPA addresses the circumstances under which one state must give full faith and credit to custody or visitation decrees of another state. The PKPA applies to custody or visitation determinations made consistently with the provisions of the PKPA by the court of another state. Custody determination is defined as a court order providing for the custody of the child, including permanent and temporary orders, and initial orders and modifications. Visitation determination is defined as a court order providing for the visitation of a child, including permanent and temporary orders and initial orders and modifications.

B. Notice Provisions

Both the UCCJA and the UCCJEA require that the contestants be given notice and an opportunity to be heard. The PKPA requires that notice and an opportunity to be heard must be given in order for the full faith and credit provisions of the PKPA to apply. An order that is entered without giving a party adequate notice and an opportunity to be heard is not considered a valid order and is not entitled to full faith and credit in sister states.

C. Jurisdiction to Make an Initial Child Custody Determination

After determining that the matter before the court falls within the scope provisions of the relevant statute, the next question to be addressed when addressing the issue of child custody jurisdiction is whether the court is making an initial child custody determination or is attempting to modify an existing child custody determination. The jurisdictional rules differ depending upon whether the matter involves an initial determination of custody or a modification. As will be explained below, once a court has made an initial determination of child custody, that court is entitled to retain jurisdiction to the exclusion of other states in most circumstances.

1. The Uniform Child Custody Jurisdiction Act (UCCJA)

Under the UCCJA, a court can assume child custody jurisdiction under any one of four different jurisdictional grounds, as discussed below, as long as the requirements of that particular jurisdictional ground were met. The jurisdictional grounds are not prioritized. The assumption is that if two or more states claim jurisdiction at the same time, the courts will communicate, cooperate, and determine which court is best suited to hear the matter. Unfortunately, that level of cooperation and communication was not always present. Jurisdictional conflicts arose when two or more states claimed jurisdiction and would not defer to the court best suited to make the child custody determination. For instance, one state might claim home state jurisdiction and another state might claim significant connections jurisdiction, or emergency jurisdiction. The four jurisdictional bases are defined below:

a. *Home State Jurisdiction*

A child's "home state" is defined as the state where the child has lived with a parent, or person acting as a parent, for at least six consecutive months immediately preceding the commencement of a child custody proceeding. A person acting as a parent is defined as someone who had physical custody for six consecutive months within the year prior to filing or was awarded legal custody. If the child is less than six months old, the home state is the state in which the child has lived with any of the persons previously mentioned. A period of temporary absence is not deducted when calculating time under this definition. Temporary absence, however, is not defined.

"Home state jurisdiction" is different from "home state," in that a state may continue to claim home state jurisdiction for six months after the child is removed from the home state, as long as a parent or a person acting as a parent remains in the state. The underlying rationale is that at least for the next six months after the child leaves the state, the home state is still the state with the most current, relevant information concerning the child and would, therefore, be the best forum for a child custody determination. After being removed from the home state for more than six months, another state is likely to have become a child's new home state and to be the forum with the most current, relevant information concerning the child. In order to claim home state jurisdiction after the child's removal from the state, a parent or person acting as a parent must continue to reside in the home state at the time of commencement of the proceeding.

b. *Significant Connections Jurisdiction*

A court may assume jurisdiction when it is in the best interests of the child for a court of that state to assume jurisdiction because the child and his parents, or the child and at least one contestant, have a significant connection with that state and there is available within the state substantial evidence concerning the child's present or future care, protection, training, and personal relationships. Jurisdiction under this provision of the UCCJA is generally referred to as significant connections jurisdiction. The child does not have to be physically present in the state for this jurisdictional ground to apply, but the court does have to make a determination that assuming jurisdiction would be in the child's best interest, that the child and at least one contestant have a significant connection with the state, and that substantial evidence concerning the child custody issue is available within the state.

c. *Emergency Jurisdiction*

A court may assume emergency jurisdiction if a child is physically present in a state and has been abandoned. The court may also assume emergency jurisdiction when it is necessary in an emergency to protect a child who is physically present in the state and has been subjected to, or threatened with, mistreatment or abuse, or is otherwise neglected or dependent. The physical presence of the child within the state is a requirement for emergency jurisdiction.

d. *Default Jurisdiction*

A state may assume default jurisdiction if it appears that no other state would have jurisdiction under home state, significant connections, or emergency jurisdiction. Default jurisdiction may also be assumed if another state declines to exercise jurisdiction on the grounds that the default state is the more appropriate forum, and that it is in the best interests of the child that the forum state assume jurisdiction. Physical presence of the child in the default state may, in itself, be a sufficient basis to confer default jurisdiction. Physical presence of the child, however, is not required for default jurisdiction.

2. The Parental Kidnapping Prevention Act (PKPA)

The PKPA attempted to address the jurisdictional conflict created when two or more states claimed jurisdiction under the UCCJA by providing in the PKPA that full faith and credit was required only for custody or visitation determinations made consistently with the PKPA. The PKPA further provided that a child custody or visitation determination is consistent with the PKPA only if the court has jurisdiction under the law of that state and one of four jurisdictional grounds is met. The four jurisdictional grounds are essentially the same as those set forth in the UCCJA, except that the list of parties who can extend home state jurisdiction is broader under the PKPA than under the UCCJA. The PKPA allows home state jurisdiction to be extended for six months after the removal of the child, as long as a contestant remains in the state. Contestant is defined to include grandparents. The UCCJA limits the parties who may extend home state jurisdiction to parents and persons acting as parents.

A more significant difference between the UCCJA and the PKPA is that the PKPA prioritizes jurisdictional grounds as between home state jurisdiction and significant connections jurisdiction, by providing that a state may rely on significant connections jurisdiction only where there is no state with home state jurisdiction. Unfortunately, the PKPA did not address the prioritization of emergency jurisdiction, leaving open the possibility for continuing dual claims of jurisdiction.

The PKPA was not effective in resolving the problem of conflicting claims of jurisdiction among states for several reasons. First, as previously noted, it did not address the prioritization of emergency jurisdiction. Second, there was no opportunity to resolve conflicting claims of jurisdiction in the federal district courts. In *Thompson v. Thompson*, 484 U.S. 174 (1988), the Supreme Court held that the PKPA does not create a private right of action in the federal courts to resolve conflicting jurisdictional disputes. As a result, federal enforcement of the PKPA is available to parties only after taking their cases to the highest courts of the states involved. Third, the only penalty for noncompliance with the PKPA is that the non-complying state's child custody determination is not entitled to full faith and credit in sister states. The non-complying child custody determination could, however, be deemed enforceable in the state making the determination. If the child is located in the non-complying state, the non-resident parent would have no way to enforce a child custody determination entered in a sister state consistent with the PKPA, unless the matter is pursued to the highest court of each state and then to the Supreme Court under federal question jurisdiction.

3. The Uniform Child Custody Jurisdiction and Enforcement Act (UCCJEA)

The UCCJEA attempted to address the failings of the PKPA by clarifying limitations on emergency jurisdiction and by creating, in the enforcement section of the UCCJEA, a procedure for obtaining registration and confirmation, in a sister state, of a child custody determination rendered in another state. The registration and confirmation procedure can be used by the nonresident parent to determine whether another state will give full faith and credit to the child custody determination, prior to sending the child to that state for parenting time with the other parent. If the order is registered and confirmed, the nonresident parent can safely send the child to the other state, confident that the other state will enforce the foreign decree, should the need arise.

a. Home State Jurisdiction

The definition for home state jurisdiction is the same under the UCCJEA as it is under the UCCJA and the PKPA. The difference is that under the UCCJEA, home state jurisdiction has priority over all of the other jurisdictional bases.

b. *Significant Connections Jurisdiction*

Significant connections jurisdiction has the same definition under the UCCJEA that it has under the PKPA. A state cannot proceed under significant connections jurisdiction unless there is no state with home state jurisdiction or the state with home state jurisdiction defers to the state with significant connections jurisdiction. In addition, the court must determine that the child and at least one parent, or person acting as a parent, have a significant connection with the state, other than mere physical presence, and that substantial evidence is available in that state concerning the child's care, protection, training, and personal relationships.

c. *Deferral Jurisdiction*

Deferral jurisdiction allows a state to assume jurisdiction if the state, or states, with home state jurisdiction or significant connections jurisdiction decline to exercise jurisdiction on the ground that the deferral state is an appropriate forum.

d. *Default Jurisdiction*

A court may assume default jurisdiction if no court of any other state would have jurisdiction under home state jurisdiction, significant connections jurisdiction, or deferral jurisdiction.

e. *Temporary Emergency Jurisdiction*

The basis for assuming emergency jurisdiction is the same under the UCCJEA as it is under the UCCJA and PKPA, but, unlike the UCCJA and PKPA, emergency jurisdiction under the UCCJEA is temporary. The UCCJEA makes emergency jurisdiction temporary only, in most cases, and distinguishes between emergency jurisdiction where there is no existing child custody determination (or ongoing litigation) and emergency jurisdiction where there is a prior existing child custody determination. If there is no existing child custody determination (or ongoing litigation), a court's emergency order remains valid until another valid state order is entered by a court in a state having jurisdiction under the UCCJEA. The temporary emergency order may become final in one instance, however. If no other state order is entered, the emergency order can become a final order, if it so states, and if that state later becomes the child's home state.

D. Grounds to Decline Jurisdiction—Initial Decree

Once the court of a state determines that it does have jurisdiction under one of the grounds contained in that state's law, and consistent with the PKPA, the next step is to determine whether the court may or must decline jurisdiction. Each of the acts contains both discretionary and mandatory grounds for declining jurisdiction.

1. The Uniform Child Custody Jurisdiction Act (UCCJA)

a. Mandatory Grounds

Prior pending action—There is one instance in which a court must decline jurisdiction at the time of an initial child custody determination. It is when there is a prior pending action in another state with jurisdiction under the UCCJA. The mandatory ground applies when, at the time of the filing of the petition in a state, a proceeding concerning the custody of the child is pending in a court of another state having jurisdiction under the UCCJA, unless, of course, the court with the prior pending action defers to the other state as a more appropriate forum. Parties are required to inform the court in their pleadings of any pending child custody determinations, with the goal of allowing the courts to confer and determine the more appropriate forum for making the child custody determination, consistent with the child's best interests.

b. Discretionary Grounds

Forum non conveniens—A court has discretion to decline jurisdiction under the UCCJA, if the court determines that it is an inconvenient forum, and that another state is a more appropriate forum. If the court declines jurisdiction on this basis, it has the discretion to charge the petitioner with necessary travel and other expenses, including attorney's fees, incurred by the other parties or their witnesses.

Wrongful removal, not in violation of a court order—A court also has discretion to decline jurisdiction if the petitioner for an initial child custody determination has wrongfully taken the child from another state or has engaged in similar reprehensible conduct. If the court declines jurisdiction on this basis, it has the discretion to charge the petitioner with necessary travel and other expenses, including attorney's fees, incurred by the other parties or their witnesses.

2. The Uniform Child Custody Jurisdiction and Enforcement Act (UCCJEA)

a. *Mandatory Grounds*

Prior pending action—Like the UCCJA and PKPA, there is one instance in which a court must decline jurisdiction at the time of an initial child custody determination. It is when there is a prior pending action in another state with jurisdiction under the UCCJEA. The mandatory ground applies when, at the time of the filing of the petition in a state, a proceeding concerning the custody of the child is pending in a court of another state having jurisdiction under the UCCJEA, unless, of course, the court with the prior pending action defers to the other state as a more appropriate forum. Parties are required to inform the court in their pleadings of any pending child custody determinations, with the goal of allowing the courts to confer and determine the more appropriate forum for making the child custody determination, consistent with the child's best interests.

Unjustifiable conduct—Unlike the UCCJA, the UCCJEA does not distinguish between initial decrees and petitions to modify, or between mandatory and discretionary, when addressing grounds to decline jurisdiction based on parental behavior. A court must decline jurisdiction if the state has jurisdiction because of the unjustifiable conduct of the petitioner. Exceptions to the mandatory rule are recognized where all of the parties acquiesce in the court's jurisdiction, where a court that would otherwise have jurisdiction defers to the court that would otherwise have to decline jurisdiction, or where no court of another state would have jurisdiction under the UCCJEA. If the court declines jurisdiction under this section, it may fashion a remedy to ensure the safety of the child and to prevent a repetition of the unjustifiable conduct, including staying the proceeding until a child custody proceeding is commenced in a state with UCCJEA jurisdiction. If a court dismisses a petition or stays a proceeding because of unjustifiable conduct, it must assess expenses against the culpable party, unless the court finds that it would be clearly inappropriate to do so.

b. Discretionary Grounds

Forum non conveniens—Like the UCCJA, the UCCJEA gives a court discretion to decline jurisdiction if the court determines that it is an inconvenient forum and that another state is a more appropriate forum.

3. The Parental Kidnapping Prevention Act (PKPA)

Prior pending action—The PKPA mandates declining jurisdiction, where there is a prior pending action. The PKPA provides that a court of a state shall not exercise jurisdiction commenced during the pendency of a proceeding in a court of another state where that other court is exercising jurisdiction consistently with the PKPA, to make a custody determination.

E. Jurisdiction to Modify an Existing Child Custody Determination

Once a court makes an initial child custody determination, that court generally retains jurisdiction for the duration of the child's minority under the *parens patriae* doctrine. Because of this continued interest of the court in the child's welfare, the PKPA and UCCJEA recognize continuing, exclusive jurisdiction (CEJ) in the court that makes the initial determination, under some circumstances. The UCCJA does not recognize CEJ.

1. The Uniform Child Custody Jurisdiction Act (UCCJA)

The UCCJA does not recognize CEJ, but the UCCJA does provide that a UCCJA court may not modify the decree of another state as long as the court of the decree-rendering state continues to have jurisdiction or declines to exercise that jurisdiction. Again, as with initial decrees, the court in a UCCJA state must also have jurisdiction to modify a child custody determination under any one of the four jurisdictional bases of the UCCJA. Because UCCJA courts could continue to claim jurisdiction under any of the four jurisdictional bases, it became difficult for another state to ever be in a position to modify a decree rendered in a UCCJA state. As with initial decrees, this approach resulted in continued forum shopping and parental kidnapping.

2. The Parental Kidnapping Prevention Act (PKPA)

The PKPA sought to address the jurisdictional conflicts existing under the UCCJA regarding petitions to modify by providing that a state could modify another state's child custody determination only if the modifying court has jurisdiction to make a child custody determination and the original state no longer has jurisdiction or declines to exercise that jurisdiction. The PKPA further provided that the state issuing the initial child custody determination continues to have jurisdiction (CEJ) as long as that court meets the jurisdictional requirements of that state and at least one contestant or the child remains a resident of that state. Thus, a UCCJA court could no longer claim continuing jurisdiction under significant connections or emergency jurisdiction if none of the parties or the child remained in the state. A UCCJA state would, however, be able to continue to claim CEJ, as against a UCCJEA state that had become the child's home state, indefinitely, as long as one contestant remained in the UCCJA state. (The child would be in the UCCJEA state in order for it to become the home state).

3. The Uniform Child Custody Jurisdiction and Enforcement Act (UCCJEA)

The UCCJEA adopted the CEJ approach of the PKPA, but only under the prioritized jurisdictional grounds for the initial decree, unlike the PKPA, which deferred to state law of the court rendering the initial decree. The UCCJEA recognizes continuing, exclusive jurisdiction in the decree-rendering state as long as that court initially met the jurisdictional requirements of the UCCJEA (prioritized), that state still has significant connections, and at least one party or the child remains a resident of that state. The UCCJEA also addresses the question of which court makes a determination of CEJ. Either the decree rendering court or the modifying court may determine whether all of the parties and the child no longer reside in the decree rendering state, but only the decree rendering state can determine that it no longer has sufficient connections to retain CEJ. The effect is that UCCJEA states do not have to defer to CEJ claims of UCCJA courts whose initial decrees were not in compliance with the prioritized jurisdictional grounds of the UCCJEA.

F. Grounds to Decline Jurisdiction—Modification

1. The Uniform Child Custody Jurisdiction Act (UCCJA)

a. Mandatory Grounds

Prior pending action—The UCCJA recognizes two instances in which a court must decline jurisdiction to hear a modification petition. One instance is when there is a prior pending action in another state with jurisdiction under the UCCJA. The mandatory ground applies when, at the time of the filing of a petition to modify in a state, a proceeding concerning the custody of the child is pending in a court of another state having jurisdiction under the UCCJA, unless, of course, the court with the prior pending action defers to the other state as a more appropriate forum. As before, parties are required to inform the court in their pleadings of any pending child custody determinations, with the goal of allowing the courts to confer and determine the more appropriate forum for making the child custody determination consistent with the child's best interests.

Wrongful removal, in violation of a court order—Unless required in the interests of the child, a court must decline jurisdiction if the petitioner in a modification proceeding has wrongfully taken the child from another state or has engaged in similar reprehensible conduct in violation of a valid court order. If the court declines jurisdiction on this basis, it has the discretion to charge the petitioner with necessary travel and other expenses, including attorney's fees, incurred by the other parties or their witnesses.

b. Discretionary Grounds

Forum non conveniens—This discretionary ground is the same, under the UCCJA, for initial decrees and petitions to modify. A court has discretion to decline jurisdiction under the UCCJA if the court determines that it is an inconvenient forum and that another state is a more appropriate forum. If the court declines jurisdiction on this basis, it has the discretion to charge the petitioner with necessary travel and other expenses, including attorney's fees, incurred by the other parties or their witnesses.

Violation of a court order, other than wrongful removal—A court also has discretion to decline jurisdiction if the petitioner for a modification of a child custody determination has violated a court order with conduct less serious than parental kidnapping. If the court declines jurisdiction on this basis, it has the discretion to charge the petitioner with necessary travel and other expenses, including attorney's fees, incurred by the other parties or their witnesses.

2. The Uniform Child Custody Jurisdiction and Enforcement Act (UCCJEA)

The grounds for declining jurisdiction under the UCCJEA are the same with a petition to modify as they are with an initial petition.

a. Mandatory Grounds

Prior pending action—Like the UCCJA and PKPA, there is one instance in which a court must decline jurisdiction to modify another court's decree. It is when there is a prior pending action in another state with jurisdiction under the UCCJEA. The mandatory ground applies when, at the time of the filing of the petition in a state, a proceeding concerning the custody of the child is pending in a court of another state having jurisdiction under the UCCJEA, unless, of course, the court with the prior pending action defers to the other state as a more appropriate forum. Parties are required to inform the court in their pleadings of any pending child custody determinations, with the goal of allowing the courts to confer and determine the more appropriate forum for making the child custody determination, consistent with the child's best interests.

Unjustifiable conduct—Unlike the UCCJA, the UCCJEA does not distinguish between initial decrees and petitions to modify, or between mandatory and discretionary, when addressing grounds to decline jurisdiction based on parental behavior. A court must decline jurisdiction if the state has jurisdiction because of the unjustifiable conduct of the petitioner. Exceptions to the mandatory rule are recognized where all of the parties acquiesce in the court's jurisdiction, where a court that would otherwise have jurisdiction defers to the court that would otherwise have to decline jurisdiction, or where no court of another state would have jurisdiction under the UCCJEA. If the court declines jurisdiction under this section, it may fashion a remedy to ensure the safety of the child and to prevent a repetition of the unjustifiable conduct, including staying the proceeding until a child custody proceeding is commenced in a state with UCCJEA jurisdiction. If a court dismisses a petition or stays a proceeding because of unjustifiable conduct, it must assess expenses against the culpable party, unless the court finds that it would be clearly inappropriate to do so.

b. Discretionary Grounds

Forum non conveniens—Like the UCCJA, the UCCJEA gives a court discretion to decline jurisdiction if the court determines that it is an inconvenient forum and that another state is a more appropriate forum.

3. The Parental Kidnapping Prevention Act (PKPA)

Prior pending action—The PKPA grounds for declining jurisdiction do not distinguish between initial decrees and petitions to modify. The PKPA mandates declining jurisdiction where there is a prior pending action. The PKPA provides that a court of a state shall not exercise jurisdiction commenced during the pendency of a proceeding in a court of another state where that other court is exercising jurisdiction consistently with the PKPA to make a custody determination.

G. Enforcement Provisions

Neither the UCCJA nor the PKPA contained much in the way of enforcement provisions. One of the major contributions of the UCCJEA is the section on enforcement provisions.

1. The Uniform Child Custody Jurisdiction Act (UCCJA)

The UCCJA provided that the initial or modification decrees of another state, consistent with the provisions of the UCCJA, would be recognized and enforced. It also permitted a certified copy of a custody decree from another state to be filed in the clerk's office and enforced like any other custody order rendered by the forum state. Finally, it provided for the court to impose travel or other expenses, including attorney's fees, incurred by the party entitled to custody, on the party violating a custody decree and making it necessary to enforce the foreign decree in the forum state.

2. The Parental Kidnapping Prevention Act (PKPA)

The PKPA contains general language directing states to enforce child custody determinations made consistent with the provisions of the PKPA. It also authorizes use of the Federal Parent Locator Service in connection with enforcement of child custody orders and makes interstate or foreign parental kidnapping a federal crime punishable by a fine of not more than $5,000 or five years in prison, or both.

3. The Uniform Child Custody Jurisdiction and Enforcement Act (UCCJEA)

Drafters of the UCCJEA noted that there was, at that time, no uniform method of enforcing custody and visitation orders validly entered in another state, despite the fact that both the UCCJA and the PKPA direct the enforcement of those orders. The lack of uniformity regarding enforcement procedures and remedies increases the cost of the enforcement actions, decreases the certainty of outcome, and can result in a long and drawn-out procedure. The UCCJEA sought to address those problems by drafting a number of enforcement and remedial procedures.

a. Duty to Enforce

The UCCJEA requires courts to recognize and enforce a child custody determination from a sister state if the order is entered consistent with the provisions of the UCCJEA.

b. Temporary Visitation

The UCCJEA allows courts without modification jurisdiction to address visitation issues that might arise in that state, on a temporary basis. Even though a court does not have jurisdiction to modify an existing custody order, it may issue a temporary visitation order enforcing a visitation schedule decreed by another state or enforcing the visitation provisions of another state's decree that does not provide for a specific visitation schedule. The temporary visitation order must specify a period that the court considers adequate to allow the petitioner to obtain an order from the court having jurisdiction. The temporary visitation order remains in effect until an order is obtained from the other court with jurisdiction or until the period expires.

c. *Registration and Confirmation of a Child Custody Determination*

The UCCJEA provides a mechanism for registration and confirmation of a foreign decree in a sister state, with or without a simultaneous request for enforcement. Notice must be given to parties awarded custody or visitation, giving them an opportunity to contest the validity of the order being registered. The order will be confirmed, unless the contesting party can show that the issuing court lacked jurisdiction; that the order has been vacated, stayed, or modified by a court having jurisdiction; or that the requirements of notice and an opportunity to be heard were not met. Confirmation of the order precludes any further contest of the order, regarding any matter that could have been asserted at the time of registration.

As previously noted, the registration and confirmation procedure can be used by the nonresident parent to determine whether another state will give full faith and credit to the child custody determination, prior to sending the child to that state for parenting time with the other parent. If the order is registered and confirmed, the nonresident parent can safely send the child to the other state, confident that the other state will enforce the foreign decree, should the need arise.

d. *Simultaneous Proceedings*

If a court is petitioned to enforce (not modify) an order from a sister state and learns that a proceeding to modify is pending in the sister state, the proceeding for enforcement may continue unless the enforcing court, after consultation with the modifying court, decides to stay or dismiss the enforcement proceeding.

e. *Expedited Enforcement of Child Custody Determination*

The UCCJEA provides for expedited enforcement of a child custody determination, requiring courts to issue an order directing the respondent to appear in person, with or without the child, at a hearing. The court may also enter any order necessary to ensure the safety of the parties and the child. The court is required to hold a hearing on the next judicial day after service of the order, if possible. Otherwise, the hearing must be held on the next judicial day possible. The date may be extended by the court at the request of the petitioner. The order directing the respondent to appear must also state that the court may grant the petitioner immediate physical custody of the child and may also order expenses, in addition to further appropriate relief, unless the respondent appears and establishes (1) that the child custody determination has not been registered and confirmed and that a defense to its validity exists; or (2) that a registered and confirmed order has since been vacated, stayed, or modified by another court with jurisdiction.

f. Hearing and Order

Upon finding that the petitioner is entitled to immediate physical custody, a court must order that the petitioner may take immediate physical custody of the child, unless the court enters a temporary emergency order or the respondent establishes a defense valid against the registration and confirmation of the order. The court must also award fees, costs, and expenses as authorized in the act and may grant additional relief, including a request for law enforcement officials to assist the petitioner. The court may draw a negative inference from a party's refusal to testify on the ground of self-incrimination. Parties may not invoke interspousal confidential communications privilege, interspousal immunity, or parental immunity in enforcement proceedings.

g. Warrant to Take Physical Custody of the Child

A petitioner who files a petition for enforcement may also file a verified application for the issuance of a warrant to take physical custody of the child, if the child is immediately likely to suffer serious physical harm or to be removed from the state. A hearing must be held on the next judicial day after service of the order, if possible, otherwise, on the next judicial day possible. If the court finds that a less intrusive remedy is not effective, it may authorize law enforcement officers to enter private property and take physical custody of the child. Under exigent circumstances, a court may authorize law enforcement officers to make a forcible entry at any hour. The court may also impose conditions upon placement of a child to ensure the appearance of the child and the child's custodian.

h. Costs, Fees, and Expenses

The court is required to award the prevailing party necessary and reasonable expenses, including costs, communication expenses, attorney's fees, investigative fees, expenses for witnesses, travel expenses, and childcare expenses during the course of the proceedings, unless the party charged can establish that the award would be clearly inappropriate.

i. Appeals

The UCCJEA provides for expedited appeals, but a court is not allowed to stay an order enforcing a child custody determination pending appeal, unless the court enters a temporary emergency order.

H. International Custody Disputes

1. Applicability of the UCCJEA and UCCJA

The UCCJEA provides that a court may use the UCCJEA to enforce an order for the return of the child made under the Hague Convention, as if it were a domestic custody order (a child custody determination rendered by another state).

2. The Hague Convention on Child Abduction (Hague Convention)

In 1980, the Hague Convention on the Civil Aspects of International Child Abduction was adopted to secure the return of children wrongfully removed from their country of "habitual residence." Congress passed implementing legislation in 1986, entitled, the International Child Abduction Remedies Act (ICARA). In 2014, the International Child Abduction Prevention and Return Act (ICAPRA) was adopted by Congress to enhance Hague Convention compliance and provide additional assistance to victim parents. The Hague convention is civil in nature, and the remedies under the convention are nonexclusive. An injured parent may choose to pursue a state custody action under the UCCJA or UCCJEA, instead.

The Hague Convention applies to children under the age of sixteen who were "habitually resident" of a signatory country, immediately before any breach of custody or access rights. A petition must be brought within one year from the wrongful taking or retention of the child. The court must return the child to the country of habitual residence, unless one of three defenses is shown by clear and convincing evidence:

1. Lack of actual exercise of custody by the petitioner; or petitioner's consent, or acquiescence, to the removal or retention;
2. A grave risk that return to the country of habitual residence will expose the child to physical or emotional harm or other intolerable situation; or
3. Objection to the return by a child of suitable age.

3. The International Parental Kidnapping Act of 1993 (IPKA)

The International Parental Kidnapping Act makes it a federal felony, punishable by up to three years in prison and a fine, to remove or retain a child outside the United States with the intent to obstruct the lawful exercise of parental rights. Parental rights are defined as the right to physical custody of the child. The act applies to children under the age of sixteen. There are three recognized defenses that may be shown:

1. The defendant acted within the provisions of a valid court order granting the defendant legal custody or visitation rights and that order was obtained pursuant to the UCCJA or the UCCJEA and was in effect at the time of the offense;
2. The defendant was fleeing an incidence or pattern of domestic violence; or
3. The defendant had physical custody of the child pursuant to a court order granting legal custody or visitation rights and failed to return the child as a result of circumstances beyond the defendant's control, and the defendant notified or made reasonable attempts to notify the other parent or lawful custodian of the child of such circumstances within twenty-four hours after the visitation period had expired and returned the child as soon as possible.

CHECKPOINTS

- In an effort to avoid parental kidnapping and to resolve jurisdictional disputes among states over custody issues, the National Conference of Commissioners on Uniform State Laws proposed the Uniform Child Custody Jurisdiction Act. The UCCJA was finally adopted by all 50 states, although not always in the uniform version. Before the UCCJA was adopted by all states, Congress addressed the problem by passing the PKPA, Parental Kidnapping Prevention Act. More recently, the UCCJA was amended by the UCCJEA, the Uniform Child Custody Jurisdiction and Enforcement Act, which has been adopted in 48 states.
- The UCCJA, the UCCJEA, and the PKPA all address the same issues of jurisdiction to render an initial child custody determination

and jurisdiction to modify an existing child custody determination. Where the acts are in conflict, however, federal law, the PKPA, preempts state law and is controlling.

- The only consequence of failing to follow the PKPA is that the state's decree is not entitled to full faith and credit in other states.
- The Supreme Court ruled that the PKPA does not create a private cause of action for noncompliance, so a party cannot file an action in federal district court. Instead, the only way to get federal review is to create federal question jurisdiction.
- When trying to determine whether a court may assume jurisdiction to hear a custody matter, the first question is whether the UCCJEA applies and whether the other state or states involved have passed the UCCJEA.
- If the UCCJA or UCCJEA applies, the next question to ask is whether the issue involves an initial decree or a modification of a prior existing decree.
- In addition to meeting the custody requirements under the relevant acts, for a decree to be valid, there must be proper notice to the defendant with an opportunity to be heard, consistent with procedural due process.
- If any of the parties are not parents, they must meet the definition of a "person acting as a parent," having had physical custody for six consecutive months within the year prior to filing or having been awarded legal custody.
- The UCCJA does not prioritize jurisdictional grounds.
- The PKPA gives priority to home state jurisdiction over significant connections jurisdiction.
- The UCCJEA prioritizes all jurisdictional grounds.
- Even though a court may have jurisdiction to make a child custody determination, there may be mandatory or discretionary grounds to decline that jurisdiction.
- The PKPA recognizes continuing jurisdiction after a court makes an initial child custody determination, so long as the state remains the residence of the child or any contestant.

- The UCCJEA limits exclusive continuing jurisdiction to decrees entered by courts with jurisdiction consistent with the UCCJEA, where the court retains significant connections, and a parent or person acting as a parent continues to reside in the state.
- The UCCJEA provides a number of enforcement and remedial mechanisms.

CHAPTER 11

Divorce Custody Determinations

ROADMAP

After reading this chapter, you should understand:

- The various types of custody;
- The various standards for determining custody, including those that are impermissible;
- The relevant factors that may be considered in determining custody;
- The standards for modifying custody; and
- The means of enforcing a custody order.

Custody decisions are some of the most difficult decisions that courts are called upon to make. Historically, custody was the prerogative of the father as the children were considered his property. Gradually, states began to adopt the tender years presumption, finding that young children should presumptively be placed in the mother's custody. The tender years doctrine expanded in many states to include all minor children at the time of the divorce.

Our court systems have always considered the best interests of the child to be paramount in making custody determinations. Courts and legislatures have struggled over the years, however, trying to define standards for determining custody, consistent with the best interests of the child.

A. Terminology

Courts and legislatures traditionally used the terms custody and visitation when making decisions concerning children at the time of divorce. These terms grew to have negative connotations, however. The "good" parent was awarded custody, and the "bad" parent received visitation. The custodial parent was the "real" parent, while the noncustodial parent was just a "visitor."

In an effort to remove some of the stigma attached to the role of noncustodial parent and to facilitate more cooperation and joint parenting following divorce, some states have adopted more parent-friendly, inclusive terms such as primary residential parent instead of custodial parent; allocation of parenting responsibilities and residential time, or parenting time, instead of custody and visitation; and alternate residential parent, rather than noncustodial parent.

In the materials below, however, the terms custody and visitation will be used for purposes of clarity and simplicity, as many states still use these terms.

B. Types of Custody

1. Sole Custody without Visitation

One type of custody is sole custody without visitation to the other parent. In this arrangement, the custodial parent makes all of the decisions regarding the child. The other parent has no right to make decisions for, or spend time with, the child. Orders of this type are unusual today, unless the court has determined that contact with the other parent would be harmful to the child, or unless agreed to by the parties.

2. Primary Custody with Visitation

Primary custody with visitation is probably the most common form of custody order, whether ordered by the court or agreed to by the parties. Under this arrangement, the child lives primarily with one parent and spends time with the other parent. The time with the other parent generally includes significant parental time including overnight visits and time during the summer and on alternate holidays, but it generally does not come close to equal time spent with each parent.

3. Joint (Shared) Custody

Joint custody can mean different things, depending upon the court, or the parties. It may refer only to joint physical custody, meaning that the child spends approximately equal time with each parent. The child may alternate weeks, or months, or some other time interval, between parents' homes. In some cases, the child stays in the home and the parents move in and out. The core concept, however, is that the child spends a substantially equal amount of time with each parent.

The term may refer only to joint legal custody, which is decision-making authority regarding the child's health, education, religion, and other matters. With joint legal custody, each parent has equal decision-making authority, making it important to have some procedure for tiebreaking, when the parents are unable to agree, rather than having to return to court each time.

The term may also apply to both physical and legal custody, sometimes referred to as shared custody or equally shared custody. Unfortunately, courts, parties, and legislatures are not always clear about their intentions when using the term, joint custody. In recent years, some legislatures and some courts have adopted a preference, or even a presumption, for joint custody or maximum participation by both parents, on the assumption that it is in the child's best interest. Again, the term means different things in different states. Generally, a state or a court mandated preference for joint custody refers to joint legal custody. But there are instances in which it means both joint legal custody as well as joint physical custody.

Other states take the opposite view and assume that joint physical as well as joint legal custody are not in the child's best interest but will generally allow it if the parties themselves agree to it, on the assumption that they know what is best for their situation. The rationale behind not preferring joint custody is the assumption that the parties are not able to get along well enough post-divorce to co-parent equally. Ordering joint custody over the parties' objections, or over the objection of one party, would put the child in the middle of ongoing parental conflict, which would not be in the child's best interests.

4. Split Custody

Split custody is an option where there are two or more children. With split custody, one parent is the custodial parent of one child and the other parent is the custodial parent of the other child or children. Courts are reluctant to split custody, because it means separating siblings, but may approve split custody if the parties agree to it, and the needs of the children are unique.

5. Subject Specific Custody

The court may order, or the parties may agree to, subject specific custody, such as custody for health care decisions or religious custody, etc. With subject specific custody, one parent is named the custodial parent who will make most of the decisions regarding the child and with whom the child will live primarily, but the other parent will have decision-making authority regarding health care decisions, for instance, or matters regarding religion, etc. This approach is rare.

C. Standards for Determining Custody

Over the years, courts and legislatures have tried different standards for determining custody. The advantage of having a clear standard or presumption is that it leads to greater predictability, which leads to more agreements on custody. The greater the indeterminacy, the greater the likelihood that the custody issue will be litigated or at least used strategically in the bargaining process between the parties. Contested custody battles and strategic bargaining can make the child a pawn in the parents' ongoing conflict, to the detriment of the child.

Courts encourage couples to reach an agreement regarding custody and visitation issues because the parents generally know better than the court what is best for their family. Any agreement must, however, be approved by the court, based on a best interest standard.

1. Presumptions

a. Tender Years

The tender years presumption was followed by most states, until it was successfully challenged on equal protection grounds in the 1980s. The underlying rationale for the doctrine is that children of a tender age are better cared for by the mother. The tender years presumption applied not only to children of tender years, but to older children as well, generally resulting in custody being given to mothers routinely. In many states, the presumption could be overcome only by showing that the mother was unfit. Gradually, however, some states began to weaken the presumption and allow it to be overcome by a showing that custody with the father, or joint custody, would be in the child's best interests.

b. Primary Caretaker

When courts and legislatures were not able to rely upon the tender years presumption, some chose to substitute a presumption in favor of the primary caretaker of the child. Other states simply added the primary caretaker as a factor to be considered in a custody determination based on the comparative fitness of the parents.

c. Psychological Parent

The concept of the psychological parent looks at the relationship between the child and each of the parents to determine which parent has a closer emotional and psychological bond to the child. The underlying rationale is that it is in the child's best interests to have custody awarded to the parent to whom the child is most closely bonded.

d. Joint Custody

As discussed above, some states have moved toward a presumption in favor of, or at least a preference for, joint custody. In some cases, joint custody means joint legal custody and in others it means both joint legal custody as well as joint physical custody. Other states have moved in the opposite direction and oppose joint custody unless it is expressly agreed to by the parties or the court makes an affirmative finding that joint custody is in the child's best interest.

2. Random Selection

Some scholars have taken the position that there is no way, in most cases, for a court to know what is truly in a child's best interest. The answer, then, is simply to make a random selection between the two fit parents. The benefit to the child is the elimination of the trauma of a custody fight and the preservation of family resources that can be spent on the child rather than on custody litigation. It also precludes a contest between the fit parents to determine who is "more fit."

3. Comparative Fitness

Many states currently follow a comparative fitness approach to determine custody of children. The courts are generally required to consider a number of statutory factors in making a best interest determination. The court will also determine what type of custodial arrangement is in the child's best interest.

4. Historical Allocation of Parental Responsibilities

The American Law Institute's Principles of the Law of Family Dissolution: Analysis and Recommendations (ALI Principles), promulgated in 2000, recommends that the court try to replicate in its custody decision the same allocation of parenting responsibilities that the parents shared prior to the divorce. The underlying theory is that stability and continuity of care is in the child's best interest. (See further discussion of ALI Principles below.)

D. Relevant Factors

Most courts are required to consider a number of statutory factors in making a custody determination. Some of the most common factors will be reviewed below, along with some factors that used to be considered and are no longer permissible considerations.

1. Gender

The gender of the parents is no longer a permissible factor in making a custody determination, following the equal protection challenges to the tender years presumption discussed above, where maternal custody was presumed to be in the child's best interest. It was not uncommon, in the past, for courts to consider gender in a different way, for older children, by taking the position that older children needed the same gender parent as a role model for adult behavior, giving the same gendered parent an advantage in the custody determination.

2. Sexual Activities

Courts historically have taken three approaches to parental sexual behavior and its effect on custody. One approach is the per se approach, which considers inappropriate sexual conduct, whether heterosexual or homosexual, as per se evidence of parental unfitness. The second approach is the nexus approach. This approach requires a showing of some nexus between the parental sexual activity and a detrimental or harmful effect on the child. The third approach is the factor approach. It simply treats parental sexual behavior as one more factor in the list of many factors that the court can take into account in making a best interest determination. Most states have moved away from the per se approach in favor of the nexus or factor approach.

3. Sexual Orientation

Parental homosexuality, at one time, was treated as per se evidence of parental unfitness by some courts. Since *Lawrence v. Texas*, 123 S. Ct. 2472 (2003), and certainly since *Obergefell v. Hodges*, 576 U.S. 644 (2015), courts have increasingly moved away from considering sexual orientation as a factor in child custody decisions. Today, most courts take the position that sexual orientation, in and of itself, is not a sufficient basis to deny custody or visitation. The sexual activities of the parent, however, may be considered, as noted above.

4. Work Obligations

As more women sought to have a career in addition to being the custodial parent, some courts saw career demands as a negative factor in determining a mother's parental fitness. A court was especially likely to make this negative inference if the father had someone available to care for the child full-time in the home, while the mother was planning to rely on childcare. Currently, most courts do not consider the work demands of parents in making a custody determination, except in unusual circumstances where the work demands would seriously interfere with the parent's custodial obligations. However, several states in moving toward a more comprehensive shared parenting approach, have adopted either statutory or informal decision-making that favors maximum participation by both parents over care by third parties.

5. Religious Activities

Parents have a right to practice their own religious beliefs and to introduce the child to their religious beliefs, as long as there is no danger of harm to the child. Courts apply different standards for determining when religious activities may be taken into account in making a custody award. Most courts require a showing of harm or detriment to the child. Other courts consider it a factor among many that the court may consider in making a comparative fitness determination.

6. Incarceration

A parent's incarceration, obviously, may be a factor in awarding physical custody, particularly if the parent will be incarcerated for a long period of time. Even though a parent is incarcerated, that parent could be awarded joint legal custody, as long as doing so is consistent with the child's best interest.

7. Race

Race is an impermissible factor in determining custody. It is impermissible to consider race of the parent as well as the race of someone that parent is dating. The Supreme Court, in *Palmore v. Sidoti*, 466 U.S. 429 (1984), held that race cannot be a factor in awarding custody.

8. Domestic Violence

Until fairly recently, many states did not consider domestic violence between the parents as relevant to the issue of custody. Courts took the position that domestic violence was an issue between the parents, as long as the domestic violence was not directed toward the children. Most states now realize that being exposed to domestic violence between the parents can be emotionally harmful to children and can model behavior that the children may emulate as adults, either as a future victim or a future abuser. Some courts limit or deny parental contact between the abuser and the child where domestic violence is found. Some states have a rebuttable presumption against awarding custody to a parent with a history of committing domestic violence. Some courts take the position that even the victim is not a suitable parent to have custody, based on the victim's inability to prevent the children's exposure to domestic violence.

9. Friendly Parent Provision

Some social science research has demonstrated a correlation between post divorce parental cooperation and healthy outcomes for children. Children who have a loving relationship with both parents are more likely to develop into well-adjusted adults. Some courts consider whether a parent is willing to cooperate with the other parent, and that level of cooperation is a factor in determining custody.

10. Parental Health

Most courts will consider the physical and mental health of each parent in making a custody determination. Obviously, to the extent that the parent is physically or mentally unable to care for the child, the court may find that it is not in the child's best interest to award custody to that parent. On the other hand, the mere fact that a parent may be physically disabled or somewhat mentally challenged, does not usually preclude custody, as long as the child is not exposed to a dangerous or potentially harmful situation. Some lower courts have denied custody to physically handicapped parents in the past, but those decisions were generally overturned on appeal, on the theory that parenting is more about the emotional bond between the parent and child than about the ability to throw a football. On the other hand, a court would also be reluctant to grant custody to a handicapped parent where the evidence was clear that the child was going to be more of a caretaker to the parent than the other way around.

11. Child Abuse

A finding of child abuse by a parent would, in most instances, preclude granting custody to the abusive parent. It would not matter whether the abuse was physical, emotional, or sexual. Mere allegations of abuse, on the other hand, cause a great deal more difficulty for courts because of the concern that false allegations may be made by one parent in order to gain a strategic advantage in the divorce proceeding. Unfortunately, sexual abuse is very difficult to prove or disprove. What may be considered physical abuse to one parent may be parental discipline to the other. What may be seen as emotional abuse to one parent may be considered teasing or discipline to the other.

12. Child's Preference

Courts are generally reluctant to draw children into the custody determination, for fear of putting the child in a no-win position of choosing between the parents. However, many states do have statutory provisions that allow a child of a certain age to be heard regarding their preference. The court will generally hear from the child in camera, with attorneys for each side present. If the attorneys are excluded, they are typically given a transcript of the interview. The child's preference, however, is not outcome determinative. The court will give the child's testimony whatever weight is deemed appropriate by the court.

13. Siblings

Courts generally like to keep siblings together, if at all possible. There may be unusual circumstances where it may be in the children's best interests to be separated, however, particularly where there may be a great deal of jealousy or animosity between children.

14. Expert Opinion

Courts are increasingly likely to consider expert testimony from counselors, psychologists and psychiatrists regarding the parties as well as the child, where that information is relevant to a custody determination. The evidence of the expert is not outcome determinative, however. The ultimate decision is one for the court to make. The court may give the expert's testimony whatever weight the court deems advisable, which includes ignoring it altogether.

E. Modification Standards

1. General Standards

Once a custody determination has been made, courts are reluctant to reopen that matter. Without some limitations, some litigious parents would continue to battle over custody throughout the child's minority. Custody battles between parents can take a terrible toll on the children involved. Courts try to limit that type of negative exposure for the child, where possible, consistent with the child's best interest. Some courts place a specific minimum time limit on modification petitions, for instance, two years following the initial award of custody, subject to exigent circumstances. Other courts impose a threshold test for hearing a petition to modify such as a substantial and material change of circumstances. Some states do both.

Some states have held that the change of circumstances generally must pertain to facts not contemplated by the parties or the court at the time of the original decree. Some states, however, acknowledge that even contemplated facts, such as a child's age, could cause a change in the child's best interest and should permit modification. If the original decree is based on an agreement of the parties rather than a contested hearing, the court may allow facts existing at the time of the agreement to be considered, because those facts have not previously been litigated before the court.

2. Change of Custodial Parent

Courts are reluctant to change the designation of custodial parent from one parent to the other, absent a very good reason to do so. The social science evidence supports the importance of stability and continuity of care in the child's life. The approach of many courts is that once a determination of custody has been made, that arrangement should remain in place, absent a substantial and material change of circumstances that would justify reopening the matter. If, however, the court determines that the threshold test has been made for reconsidering custody, it may, at that point, apply a general best interest of the child standard to determine whether a modification is warranted. Some courts impose a higher standard, i.e., changing custody only where failing to do so would expose the child to some danger of harm.

If there has been a de facto change of custody, where the parties have acquiesced in allowing the child to live primarily with the noncustodial parent, courts will generally require a lesser threshold standard to hear a modification petition seeking to modify the court order to reflect the reality of the custodial arrangement.

3. Modification of the Type of Custody

Courts may be more likely to revisit the type of custody ordered, particularly when the arrangement was agreed to by the parties rather than ordered by the court, at least in those states without a presumption in favor of joint custody. For instance, if the parties agreed to joint (shared) custody and one of the parties later decides it isn't working out, the court might be willing to hear the petition and make a determination that would serve the child's best interest. In such cases, the petitioner may not have to meet the threshold standard of showing changed circumstances.

4. Relocation

Relocation decisions have been very difficult issues for the courts. Most states have changed the applicable standard more than once. In some states, the standard has changed multiple times with both the courts and the legislature weighing in. The noncustodial parent often objects to the relocation because of the detrimental effect that relocation will have on that parent's access to the child. The custodial parent, on the other hand, argues that he or she should be free to pursue other opportunities, and not be held captive by the non-custodial parent. Obviously, the custodial parent is free to move, the real question is whether the custodial parent can relocate with the child in question. Frequently, the custodial parent will have remarried and may want to relocate to be with the new spouse and perhaps with children of the later marriage. The relocation may be necessary to pursue a degree program in order to increase the custodial parent's earning capacity. On the other hand, the relocation may be designed simply to deprive the noncustodial parent of access to the child.

Some states put the burden on the relocating parent to show that a move would be in the child's best interest. This approach is supported by social science research demonstrating the benefits to the child of regular, ongoing contact with both parents. Other states put the burden on the noncustodial parent to show that the relocation would be harmful to the child. Some states share the burden by requiring the relocating parent to show a legitimate purpose for the move and that the location is reasonable in light of that purpose. Then the burden shifts to the noncustodial parent to show that the move would not be in the child's best interest.

Some states recognize a presumption in favor of relocation, based on social science evidence supporting the importance of stability and continuity of care. Other states recognize a presumption in favor of relocation only in cases where there is a primary residential parent. In those states, if both parents are actually spending substantially equal parenting time with the child, no presumption attaches and the court makes a best interest determination regarding the relocation. Typical grounds to overcome the presumption in favor of relocation include a vindictive motive for the relocation, or a showing of potential harm or danger to the child. Some states impose no presumption and simply apply a best interest analysis to a relocation petition, treating it like any other custody modification petition.

Finally, some states separate the relocation decision from the ultimate custody decision, while others do not. Some states will condition custody on relocation, ordering that custody will change to the non-relocating parent if the custodial parent relocates. Other states allow the court to decide first whether relocation should be allowed. If the court decides that relocation should not be allowed, but the custodial parent decides to move anyway, the court will then address the custody arrangement in light of those new facts, to determine whether the child is better off relocating or having custody change to the non-relocating parent.

5. Parental Alienation Syndrome (PAS)

If one parent undertakes deliberately to destroy the relationship between the child and the other parent, the court may decide not to award custody to the alienating parent, on that basis alone. As previously stated, social science evidence supports the need for a child to have a close, loving relationship with both parents, if at all possible.

6. Military Deployment

A number of states have recently passed legislation addressing the issue of parents who are in the military and receive orders to deploy. Most statutes provide that the courts may not deprive a parent of custody solely on the basis of deployment. The court may, however, make temporary arrangements for custody of the child, while the military parent is deployed, with a goal of returning custody of the child to the military parent at the end of the deployment.

F. Agreement by the Parents

Courts encourage the parties, where possible, to reach their own agreements concerning custodial arrangement for the children of the marriage. Any agreement that the parties make must be approved by the court, however. The court will review the agreement to determine if it is consistent with the child's best interest. In most cases, the court will defer to the judgment of the parties concerning the best arrangements for their family.

G. Mediation

Courts have shown a great deal of interest, in recent years, in alternative dispute resolution as a way to resolve conflicts without having to resort to litigation. Litigation is costly, time-consuming, and, because it is adversarial, does not generally facilitate co-parenting following divorce. Mediation is the type of alternative dispute resolution most often used in conjunction with divorcing parties. Some courts encourage mediation, while other courts mandate it. In mandated, (court annexed) mediation, the court often requires special training for court-appointed mediators. Oftentimes, the court-appointed mediators will have to agree to provide some pro-bono mediation, which the court can use for indigent clients. Some studies indicate that mediation correlates with better cooperation between the parents following divorce.

H. Parenting Plans

Historically, custody orders generally named one parent as the custodial parent and awarded reasonable visitation to the other parent. More recently, courts have begun to require much greater specificity as to parenting arrangements between the parties, in part to lessen opportunities for future conflicts, and in part to preserve judicial resources. Parenting plans are now required in some states, which must be approved by the court. The parenting plans are generally forms provided by the court, which allow the parties to address many of the co-parenting issues that will arise post divorce. Parenting plans generally require the parties to decide which parent will have responsibility for the child on any given day: how holidays and vacation time will be allocated; how parental decisions will be made; and how disputes will be resolved, prior to returning to court. Again, studies have shown that parents are much more compliant when they are involved in addressing these issues themselves, rather than having the court make the decision for them.

I. Parent Education Programs

A number of states now require parents to attend parent education programs while the divorce is pending. These programs are generally fairly short, usually several hours in length. The programs attempt to address some of the main parenting issues that arise in most divorces, with the goal of protecting the children of the divorce. The underlying rationale is that most parents love and want to protect their children, but are simply not aware of how divorce affects children. These programs attempt to educate the parents so that they, in turn, can do what is best for their children. Typical examples include helping parents with conflict resolution skills and advising parents not to disparage the other parent in front of the child or allow others to do so and not to make the child a messenger for communications between the parents (i.e., "Tell your mom/dad that her/his child support is due.").

Failure to attend the parent education programs can be grounds for contempt, but generally cannot be grounds to deny the divorce. Some states allow the court to consider refusal to attend the parent education program when determining custody. In some states, however, the parent education programs are optional.

J. Case Management

In high conflict divorces, particularly those with minor children, the court may employ certain case management techniques, also known as differential case management or high conflict case management, in an effort to diffuse the animosity between the parties and to move the case toward resolution. The theory is that early intervention by the court and early referrals to mediation or other forms of alternative dispute resolution may lessen the acrimony between the parties and better protect the children involved.

K. Parenting Coordinators

A parenting coordinator may be appointed by the court to assist with implementation of court orders by making recommendations to the court regarding implementation, clarification, modification, and enforcement of custody and parenting plans. Courts are most likely to appoint a parenting coordinator when:

1. The parents are persistently in conflict with one another;
2. There is a history of substance abuse by either parent or family violence;

3. There are serious concerns about the mental health or behavior of either parent;
4. A child has special needs; or
5. It would otherwise be in the children's best interests to do so.

Parents may consent to use a parenting coordinator and may agree to a specific person, subject to approval by the court, or the court may choose the person to serve as the parenting coordinator. The parenting coordinator must be an individual with appropriate training and qualifications. Oftentimes, a family counselor, psychiatrist, or psychologist is appointed. The court may also appoint an experienced family law practitioner to serve in a guardian ad litem role. The parenting coordinator may simply act as a facilitator or may have some decision-making authority. The decision-making authority is generally granted by the parties, rather than the court.

L. Enforcement of Custodial Rights

Interference with custodial rights is a serious matter. There are a number of remedies both civil and criminal designed to deter such conduct, to provide remedies for the custodial parent, and, most importantly, to protect the child.

1. Contempt

Intentional interference with the custody order is punishable by contempt. Courts generally recognize an exception, however, where the contemptuous parent is fleeing domestic violence or otherwise attempting to protect the child from the custodial parent.

2. Tort Remedies

Tortious interference with custody is a recognized tort claim in a number of states. The RESTATEMENT (SECOND) OF TORTS § 700, TITLED INTENTIONAL INTERFERENCE WITH CUSTODY, provides that one parent may be liable to the other for intentional interference with the custody of the child, including enticing the child away from a parent or harboring a child who has left home against a custodial parent's wishes.

3. UCCJA, PKPA, and UCCJEA Enforcement

The UCCJA, PKPA, and UCCJEA all address the recognition of custody decrees entered in a sister state. These acts are discussed in the chapter on Child Custody Jurisdiction and Enforcement. There are a number of enforcement tools and remedies under the UCCJEA enforcement section, which are also discussed in the chapter on Child Custody Jurisdiction and Enforcement.

4. Criminal Sanctions

a. Custodial Interference

A number of states criminalize intentional interference with the custodial rights of the other parent. In some cases, the crime is a felony and includes both imprisonment and a fine.

b. International Parental Kidnapping Crime Act of 1993

The International Parental Kidnapping Crime Act makes it a federal felony, punishable by up to three years in prison and a fine, to remove or retain a child outside the United States with the intent to obstruct the lawful exercise of parental rights. Parental rights are defined as the right to physical custody of the child. The act applies to children under the age of sixteen. There are three recognized defenses that may be shown:

1. The defendant acted within the provisions of a valid court order granting the defendant legal custody or visitation rights and that order was obtained pursuant to the UCCJA or the UCCJEA and was in effect at the time of the offense;
2. The defendant was fleeing an incidence or pattern of domestic violence; or
3. The defendant had physical custody of the child pursuant to a court order granting legal custody or visitation rights and failed to return the child as a result of circumstances beyond the defendant's control, and the defendant notified or made reasonable attempts to notify the other parent or lawful custodian of the child of such circumstances within twenty-four hours after the visitation period had expired and returned the child as soon as possible.

M. Counsel for the Child

Very few states have clearly defined guidelines addressing when counsel will be appointed for the child in a custody determination. Even fewer states have clear guidelines concerning the role of the child's representative. States, and even courts within a state, differ on the terminology used and what the individual terms mean. Several of the possible models will be discussed below. Regardless of the names used, the issues generally center on whether the child's representative represents the child or advocates for the child's best interest or is simply a fact finder for the court.

1. Guardian ad Litem

Guardian ad litem is probably the term most often used to designate someone who represents the child's best interests in a custody hearing. The Guardian ad litem may be required to be a lawyer, but often, need not be. Sometimes the Guardian ad litem is more of a fact finder for the court, charged with investigating the case and providing the court with a report and recommendation. Other times, the Guardian ad litem may be an attorney representing the child's best interests, who calls witnesses and advocates on behalf of the child's best interests.

2. Attorney ad Litem

The Attorney ad litem is, by definition, an attorney. The Attorney ad litem generally represents the child as a client and advocates for the child's wishes. In some cases, however, the Attorney ad litem will be charged to advocate for the child's best interests and to simply make the court aware of the child's wishes, to the extent that they differ from the position that the Attorney ad litem is advocating. The Attorney ad litem may also be appointed when the child has a guardian ad litem advocating for her best interest but has expressed a different position, thus creating a conflict of interest that the court often resolves by appointing an attorney ad litem to advocate the child's position, while leaving the guardian ad litem to advocate the child's best interest.

N. Custody Claims by De Facto Parents

Sometimes a court will be presented with a claim for custody by someone other than a legal parent. Possible claimants include relatives, parental paramours, stepparents, and other caregivers, to name a few. Typically, courts will give a strong preference to the legal parent. In some states, the doctrine is referred to as the natural parent preference. Other states recognize a state constitutional right to parent one's child, absent a showing of harm or potential harm to the child. In those states recognizing a presumption in favor of the natural parent, the standards for overcoming the presumption vary from state to state. Some states make a best interest determination, while others require a showing of harm to the child and still others require a showing of parental unfitness to overcome the presumption in favor of the parent.

O. Uniform Laws

1. Uniform Marriage and Divorce Act (UMDA)

The Uniform Marriage and Divorce Act (UMDA), promulgated in 1970 by the National Conference of Commissioners on Uniform State Laws (NCCUSL), has been adopted, at least in part, by a number of states. The UMDA requires the court to make a custody determination based on the best interests of the child, after considering relevant statutory factors including parental preferences; the child's wishes; the relationship between the child and the parents, and any other persons who may significantly affect the child's best interests; the child's adjustment to his home, school, and community; and the mental and physical health of all individuals involved. The court cannot consider parental conduct that does not affect the parent-child relationship.

The UMDA prohibits modification petitions within two years of a custodial decree absent affidavits that give the court reason to believe that the child's present environment may endanger seriously the child's physical, mental, moral, or emotional health. The threshold test for considering a parent's modification petition is a change of circumstances, based on facts that have arisen since the prior decree, or that were unknown to the court at the time of the entry of the prior decree, such that modification is necessary to serve the best interests of the child. The court shall, however, retain the custodial appointment made in the prior degree, unless one of three circumstances, known as consent, integration, or endangerment is found:

1. The custodian agrees to modification;
2. The child has been integrated into the family of the petitioner with consent of the custodian; or
3. The child's present environment endangers seriously his physical, mental, moral, or emotional health, and the harm likely to be caused by a change of environment is outweighed by its advantages to him.

The court is also required to assess attorney fees and costs against the party seeking modification if the court finds that the petition is vexatious and constitutes harassment.

2. American Law Institute Principles of the Law of Family Dissolution (ALI Principles)

The American Law Institute's Principles of the Law of Family Dissolution: Analysis and Recommendations (ALI Principles), was promulgated in 2000. In almost three decades since its passage, legislators and courts alike have failed to formally adopt its recommendations. The ALI, though, is still persuasive in its functional approach to family law. The ALI Principles recommend parental agreement using parenting plans. In contested cases, the court is advised to award custody in such a way as to approximate the portion of caretaking undertaken by each parent prior to the separation or the filing of the action, if not married. Exceptions to the approximation standard apply in certain circumstances:

1. To permit the child to have a relationship with each parent;
2. To accommodate the wishes of an older child;
3. To keep siblings together;
4. To protect the child's welfare;
5. To take into account a prior agreement of the parties;
6. To avoid an allocation that would be impractical or would create instability for the child;
7. To provide for visitation in the case of relocation; or
8. To avoid harm to the child.

There are a number of factors that the court may not consider including:

1. Race or ethnicity of the child, parent, or other member of the household;
2. The sex of a parent or the child;
3. The religious practices of a child or parent, except to protect the child from harm or to protect the child's ability to practice a religion that has been a significant part of the child's life;
4. The sexual orientation of a parent;
5. The extramarital sexual conduct of a parent, absent a showing that it causes harm to the child; or
6. The parents' relative earning capacities or financial circumstances.

The court should, however, consider any limiting factors and take steps to protect the child and the other parent. Limiting factors include:

1. Child abuse, neglect or abandonment;
2. Domestic violence;
3. Drug or alcohol abuse; or
4. Persistent and unjustified interference with the other parent's access to the child.

Joint legal custody is presumed to be in the child's best interests, unless rebutted. The presumption is rebutted if there is a history of domestic violence or child abuse, or if it is shown that joint legal custody is not in the child's best interests.

The court may order a written investigation or evaluation to assist it in determining any issue related to custody. The court may also appoint a Guardian ad litem to represent the child's best interests or an Attorney ad litem to represent the child or to represent the Guardian ad litem. The court should consider the parties' financial resources when deciding whether to make such appointments and should allocate the costs equitably.

The ALI Principles argue that parents by estoppel should be treated equal to legal parents in custodial decisions. A parent by estoppel is defined as a person who is not a legal parent under state law, but who:

1. Is obligated to pay child support; or
2. Lived with the child for more than two years and during that time had a reasonable good faith belief that he was the father and assumed parental responsibilities, even if he later learned the true facts; or

3. Lived with the child since the child's birth, holding out and accepting full and permanent parental responsibilities, as part of a prior co-parenting agreement with the child's legal parent or parents, when the court finds that recognition of the individual as a parent is in the child's best interests; or
4. Lived with the child for at least two years, holding out and accepting full parental responsibilities pursuant to an agreement with the child's parent or parents, when the court finds that recognition of the individual as a parent is in the child's best interests.

CHECKPOINTS

- There are a number of different custodial arrangements, including sole custody without visitation, primary custody with visitation, joint (shared) custody, split custody, and subject specific custody.
- Some states have eliminated old custodial terminology in favor of more parent inclusive terms such as parenting time, primary residential parent, alternate residential parent, parental decision making authority, and parental obligations.
- Many states base custody determinations on the comparative fitness of the parents, but some states recognize a presumption in favor of joint custody.
- Many states have a list of statutory factors that a court may or must consider in making a custody determination. Race cannot be a decisive factor.
- Courts may not apply a custodial presumption based on the gender of the parent.
- The preference of an older child may be considered, but is not outcome determinative.
- Courts encourage the parents, where possible, to reach an agreement on custody. Such agreement, however, is always subject to court approval, based on the child's best interests.
- Modification of a custody order generally requires a showing of a substantial and material change of circumstances not contemplated

at the time of the existing decree, such that the welfare of the child requires a change in custody.

- Some courts apply a different standard for relocation cases, recognizing a presumption in favor of relocation in some cases.
- Custodial rights can be enforced under the UCCJEA, by a contempt petition, a tort claim, and by criminal sanctions.
- A child may be represented in some cases by a guardian ad litem or an attorney ad litem. The guardian ad litem generally represents the best interests of the child while the attorney ad litem generally represents the child or the guardian ad litem.
- Most states recognize a presumption in favor of legal parents in custody disputes between legal parents and de facto parents.

CHAPTER 12

Visitation

ROADMAP

After reading this chapter, you should understand:

- The standards for granting, limiting and denying visitation to a legal parent;
- The rights that are generally granted to a noncustodial parent;
- The grounds for modifying visitation;
- The special rules applicable to relocation;
- The various means of enforcing visitation; and
- The rights of certain third parties to seek visitation.

A. Terminology

Visitation is the term traditionally used for the time that the noncustodial parent is allowed to spend with the child following divorce. In an effort to remove the connotation that the noncustodial parent is a mere visitor, vis-à-vis the child, some states have begun to use more parent-friendly terminology. Visitation is often referred to as parenting time or residential time or an allocation of parental responsibilities or custodial responsibilities. The non-custodial parent is often referred to as the alternate residential parent or the nonresidential parent. For the sake of convenience, however, the traditional term, visitation, will be used in this chapter.

B. Parental Visitation

1. Standards for Determining Visitation

a. Generally

Parents divorce each other, but they do not divorce their children. Social science research shows that children benefit from having a close, loving relationship with both parents following the divorce. In recognition of that fact, courts and legislatures attempt, where consistent with the child's best interests, to foster the relationship between the child and each parent.

Some states have a presumption of joint physical custody, resulting in each parent having the same amount of residential time with the child, so that the typical custody/visitation model does not apply. In most states, however, there is no presumption in favor of joint physical custody, and the courts, in contested cases, generally award custody to one parent and visitation to the other. Visitation varies considering the circumstances of the parties, but a traditional award of visitation might include every other weekend, one overnight during the week, alternating holidays, and two or more weeks during the summer. But since at least 2020, there has been a noticeable shift away from traditional custody schedules, toward more balanced arrangements. The parties themselves, of course, are free to agree on a visitation schedule, and are encouraged to do so. Any such agreement by the parties would be subject to court approval, based upon a best interest standard.

b. Restricted Visitation

In some instances, it may not be in the child's best interests to have general visitation privileges. If there are credible allegations of abuse, for instance, the court may order supervised visitation. Supervised visitation means that the parent will have contact with the child but only in the presence of a third party designated or approved by the court. The court might also prohibit overnight visitation if the court deems that such visitation might be harmful to the child, as in cases where the noncustodial parent shares a home with someone who has a history of violent behavior. Alternatively, the court may order that the noncustodial parent may not have overnight adult visitors if the child is present. The court may place any restrictions on visitation that are deemed necessary to protect the child.

c. *Denial of Visitation*

Fit parents have a constitutionally protected right to parent their children. Consequently, a court will not deny visitation altogether unless it can be shown that any such contact would be likely to endanger the child's physical or emotional health. Even if a parent is incarcerated, the court is likely to allow contact through letters, phone calls, and possibly prison visits, if the child is willing. Some courts make an exception, and deny visitation altogether, where the incarceration is the result of one parent killing the other parent. Another ground for denial of visitation would be a finding of child abuse, whether physical, emotional, or sexual.

2. Decision Making During Visitation

Courts generally allow the non-custodial parent to exercise decision-making authority during visitation as to parental issues that arise in the normal course of the visitation. The non-custodian parent would not be allowed, however, to use visitation to make parental decisions unrelated to the visitation, unless that parent was given legal custody as well. For instance, a non-custodial parent cannot decide to change a child's school location while the child is on an overnight or weekend visit, but that parent will be able to decide what the child can eat and what time the child will go to bed. Usually, a parent may take the child to religious services during visitation, absent a showing of harm to the child.

3. Visitation Bill of Rights

A number of states have codified a noncustodial parent's Bill of Rights, which includes such things as:

1. The right to unimpeded telephone conversations with the child at reasonable times and for a reasonable duration;
2. The right to send mail to the child which the other parent cannot open or censor;
3. The right to receive notice and relevant information as soon as practicable, of any hospitalization, major illness, or death of the child;
4. The right to receive information from the child's school including report cards, attendance records, test scores, and other information customarily made available to a parent;

5. The right to receive copies of the child's medical, health, and other treatment records directly from the physician or health care provider;
6. The right to be free of derogatory remarks made by the other parent to or in the presence of the child;
7. The right to reasonable notice of extracurricular activities involving the child, and the opportunity to participate or observe school activities, athletic activities, church activities, and other activities in which the child is involved;
8. The right to receive an itinerary from the other parent who leaves the state with the child for more than two days, including telephone numbers for use in the event of an emergency; and
9. The right to participate in the child's education, including the right of access to the child for lunch and other activities, on the same basis that is provided to all parents.

Additional rights may be added, or removed by the court, based on the best interests of the child. Some scholars, including this author, have advocated for a more child-centered approach, particularly since courts are moving toward shared parenting.

4. Modification of Visitation

Courts recognize that children's and families' needs change over time so that a visitation order or parenting plan entered at the time of the divorce may need to be modified as the children grow older or other circumstances change. Some states have the same standard for modification of visitation that applies to modifications of custody, the substantial and material change of circumstances standard. Other states have a lesser threshold standard for modifications of the parenting plan that do not involve a change in the designation of custodial parent. The standard may simply be a best interests test, requiring a showing that the best interests of the child require a modification of the visitation order or parenting plan.

5. Relocation

Relocation of either parent necessarily involves a modification of visitation. Courts typically will try to modify visitation in the event of relocation to preserve the parent-child relationship with the noncustodial parent. If the custodial parent relocates with the child, some states allow the court to consider reducing the noncustodial parent's child support obligation, in light of the increased costs associated with visitation resulting from the relocation.

6. Enforcement

a. Relationship between Visitation and Child Support

Oftentimes, a custodial parent will withhold visitation if the child support payments are delinquent, or the noncustodial parent will withhold child support payments if visitation is denied. Most courts, however, treat visitation and the child support obligation as independent obligations. While each parent's time with the child will likely factor into the amount of support due, neither parent is allowed the self-help remedy of withholding child support or visitation because each of those obligations is for the benefit of the child, not the other parent. The parent's remedy is to seek redress in the court for delinquent child support or denial of visitation. Exceptions exist, of course, to protect the child from imminent danger, such as the noncustodial parent arriving to pick up the child with the intent of driving with the child in the car while under the influence of alcohol or other drugs.

b. Remedies for Denial of Visitation

If the custodial parent refuses to comply with the visitation order, the noncustodial parent may seek to have the custodial parent held in contempt and can also petition the court to order additional visitation time to compensate for the denied visitation, sometimes referred to as alternate visitation, replacement visitation, or compensatory visitation. Some courts will allow attorney fees and costs, as well. Some states also allow license suspension or revocation for noncompliance with a visitation order. It is generally not a defense that the child did not want to visit. The custodial parent is usually required to encourage the child to visit and to make the child available at the appointed time. The situation is more difficult with teenagers so the court may sometimes defer to the child's wishes, but the court is not required to do so.

c. PAS (Parental Alienation Syndrome)

If the custodial parent's interference with visitation is directed toward alienating the child from the other parent, the court will probably try first to address the problem through counseling, replacement visitation time, fines, and even jail time. When the situation is severe and other remedies are not effective, the court may change custody to the non-alienating parent, if the court finds such a change to be consistent with the best interests of the child. Such cases are not common.

C. Third Party Visitation

The right to visitation generally belongs only to the non-custodial parent. There are instances, however, when non-parents may seek visitation from the court. Lack of standing may be an issue in many of these cases where the visitation statute is narrowly drawn to exclude petitions by persons other than legal parents.

1. Stepparents

Stepparents are not legal parents. As such, they have no continuing obligation of support or right to visitation following a divorce or death of the child's parent, as a general rule. Some states, however, do allow the court to order visitation to stepparents, if consistent with the child's best interest, where the stepparent has contributed to the child's support during the marriage and continues to do so following the divorce. In such cases, the stepparent may be found to have acted *in loco parentis*.

2. Grandparents

All fifty states have statutes allowing courts to grant visitation rights to grandparents in certain circumstances, consistent with the best interests of the child. The issue for the courts, however, is the amount of deference the court must give to the parental decision regarding grandparent visitation. In *Troxel v. Granville*, 530 U.S. 57 (2000), the Supreme Court held that a state must give some deference to the parental decision, but the Court did not specify how much weight must be given because the statute at issue gave no weight or deference to the mother's decision regarding grandparent visitation. The Washington statute allowed any person to seek visitation at any time, subject only to a best interest determination by the court. The Court relied on a long recognized due process right of parents to make decisions regarding the nurturing, upbringing, companionship, care, and custody of their children under the Due Process Clause of the Fourteenth Amendment.

Some states also recognize a state constitutional right of privacy regarding parental decision making. Typically, the court cannot intrude into the privacy of the family absent some justification, such as the need to protect the child from harm. Only after establishing the threshold test of harm or danger to the child, is the court then able to make a best interest determination regarding grandparent visitation. However, many states have adopted a very lenient view of harm, particularly when the grandparent's own child is absent, often requiring only a showing of a close bond between the grandparent and the child, the loss of which would be harmful to the child and discordant with the child's best interest.

3. Other De Facto Parents

Courts are quite reluctant, in most instances, to allow other parties to claim de facto parental status and obtain visitation. There are, however, instances when the court has found such visitation to be in the best interests of the child. Older decisions allowing such visitation would now have to be read in light of the standard of parental deference set out in *Troxel*.

D. Uniform Laws

1. Uniform Marriage and Divorce Act (UMDA)

The Uniform Marriage and Divorce Act (UMDA), promulgated in 1970 by the National Conference of Commissioners on Uniform State Laws (NCCUSL), has been adopted, at least in part, by a number of states. The UMDA reflects the general approach taken by the courts regarding visitation at that time. It states only that a parent who is not granted custody is entitled to reasonable visitation rights. Those rights may be denied, however, if the court, following a hearing, finds that visitation would seriously endanger the child's physical, mental, moral, or emotional health.

2. American Law Institute Principles of the Law of Family Dissolution (ALI Principles)

The American Law Institute's Principles of the Law of Family Dissolution: Analysis and Recommendations (ALI Principles), was promulgated in 2000. In almost three decades since its passage, legislators and courts alike have failed to formally adopt its recommendations. The ALI, though, is still persuasive in its functional approach to family law. It reflects a more modern approach to visitation. The ALI Principles use the parent-friendly term custodial responsibility rather than visitation. The ALI Principles propose allocating custodial responsibility according to the allocation actually maintained by the parties prior to their separation, where it is feasible to do so and in the child's best interests. The ALI Principles also endorse the use of parenting plans. Under the ALI Principles, a court should take steps to protect the child if certain limiting factors are found to be present, which include child neglect, abuse or abandonment; domestic violence; alcohol or drug abuse; or persistent unjustified interference with the other parent's access to the child. The steps the court may consider include, but are not limited to, reducing or eliminating a parent's custodial responsibility; ordering supervised custodial responsibility; setting up the exchange of the child in a protected setting; restraining a parent's communication with or proximity to the other parent or the child; ordering the parent to abstain from alcohol or other drugs; denying overnight custodial responsibility; restricting the presence of specific persons while the parent is with the child; requiring the parent to post a bond to secure the return of the child; or requiring the parent to complete a treatment program.

The ALI Principles recognize visitation for de facto parents. A de facto parent is someone who, for two years or longer:

1. Lived with the child and:
2. For reasons primarily other than financial compensation, and with the agreement of a legal parent, or due to the complete inability of any legal parent to perform caretaking functions,

    a. Regularly performed most of the caretaking for the child, or
    b. Regularly performed as much caretaking as the custodial parent.

CHECKPOINTS

- Both parents will usually be awarded some contact with the child post divorce because it is generally thought that contact with both parents is consistent with the child's best interests and because fit parents have a constitutionally protected right to parent their children.
- The court will, however, limit or deny visitation if it would endanger the child.
- A parent generally has the right to make parenting decisions during visitation.

- Unless the parent has at least joint legal custody, that parent should not make major decisions concerning the child without the custodial parent's consent.
- The noncustodial parent generally has the right to contact the child and to participate fully as a parent in the child's school and other activities, even during non-visitation times.
- If the custodial parent relocates with the child, visitation will generally be modified to allow the noncustodial parent to maintain a relationship with the child.
- The noncustodial parent may not withhold child support if visitation is denied. The noncustodial parent's remedy lies with the court in the form of alternate visitation, contempt, etc.
- Third parties may be granted visitation over a parent's objection, as long as the court gives some deference to the parent's decision, consistent with Troxel.

CHAPTER 13

Child Support

ROADMAP

After reading this chapter, you should understand:

- The scope of the child support obligation;
- The standards for establishing and modifying child support orders;
- The various methods for enforcing child support obligations;
- The defenses available to the child support obligor; and
- The procedure for interstate enforcement of child support.

A. Obligation of Support

1. Natural and Adoptive Parents

Parents have a co-equal duty to support their children according to their ability. This duty is assumed by adoptive parents as well. The obligation of support generally exists throughout the child's minority.

Many states have passed filial responsibility statutes which make adult children liable for the support of indigent parents, but the statutes are not routinely enforced. To the extent that they have been enforced, the statutes have been found to be constitutional.

2. Stepparents

Stepparents generally do not have an obligation of support during the marriage or after divorce, although some states do allow visitation to be granted post divorce to stepparents who support children during the marriage and who continue to contribute child support following divorce. Additionally, some states recognize equitable estoppel to impose support obligations on stepparents whose representations or conduct regarding child support led to reliance by the custodial parent or children to their detriment such that the stepparent should be estopped from denying the obligation of support, post divorce. The detriment may be shown where the stepparent's conduct results in the natural parent being unavailable as a source of support for the children. If the natural parent is available for support, most courts will not apply equitable estoppel against the stepparent.

3. Unmarried Parents

Unmarried parents generally have the same child support obligations that married parents have. However, a child born to a married couple will, upon birth, have two legal parents who have a legal obligation of support. When the parents are unmarried, until a biological father is determined to be a legal parent, no such obligation exists, often causing delay in support.

4. Underage Parents

All parents have an obligation to support their children, even when the parents are themselves still children. Some states provide that an adult noncustodial parent may also be obligated to pay support for an underage custodial parent in addition to having to pay support for the child of the parties.

B. Jurisdiction over the Obligor

The court must have personal jurisdiction over the obligor in order to issue a child support order. Personal jurisdiction over the obligor can be obtained through personal service within the jurisdiction or through valid long arm service, consistent with the minimum contacts sufficient to satisfy due process requirements. Alternatively, the custodial parent may initiate a proceeding *quasi in rem* by attaching any property owned by the obligor that is located within the jurisdiction. The court can issue a child support order, but only to the extent of the property attached.

C. Duration of Support

1. Age of Majority

The obligation of support generally terminates when the child attains the age of majority in the state. The age of majority is usually between eighteen and twenty-one. Exceptions are often recognized when the child is still in high school after attaining the age of majority, assuming that child's entering cohort remains in school as well. No valid distinction may be drawn between the age of majority for male and female children. *Stanton v. Stanton*, 421 U.S. 7 (1975).

2. Emancipation

The obligation of support can be terminated prior to the age of majority when the child is emancipated. Emancipation can occur through marriage, by joining the military, or through court order.

3. Death

The obligation of support ends when the child dies prior to attaining the age of majority. The support obligation generally ends upon the death of the parent as well, absent agreement or court order to the contrary. Some states, however, take the opposite view that the child support obligation survives the death of the parent, unless otherwise agreed by the parties or ordered by the court. The parties or the court may address the issue by requiring the parent to maintain life insurance with the child as the beneficiary.

4. Retroactive Support

When the court is entering the initial child support order, it can order support retroactive to the time of abandonment by the obligor, or in the case of establishing paternity, to the time of birth. Exceptions can be made in some cases based on the equities of the situation, such as cases where the custodial parent hid the existence of the child from the obligor for some period of time.

5. Post-Majority Support

Some states impose an obligation on parents for post-majority support, especially post-majority educational support. Most states, however, do not extend liability beyond the age of majority in the normal case. A few exceptions are recognized even under the general rule where, for instance, the parents themselves agree to pay post-majority support. Such obligations, generally found in the terms of the divorce settlement agreements, are enforced as contract provisions in most cases. Some courts also allow post majority educational support to be ordered by the court, during the child's minority, by ordering the obligor to contribute to an educational trust fund for the child. If the funds are not used for any reason they generally revert to the obligor.

6. Disabled Child

The support obligation can extend beyond the age of majority in the case of a severely disabled child. The support obligation in such cases can extend indefinitely, for the life of the child. Some states allow a more limited support obligation to be imposed for less severely disabled children. For example, support may be extended to age twenty-one, rather than eighteen, where the child is disabled as defined by the Americans with Disabilities Act.

D. Establishment of the Support Obligation

1. Child Support Guidelines

Typically, child support orders are alleged to be both more than the obligor can readily afford and less than is reasonably needed for the support of the child or children subject to the support order. There is some truth to both allegations. Following divorce, the couple loses the benefit of economies of scale. There are now two rent or mortgage payments rather than one, two utility bills, etc., with no corresponding increase in income.

Child support guidelines fall mainly into two categories, income shares and straight percentage models. Under the income shares model, the income of both parents is considered and each is responsible for a pro rata share of the child support generated by considering the income of both parents. Generally, the noncustodial parent is ordered to pay his or her share to the custodial parent. It is possible that a high earning custodial parent could owe support to a non-custodial parent. Under the straight percentage model, only the income of the obligor (noncustodial parent) is considered and a straight percentage of that income is ordered as child support, taking into account the number of children (*e.g.*, 21% for one child, 34% for two children). Currently, forty-one states use the income shares model, followed by the straight percentage model, but there are a few states that use a hybrid or unique formula.

2. Deviations from the Child Support Guidelines

Courts generally have very little discretion to deviate from the amount of child support presumptively due under the child support guidelines. In order to deviate, the court usually has to find that application of the child support guidelines is not in the best interests of the child or equitable between the parties. The court may also have to provide the factual basis for the deviation in the order along with the amount of support that would have been due under the child support guidelines. Typical areas in which courts are routinely allowed to deviate from the guidelines include very high-income obligors, cases involving more than average visitation or less than average visitation, and cases involving children with exceptional medical or educational needs.

3. Determining Income

a. Lottery Winnings

Courts generally include income from all sources, even lottery winnings, on the theory that children are entitled to share in the parent's lifestyle. The payments are generally averaged out over the time in which they are received.

b. Personal Injury Recovery

Child support guidelines are generally worded broadly to include personal injury recoveries, especially to the extent that the award replaces past or future earnings. Some definitions of income are limited to "ongoing sources" and would not include personal injury recoveries. Finally, some courts exclude any portion of the award that is designated for pain and suffering.

c. Inheritance

Some states include inheritances in the definition of income. Other states include only the income from the inherited property, or in some cases the imputed income, as income for purposes of setting up or modifying child support.

d. Debt

The obligor's debt is usually not considered in establishing the amount of income available for determining child support. Even where the monthly expenses exceed the obligor's income, the court's usual approach is to tell the obligor to reduce debt. The obligation to support one's child is paramount.

e. Payments-In-Kind

Many definitions of income include the value of payments-in-kind, such as a company provided automobile, or on-base housing for military obligors. The test is usually whether the in-kind payments have the effect of reducing one's usual monthly living expenses which are factored into the child support guidelines.

E. Modification of the Child Support Obligation

1. The General Standard

a. Changed Circumstances

The general standard for considering a petition to modify child support is a showing of a substantial and material change of circumstances since the last child support order. That standard has been replaced in some states by a significant variance requirement, discussed below.

b. Significant Variance

Some states require that a petition for a child support modification cannot be heard unless there is a threshold showing of a significant variance between the support currently being paid and the support that would currently be due under the child support guidelines. Each state defines "significant variance," with many using 15% of the current support amount as the threshold.

c. Retroactive Modification

All states have passed legislation prohibiting retroactive modifications of child support obligations. Congress mandated such action in the Bradley Amendment, passed in 1986. This law presents a hardship for the obligor who delays in seeking a modification as the court's jurisdiction to modify begins after the petition to modify is filed and notice is given to the other party.

2. Underemployment/Nonemployment

The basic issue for the court when the obligor loses a job and seeks a modification in the child support obligation is whether the obligor is in any way responsible or at fault for the job loss. If the obligor's culpable behavior led to the job loss, the court may refuse the modification. An obligor cannot avoid paying child support by becoming or remaining unemployed. The court will impute income in such circumstances based on the obligor's earning capacity.

Once the court has set child support, it is reluctant to allow the obligor to obtain a modification simply because the obligor elects to change jobs or careers. The court will generally find that the obligor's primary obligation is to support the child or children involved. If the change has a legitimate purpose, perhaps health related, for example, the court may allow the modification. Courts have refused to allow modifications where the obligor gave up employment to stay home and care for children from her later marriage, to the detriment of her older children who were the subject of the existing child support order. Other courts do not impute income in such situations if the decision to stay at home and care for children is reasonable under the circumstances. If the underemployment is related to a decision to return to school in order to enhance one's earning capacity, which will ultimately inure to the children's benefit, the court may decline to find voluntary underemployment.

3. Increased Income

Unlike alimony modifications, increased income alone generally is a sufficient basis for a child support modification. The rationale is that the child is entitled to share in the parent's lifestyle. To the extent that the parent has a significant increase in income, the child is entitled to share in that increase. The increase generally has to meet some minimum standard, such as the significant variance standard discussed above. Title IV-D cases (state enforced cases that involve a parent who receives state or federal funded financial assistance) are reviewed every three years to determine whether a modification is warranted.

4. Escalator Clauses

The parents may include an escalator clause in the settlement agreement providing for support to increase periodically based on some agreed standard. That standard may be external to the parties, such as the rate of inflation or cost of living increases or it may be related to the parties, such as a percentage of the obligor's current or future income. In any case, the agreement will be reviewed by the court, based on the best interests of the child.

5. Second Families

Initially, many courts took the position that child support orders could not be modified simply because the obligor became legally obligated to support other children. The theory was that a voluntary assumption of new child support obligations by the obligor should not work a detriment on the child already protected by a support order. In light of the trend toward the income shares model, courts are now more frequently required to recognize that all of the children are entitled to support from the same obligor on the theory that a child's right to support should not depend on birth order. Courts differ on the extent to which support of stepchildren can be considered. Generally, if state law imposes a support obligation on the obligor, the stepchild support will be considered. Some states consider actual support of stepchildren, but to a lesser degree than support of natural children, *e.g.*, only 75% of the actual support paid may be considered in some cases.

6. Pregnant Obligor/Nurturing Parent Doctrine

Some courts will relieve one parent of support obligations if that parent is staying at home to nurture the child or children, as long as doing so is reasonable under all the circumstances of the case. The rationale is that the purpose of a support order is the furtherance of the welfare and best interests of the child. Courts recognize the non-monetary contributions made by the non-working parent. If the obligor is pregnant with a child not related to the custodial parent, the court will generally relieve the obligor of her support obligations during the period that she is unable to earn support because of her pregnancy and delivery. Whether the obligor will then be able to rely on the nurturing parent doctrine to stay at home with the newborn who is not the subject of the child support order will depend on the circumstances of the case, most importantly the ability of the custodial parent to support the child who is the subject of the support order without the aid of the obligor parent. In these cases, the court notes that the child being nurtured is not the child who is the subject of the court ordered child support. This distinction is generally not dispositive, however.

7. Change in the Obligor's or Child's Health

The child's special medical needs, not covered by insurance, generally warrant a modification hearing without regard to the threshold standard otherwise applicable to modification petitions. A change in the obligor's health may support a modification if the change results in reduced income that otherwise meets the threshold standard applicable to modification petitions.

8. Incarceration

Some states refuse to relieve obligors from their support obligations simply because they are incarcerated. The arrearages will accrue while the obligor is incarcerated and unemployed. Other states do allow modifications if it is shown that the obligor will not be able to meet the support obligations while incarcerated and has no assets from which the obligation can be satisfied, including any income earned while incarcerated.

9. Unclean Hands

The common law unclean hands doctrine prevented obligors from seeking modifications while still in arrears. The theory was that the obligor had to be current on the court ordered child support obligation (clean hands) before asking the court for relief in the form of a modification. Most states will allow modifications even when the obligor is in arrears, but may still deny relief if the court finds that the nonpayment of support is willful or intentional.

10. Inflation

In order to address the effects of inflation, some parties may agree to cost of living adjustments (COLA's) to the child support order. Courts generally retain jurisdiction to approve such adjustments in light of the parties' actual financial circumstances.

11. Agreement of the Parties

Parties are encouraged to reach agreement on child support modifications, just as they are encouraged to reach agreement on the initial order. All such orders are subject to court approval and may not be adverse to the child's interests. Generally, the agreed amount must be at least equal to the amount due under existing child support guidelines. Subsequent modifications agreed between the parties are not enforceable absent court approval.

F. Enforcement Provisions

1. Incarceration

Incarcerating delinquent parents has been shown to be very effective in some studies. The approach is criticized, however, as being disproportionately visited upon minorities; as leading to job losses, which ultimately result in greater arrearages; and as instigating or exacerbating instances of domestic violence. Incarceration has withstood constitutional challenges that it amounts to imprisonment for debt or involuntary servitude. The justification is that child support is not a debt but rather a parental responsibility and the relationship between the obligor and child is much more than the ordinary relationship between debtor and creditor.

2. Income Withholding

Direct wage withholding has been shown to be the most effective child support enforcement mechanism. The Federal Office of Child Support Services provides an Income Withholding (IWO) form that must be used in all support orders post-1994, unless agreed otherwise by the parties. Income withholding is not an option, however, in the case of the self-employed obligor. Courts can now require the self-employed obligor to set up a bank account with an automatic draw each month for child support.

3. Action against Employer for Noncompliance

The employer must comply with a valid request for wage withholding. If the employer fails or refuses to comply, the employer can be held liable for resulting arrearages as well as punitive damages.

4. Marriage Restriction

In *Zablocki v. Redhail*, 434 U.S. 374 (1978), the state of Wisconsin attempted to enforce child support compliance by restricting the right of noncustodial parents to marry, absent proof of compliance with court ordered child support obligations and proof that the children "are not then and are not likely thereafter to become public charges." Marriages in violation of the statute were void and violators could be subject to criminal penalties. The Supreme Court struck down the statute, holding that when a statute significantly interferes with the right to marry it must be supported by sufficiently important state interests and closely tailored to effectuate only those interests. Assuming, arguendo, that the state's two interests: (1) providing an opportunity to counsel the applicant as to the need to fulfill his existing child support obligations, and (2) protecting the welfare of noncustodial children, were legitimate and substantial, the Court held that the means selected by the state for achieving these interests unnecessarily impinged on the right to marry and could not be upheld. Assuming that counseling takes place, a fact not established in the record, there is no state interest in withholding permission to marry after counseling is completed. Further, the Court found no clear connection between the state's interest and the statute's requirements. The Court held that the state's "collection device" rationale could not justify the statute's broad infringement on the right to marry.

5. Civil Contempt

Civil contempt is remedial in nature. It involves the use of the court's contempt powers to provide relief to the custodial parent by jailing the obligor until payment is received. Civil contempt is a civil proceeding that requires proof of willful noncompliance, that the obligor has the ability to pay but chooses not to do so. The court sentences the obligor to jail for an indefinite period until the obligor complies with the court order and pays the child support. The obligor is said to hold the keys to the jail because the obligor is free to leave at anytime, upon complying with the court's child support order. If the obligor "stands committed unless and until he performs the affirmative act required by the court's order" the proceeding is for civil contempt. "If the relief provided is a fine, it is remedial when it is paid to the complainant, and punitive when it is paid to the court, though a fine that would be payable to the court is also remedial when the defendant can avoid paying the fine simply by performing the affirmative act required by the court's order." *Hicks v. Feiock*,

485 U.S. 624, 632 (1988). However, if the obligor remains incarcerated for a substantial period of time, such usually acts as evidence that the obligor does not have the present ability to pay the "purge payment," potentially triggering constitutional implications.

6. Criminal Contempt

Criminal contempt is not designed to provide a remedy to the custodial parent. Criminal contempt is punitive in nature. It is designed to vindicate the court's authority where the obligor is found to have intentionally failed to comply with the court's order regarding child support. The proceeding is criminal in nature with the corresponding constitutional protections and burden of proof beyond a reasonable doubt. The sentence is for a determinate period. Unlike civil contempt, the criminal contempt sentence cannot be satisfied by paying child support or otherwise complying with the court's order. *Hicks v. Feiock*, 485 U.S. 624, 632 (1988). Moreover, while serving the sentence purges the contempt, the arrears for the unpaid support are still due and payable.

7. Security/Bonds

States are required to provide procedures for using bonds as security for child support payments when appropriate, such as in cases where direct withholding of payments from the obligor's salary is not an option, as in the case of self-employed obligors.

8. Liens

Federal law requires states to adopt procedures under which liens can be imposed against real and personal property for child support arrearages. If a lien is imposed on a parcel of realty, it cannot be transferred unless or until the lien is satisfied.

9. License Revocation

An effective enforcement device is the revocation of the obligor's state issued license. The license may be a driver's license or a license to practice law or medicine, for instance. The license will be revoked until the obligor complies with the child support order.

10. Disability Benefits

Parents have an obligation to support their children even if their only source of income is disability benefits. The Supreme Court held that the state statute on which the court relied in ordering the disabled obligor to pay child support and later finding him in contempt was not preempted by the Supremacy Clause as the statute did not conflict with federal law. *Rose v. Rose*, 481 U. S. 619 (1987).

11. The Child Support Recovery Act (CSRA)

In 1992, for the first time, Congress made nonpayment of child support a federal crime. The elements of the crime are willful nonpayment of child support for a child who resides in another state where the arrearage has remained unpaid for more than one year or where the arrearage amount is $5,000 or more. It is also a crime to travel in interstate or foreign commerce with the intent to evade child support obligations. The penalties increase with multiple offenses or where the obligation remains delinquent for more than two years or where the arrearage amount is $10,000 or more.

In 1998, the CSRA was amended by the Deadbeat Parents Punishment Act of 1998, which increased the penalties and created a rebuttable presumption that delinquent obligors have the ability to pay the child support obligation, thus shifting the burden of proof to the obligor. The Department of Justice has primary authority over these cases and, thus far, has prosecuted only a few high-profile cases.

12. Title IV-D Enforcement Agencies

The Family Support Act of 1974, codified as Title IV-D of the Social Security Act, required each state to designate an agency, known as a Title IV-D enforcement agency, to assist custodial parents in locating noncustodial parents, establishing paternity, and setting, enforcing, and modifying child support orders. Initially, the agency's services were available only to parents receiving public assistance. Later, services were extended to non-welfare custodial parents who are required to pay a nominal fee. As a result of the creation of the Title IV-D agencies, child support issues are increasingly handled administratively rather than judicially.

13. Parent Locator Services

The Parent Locator Service is available through the Department of Health and Human Services. It combines state and federal resources to locate obligors. The service is available to all parents seeking support and can be accessed by a parent, attorney, or agent for the child.

14. Tax Refund Intercept

State and federal tax returns can be intercepted in satisfaction of child support arrearages of $500 or more in non-public assistance cases and $150 or more in cases where the custodial parent receives public assistance. The proceeding is administrative, but the obligor must first be notified and given an opportunity to object to the amount and to identify any portion of a joint return that is owed to another person.

15. Qualified Domestic Relations Orders (QDRO's)

Qualified Domestic Relations Orders, which are routinely used to distribute pension benefits directly to the nonemployee spouse, can also be used to access pension funds to satisfy child support obligations. QDRO's are discussed more fully in the chapter on Property Division.

16. The Personal Responsibility and Work Opportunity Reconciliation Act of 1996 (PRWORA)

The Personal Responsibility and Work Opportunity Reconciliation Act of 1996 (PRWORA) made sweeping changes in the welfare system, but it also contained a number of provisions designed to assist child support establishment and enforcement. Custodial parents who receive government assistance are required to name the child's father and to cooperate with the Title IV-D agency (discussed above) in establishing paternity and enforcing child support.

a. New Hire Reporting

PRWORA established a national directory to report new hires. Employers must submit social security numbers and other identifying information on new hires which is entered into the Federal Case Registry and the federal parent locator service, discussed above. The registry and parent locator service are designed to assist in enforcing child support obligations against obligors who cross state lines and change jobs in order to avoid paying child support by helping to locate those obligors as soon as they obtain new employment.

b. Mandatory Adoption of UIFSA

PRWORA required all states to adopt the Uniform Interstate Family Support Act (UIFSA), discussed below. The act is designed to streamline establishment and enforcement of child support obligations in interstate cases and to promote cooperation between states.

c. Access to Private and Government Information

PRWORA allows Title IV-D agencies access to public state records, such as birth certificates and tax records, for purposes of locating obligors. Some access to private records, such as local utility customer records, are also available for this purpose.

d. Expedited Procedures

PRWORA provides expedited procedures for establishing paternity such as a signed voluntary acknowledgement of paternity without the requirement of any further court or administrative proceeding. The act also requires expedited genetic testing of putative fathers.

17. Passport Restrictions

Federal law requires the Secretary of State, as part of the federal Passport Denial Program, to refuse to issue a passport to an obligor who is reported as having more than $2,500 in child support arrearages. The obligor must be given notice and an opportunity to contest the allegations. If the obligor already has a passport, the Secretary of State may revoke, restrict, or limit a passport issued previously to such individual. The restrictions thus presented on international travel have been upheld. The courts have found that while the constitutional right to interstate travel is subject to strict scrutiny, the right to international travel is not so protected. Strict scrutiny does not apply, absent first amendment concerns, and the limitations on international travel are regulated within the bounds of due process.

18. Procreation Limitation as a Condition of Probation for Willful Nonsupport

At least one state, in a legally suspect, 4–3 decision, upheld a restriction on procreation as a valid condition of probation for a father of nine children who was convicted of intentional nonpayment of child support. Noting that the father would have had no procreative rights while serving six years, the court held that conditioning the obligor's procreative rights upon proof that he could support that child and his current children, was not unreasonable under the facts of the case. *State v. Oakley*, 629 N.W. 2d 200 (Wis. 2001). A strong dissent argued that the probation condition was unconstitutional because the "right to have children is a basic human right and an aspect of the fundamental liberty which the Constitution jealously guards for all Americans."

19. Termination of Parental Rights

Willful failure to support one's child can be grounds for termination of parental rights. Termination of parental rights also involves a finding that termination is in the child's best interests. Unless adoption is a possibility, the court is unlikely to find that termination of parental rights would be in a child's best interests, based only on nonsupport. Termination would relieve the obligor of future liability without providing the child with another parental source of support. As long as the obligor retains parental rights and obligations, there is always the possibility, however remote, of income for the child. (See further discussion of termination of parental rights in the chapter on Child Neglect and Abuse and the chapter on Adoption.)

20. Public Humiliation

Some states have resorted to public humiliation as a child support enforcement tool. One approach has been to put delinquent obligors' names and pictures in newspapers or on "wanted" posters. Another approach has been to "boot" the obligor's car with a pink or blue boot along with a sticker explaining the reason for the boot.

21. Privatization

Some states have privatized some, or in several states all, of that state's role in the child support collection process. The private firms take over some or all of the duties of the Title IV-D agency. Proponents argue that the private firms are more efficient and save taxpayers money.

G. Defenses to Child Support Enforcement

1. Custodial Interference

In a few states, the obligation to pay support is conditioned upon the right of visitation or access to the child. In others, custodial interference can be a basis for a child support modification. Most states, however, treat child support and visitation as independent rights and obligations. The theory is that both support and parental contact benefit the child. When the two are made dependent, the child suffers. Instead, the court should deal with the issues separately and sanction the offending parent, not the child.

With older children who refuse to visit, there are a few extreme cases in which the court has terminated the support obligation, but generally the court will not condition support upon visitation.

2. Laches

When the custodial parent delays in seeking enforcement of child support arrearages, or in establishing a child support order, the obligor may assert the equitable defense of laches. Some courts have allowed such a defense, especially when the obligor shows prejudice from the delay. Other courts do not find the existence of prejudice based on delay or refuse to recognize the defense of laches even where prejudice based on the delay can be shown. Retroactive modification of child support orders is now barred by federal law, although the courts do have some discretion to apply equitable doctrines with regard to the establishment of an initial child support order.

3. Nonpaternity

Once there has been an adjudication of paternity, some courts are reluctant to reopen or set aside the order, even with DNA evidence of nonpaternity, because of the doctrine of res judicata. A few states, however, have passed statutes allowing the issue to be addressed where the obligor learns of the nonpaternity after the initial adjudication. Even in those states that vacate a support order upon proof of nonpaternity, the order is generally prospective only, meaning that the obligor would still be liable on any existing arrearages.

4. Bankruptcy

Child support obligations are not dischargeable in bankruptcy, regardless of whether the debtor seeks a Chapter 13 or a Chapter 7 bankruptcy. Additionally, the automatic stay that applies when the debtor files a petition in bankruptcy does not apply to child support collections and enforcement proceedings.

5. Estoppel

The obligor may raise an estoppel argument if the custodial parent first agrees to forgo support in exchange for the obligor's giving up visitation and then later sues to collect child support, despite the obligor's having foregone visitation. The problem, of course, is that support and visitation are both for the benefit of the child and the parents cannot contract to the detriment of the child. Such an agreement would ordinarily be found to be against public policy. Nonetheless, some states have found that the custodial parent is estopped to assert the child support arrearages under such circumstances, especially if the obligor has changed his or her position in reliance on the agreement. Other courts have limited the estoppel argument to arrearages, but have allowed the custodial parent to enforce future child support payments. Many courts, however, do not recognize the estoppel argument, or other equitable arguments, as a defense to child support enforcement, based on a public policy or best interests of the child rationale.

6. In-Kind Payments

Courts generally disallow any credit for in-kind payments of child support, as where the obligor claims credit for direct purchases of clothing, toys, or services for the child. States require the payments to be made according to the court order in order to ensure proper accounting for payments and to allow the custodial parent to budget the support in the best interests of the child.

H. Interstate Enforcement of Support

1. Introduction

Because child support is ordered by individual states, obligors could often avoid enforcement efforts by leaving the jurisdiction. Oftentimes, the custodial parent would not be able to locate the delinquent parent or would not be able to afford collection efforts in a distant state. Even if the custodial parent was able to locate and file suit against the obligor parent, that parent could still move again, requiring the process to be started all over again.

Several uniform acts were promulgated to address the interstate enforcement of child support problem. The first was the Uniform Reciprocal Enforcement of Support Act (URESA), followed by the Revised Uniform Reciprocal Enforcement of Support Act (RURESA). The current act, approved in 1992 and amended in 2008, is the Uniform Interstate Family Support Act (UIFSA), which all states have adopted as required by the federal government in order to receive federal funding for child support enforcement. The basic provisions of UIFSA are outlined below.

2. Jurisdiction over the Obligor

One of the biggest problems in interstate child support enforcement before UIFSA was obtaining personal jurisdiction over the obligor who moved from state to state. The state statutes were not uniform and obtaining long-arm jurisdiction was tedious and time consuming. UIFSA provides a uniform long-arm statute for all states that is written very broadly. It must still comply, however, with the minimum contacts requirements for due process. *Kulko v. Superior Court*, 436 U.S. 84 (1978). (See additional discussion of jurisdiction in the chapter entitled, Jurisdiction to Divide Property and Order Support.)

3. Continuing Exclusive Jurisdiction

UIFSA provides that the court that enters a child support order will retain continuing exclusive jurisdiction to modify that order as long as the child or one of the parties continues to live in the state or unless the parties agree in writing for the matter to be heard in another state.

4. Single Order Recognition

UIFSA prioritizes multiple support orders so that only one support order is entitled to recognition at any time. Preference is given to the order, if any, that is entitled to continuing exclusive jurisdiction. If more than one state is entitled to continuing exclusive jurisdiction, the order that is entered in the child's current home state will be recognized. If there is not an order in the child's current home state, the most current order will control. If none of the courts have continuing exclusive jurisdiction, a court with jurisdiction over the parties can enter an order that will be recognized.

5. Two State Proceeding

UIFSA provides procedures for states to cooperate in establishing and enforcing child support orders. The custodial parent will usually initiate the proceedings in the issuing state. The petition will be forwarded to the responding state where the obligor is located and a support order entered. Alternatively, the custodial parent may obtain a support order in the initiating state and forward it to the responding state, where the obligor is located, for enforcement purposes.

6. Registration and Civil Enforcement

A child support order entered in one state can be registered for enforcement in a foreign state where the obligor is located. The obligor is notified and given an opportunity to object to the validity of the order. The receiving state applies its own law on procedural issues, but the substance of the order is governed by the law of the issuing state.

7. Direct Enforcement

UIFSA allows the direct enforcement of child support orders, without accessing the judicial system, by sending the order directly to the obligor's employer for immediate withholding unless the obligor objects.

8. Choice of Law

UIFSA provides that the law of the issuing state governs "the nature, extent, amount, and duration of current payments" and "the computation . . . of arrearages." In collecting arrearages, the court must apply whichever state's statute of limitations is longer. In enforcement proceedings, the responding state applies the procedures and remedies of that state and recognizes only the defenses listed in UIFSA.

9. Registration for Modification

A support order entered in one state may be registered for enforcement in another state. The support order may also be registered for modification if: (1) the issuing state no longer has continuing exclusive jurisdiction, the petitioner is a non-resident of the forum state, and the forum state has personal jurisdiction over the respondent; or (2) all the parties agree in writing to jurisdiction in the forum state.

10. Rendition

UIFSA contains a criminal rendition provision that is designed to impose criminal liability where civil proceedings have failed. This provision allows the governor in responding states to extradite parents charged with criminal nonsupport in the initiating state.

11. Full Faith and Credit for Child Support Orders Act of 1994 (FFCCSOA)

The Full Faith and Credit for Child Support Orders Act of 1994 (FFCCSOA) requires states to give full faith and credit to child support orders of sister states. States are also prohibited from modifying child support orders from other states with continuing exclusive jurisdiction. The provisions of UIFSA are consistent with the provisions of FFCCSOA.

I. Uniform Laws

1. Uniform Marriage and Divorce Act (UMDA)

The Uniform Marriage and Divorce Act (UMDA), promulgated in 1970 by the National Conference of Commissioners on Uniform State Laws (NCCUSL), has been adopted, at least in part, in a number of states. The UMDA adopts a discretionary approach to setting child support that allows the court to consider a number of factors. All states that adopted this approach have replaced it with the much less discretionary child support guidelines. Under the UMDA, the child support obligation does not terminate upon the death of the parent, unless otherwise agreed or ordered by the court. The UMDA provides that a child support order may be modified only upon a showing of changed circumstances so substantial and continuing as to make the terms unconscionable.

2. American Law Institute Principles of the Law of Family Dissolution (ALI Principles)

The ALI Principles consider the standard of living in each parent's household in addition to their income, with a supplement being added to the standard child support amount where the custodial parent has a lower standard of living than the obligor parent. Child support may be reduced where the reverse is true. The Principles require periodic review of child support awards at least every three years. Parties can avoid such review by agreement. The Principles encourage the use of self modifying terms in child support awards, such as stating the obligation as a percentage of the obligor's income. The Principles also recognize the doctrine of equitable estoppel to impose support obligations on stepparents and other third parties in certain circumstances.

CHECKPOINTS

- Parents have a co-equal duty of child support according to their ability.
- Stepparents generally are not obligated for child support, absent agreement or application of the doctrine of equitable estoppel.
- The court must have personal jurisdiction over the obligor in order to issue a child support order against him or her.

- For normal children, the support obligation usually terminates upon the child attaining the age of majority, getting married, joining the military or otherwise becoming emancipated, or dying.
- Child support liability for a severely disabled child may be extended indefinitely during the child's life.
- States differ on whether divorced parents can be held liable for post majority educational expenses, but states generally enforce parental agreements to assume post majority education expenses.
- All states have enacted child support guidelines that establish a presumptive child support amount in each case.
- Courts have limited ability to deviate from the child support guidelines but must justify the factual basis for the deviation in writing in the court's order.
- The two most common child support guideline models are the income shares model, which considers the income of both parents, and the straight percentage model, which considers the income of the obligor only.
- Income is defined very broadly under the child support guidelines.
- The obligor must generally show either a substantial and material change of circumstances or a significant variance in order to get the court to consider a child support modification petition.
- Retroactive modification of child support is prohibited.
- Many courts will not impute income to a parent who stays at home to care for the child if doing so is reasonable under the circumstances of the case.
- The most effective child support enforcement technique is direct wage withholding.
- Other frequently used enforcement techniques include the contempt powers of the court, license revocation, and tax refund intercepts.
- State and federal criminal sanctions are available for willful nonsupport.
- Courts are reluctant to recognize any defense to nonpayment of child support, except in the most egregious cases, but increasingly, courts are granting prospective relief in cases of nonpaternity.
- Child support obligations cannot be discharged in bankruptcy.

- All states have passed UIFSA to provide for more effective and efficient enforcement of child support orders in interstate cases.
- UIFSA and FFCCSOA prioritize multiple child support orders so that only one order is entitled to recognition at a given time.
- The general rule under UIFSA is a that the substantive law of the issuing court applies to the setting of and interpretation of the child support order, while the procedural law of the enforcing state applies to the process of enforcement. However, the longer statute of limitations between the affected states will control.

CHAPTER 14

Marriage Contracts

ROADMAP

After reading this chapter, you should understand:

- The role and scope of antenuptial agreements;
- The requirements for enforceability of antenuptial agreements;
- The difference between postnuptial, reconciliation, and settlement agreements; and
- The requirements for enforceability of settlement agreements.

A. Introduction

Couples may enter into agreements (contracts) at four points in their relationship: before marriage, during a stable marriage, during a troubled marriage, and at the end of the marriage. Different rules apply to the various agreements because the relationship between the parties and the assumption of trust between the parties differs in each instance.

B. Antenuptial (Premarital or Prenuptial Contracts)

Antenuptial agreements (also referred to as premarital or prenuptial contracts) are entered into in anticipation of the marriage. Antenuptial agreements generally apply both in the event of death of one of the parties and in the event of divorce. Historically, these agreements were disfavored in most states because they were thought to encourage divorce or, alternatively, to force a disadvantaged party to remain in a bad marriage. Increasingly, these agreements are finding favor in courts and state legislatures as a means to encourage marriage. The argument is that the ability to contract regarding one's property in the event of divorce or death facilitates marriages where the monied spouse is reluctant to marry and risk losing substantial assets in a divorce and where parties are reluctant to enter into second marriages which might result in their assets going to the other spouse, in the event of death, rather than to their children from a previous marriage.

1. Prerequisites for Enforceability

Many courts find a fiduciary or confidential relationship between the parties to an antenuptial agreement. As such, the agreement is subject to closer scrutiny than other contracts, particularly regarding procedural requirements. Typically, the agreement must be entered into freely, knowledgably, and absent duress or undue influence. In order to satisfy the knowledgably requirement the parties must make a full disclosure of their assets. Some states refer to this requirement as a duty to disclose material facts. The existence of the confidential relationship has led some courts to place the burden on the monied/proponent party to show that the nonmonied/opponent party was fully informed of the amount and extent of the monied/proponent party's assets. Ideally, a list of assets and their value would be appended to the agreement, but independent knowledge of the other party's assets, as where the prospective spouse is a bookkeeper for the other spouse, has been held to satisfy the requirement. Some states require that the agreement not work an injustice on one of the parties.

Obviously, it is more likely to ensure the enforceability of the antenuptial agreement if each party is represented in the negotiations, but courts have upheld agreements in which the nonmonied/opponent spouse was not represented. Some states require at least an opportunity for the nonmonied/opponent spouse to obtain counsel. Courts may also consider the relative business sophistication, experience, education, and language skills of the parties.

Cases go both ways on the timing of the agreement with some courts upholding agreements that are presented as ultimatums on the eve or even the day of the wedding, while other courts have found them to be invalid. Generally, the courts look to the totality of the circumstances to determine whether the agreement was knowingly and voluntarily entered into. If so, the fact that the dependent spouse is "faced with difficult choices" is not, alone, sufficient to invalidate the agreement.

Some states require antenuptial agreements to be in writing under the Statute of Frauds as contracts made in contemplation of marriage and require that the agreement be executed prior to the marriage. Other states are more lax and will enforce the agreement if it is made at or shortly after the time of the marriage.

In addition to the procedural requirements discussed above, some states allow the court to consider the substantive fairness of the agreement as well, permitting the court to consider the adequacy of consideration rather than merely the sufficiency of the consideration. (Typically, contract law looks only to the presence or sufficiency of the consideration rather than its adequacy. *e.g.*, A court will consider only whether the parties to a contract agree to exchange a pen for $1.00 rather than whether $1.00 is a fair price for the pen.) Some states require the court to determine the substantive fairness of the agreed consideration for an antenuptial agreement while others require only the absence of an unconscionable bargain.

The timing for the review differs too, in that some states review the fairness of the agreement at the time it is made, while other states review the fairness of the agreement at the time it is enforced. Still others consider the fairness or unconscionability of the agreement both at the time of execution and at the time of enforcement. Finally, some states distinguish between property division and spousal support, evaluating property division at the time of the execution and spousal support at the time of the divorce.

2. Subject Matter of Antenuptial Agreements

States sometimes limit the subject matter of antenuptial agreements. Some statutes permit contracting regarding separate property only. Others permit the parties to waive alimony, subject to certain limitations such as the requirement that the dependent spouse not be eligible for welfare as a result. In many states, the parties may contract regarding marital property. Any provision in the agreement pertaining to child custody would not be enforceable, absent court approval. The same limitation would generally apply to child support, especially if the amount agreed upon was less than that provided by the state's child support guidelines. Finally, antenuptial agreements are generally not enforceable to the extent that they attempt to define the personal relationship between the parties, such as allocating household chores or regulating the sexual activities of the parties.

3. Conflict of Laws

States take various approaches to the conflict of laws issue in antenuptial agreements. The problem arises when the parties include a choice of law provision in their agreement or when the agreement is made in one state, but the death or divorce occurs in another state or country.

The Uniform Premarital Agreement Act, enacted by twenty-eight states, discussed below, allows the parties to include a choice of law provision in the agreement. Many states will enforce a choice of law provision as long as it has some connection to the parties and does not violate the strong public policy of the forum state.

If the antenuptial agreement does not have a choice of law provision, states will generally apply one of two choice of law principles to determine applicable law. The first is the traditional contract approach that applies the law of the state where the contract is made to formation and enforceability issues and the law of the state where performances is to occur with regard to performance issues. The second approach is the more modern *significant relationship* test, which applies the law of the state in which the parties have the most significant relationship. Oftentimes, this approach favors the state in which the death or divorce occurs and may disappoint the expectations of one of the parties who may have relied upon the law of the state in which the contract was originally executed.

4. Uniform Premarital Agreement Act

In 2012, the Uniform Law Commission promulgated the Uniform Premarital Agreement Act. It has been widely adopted by twenty-eight states and the District of Columbia. It requires a signed writing but does not require consideration. The parties may contract as to separate and marital property, including management of same, the making of a will or trust, life insurance benefits, choice of law provisions, and any other matter that is not illegal and does not violate public policy. The agreement may not adversely affect a child's right to support. If spousal support is terminated or modified, causing one party to become eligible for public assistance, the court may require the other party to pay support sufficient to avoid that eligibility. The agreement may be contingent upon death, divorce, separation, or upon the occurrence or non-occurrence of any other event. It may be revoked or amended only by a signed writing, but, again, consideration is not required.

The agreement is not enforceable if a party proves that:

1. The agreement was not executed voluntarily; or
2. The agreement was unconscionable when executed and that prior to execution the party:
   a. Was not provided a fair and reasonable disclosure of the property or financial obligations of the other party;
   b. Did not voluntarily and expressly waive, in writing, any right to disclosure of the other party's property or financial obligations; and
   c. Did not have, or reasonably could not have had, an adequate knowledge of the property or financial obligations of the other party.

The second provision, above, is a stark departure from general contract law in that it permits enforcement of a contract found to be unconscionable when executed if the other party receives full disclosure, waives disclosure, or could have had independent knowledge of the other party's assets. If the underlying marriage is declared void, the agreement is enforceable only to the extent necessary to avoid an inequitable result.

Any statute of limitations applicable to a claim for relief under a premarital agreement is tolled during the marriage. However, equitable defenses limiting the time for enforcement, including laches and estoppel, are available to either party.

5. American Law Institute Principles of the Law of Family Dissolution (ALI Principles)

In almost three decades since its passage, legislators and courts alike have failed to formally adopts the ALI's recommendations. The ALI, though, is still persuasive in its approach to marital agreements. The ALI Principles provide that an antenuptial agreement is rebuttably presumed to be made knowledgeably and without duress upon proof that:

1. It was executed at least thirty days before the parties' marriage;
2. Both parties were advised to obtain independent legal counsel, and had a reasonable opportunity to do so, before the agreement's execution; and
3. In the case of an agreement concluded without the assistance of independent legal counsel for each party, the agreement states, in language easily understandable by an adult of ordinary intelligence with no legal training:
   a. The nature of any rights or claims otherwise arising at dissolution that are altered by the contract, and the nature of that alteration; and
   b. That the interests of the spouses with respect to the agreement may be adverse.

The court is permitted, however, to deny enforcement because of changed circumstances during the marriage in three instances, each of which requires the court to review the antenuptial agreement to ensure that enforcement would not work a substantial injustice. These three instances are where:

1. More than a fixed number of years have passed (ten is suggested);
2. A child was born to or adopted by the parties, who at the time of execution had no children in common; or
3. There has been a change in circumstances that has a substantial impact on the parties or their children, but when they executed the agreement the parties probably did not anticipate either the change or its impact.

The burden of proof is on the party claiming the injustice. In deciding whether enforcement of the agreement would work a substantial injustice, the court should consider each of the following factors:

1. The magnitude of the disparity between the outcome under the agreement and the outcome under prevailing law;
2. In marriages of limited duration, in which it is practical to ascertain, the difference between the circumstances of the objecting party if the agreement is enforced and that party's likely circumstances if the marriage had never taken place;

3. Whether the purpose of the agreement was to benefit or protect the interests of third parties (such as children from a prior relationship), whether that purpose is still relevant, and whether the agreement's terms were reasonably designed to serve that purpose; and
4. The impact of the agreement's enforcement upon the children of the parties.

6. Restatement (Second) of Contracts (1981)

Section 190 of the Restatement (Second) of Contracts, entitled *Promise Detrimental to Marital Relationship*, provides that promises made by a married person or in contemplation of marriage are unenforceable on public policy grounds if they would change some essential incident of the marital relationship (such as the obligation of support) in a way that is detrimental to the public interest in the marital relationship. An exception is recognized for enforceable separation agreements that are made after the separation or in contemplation of an immediate separation and which are fair "in the circumstances." Additionally, promises that tend unreasonably to encourage divorce or separation are also unenforceable on public policy grounds.

7. Employee Retirement Income Security Act of 1974 (ERISA)

ERISA sets standards and policies for retirement and health insurance plans in private industry, including certain requirements for administrators and participant rights. At least one court has found that ERISA governed certain provisions of a martial contract. In *In re Marriage of Rahn*, the parties executed an antenuptial agreement whereby they agreed that "all of the property now owned or hereafter acquired by husband will remain his sole and separate property throughout the marriage. Wife shall not claim or acquire any interest in any of his property if it increases in value during the marriage, jointly held property being excepted." The Colorado Court of Appeals upheld the waiver of rights other than survivor benefits, reasoning ERISA provides the explicit requirements for a spouse's waiver of rights to the qualified joint and survivor annuity and the qualified preretirement survivor annuity in a qualified ERISA plan. Regulations interpreting ERISA's statutory authority specifically state, "An agreement entered into prior to marriage does not satisfy the applicable requirements, even if the agreement is executed within the applicable election period." Thus, a waiver of a right to survivor benefits in an ERISA-qualified plan in an antenuptial agreement is ineffective, and the surviving spouse is entitled to the survivor benefits. A valid waiver can be enforced through a QDRO. *In re Marriage of Rahn*, 914 P.2d 463 (Colo. Ct. App. 1995).

C. Postnuptial (Post-Marital) Agreements

To the extent that courts differentiate, postnuptial agreements differ from reconciliation agreements in that the parties are in a viable marriage at the time of entering into a postnuptial agreement, whereas marital difficulties exist at or precede the time that the parties enter into a reconciliation agreement. Consequently, the relationship between the parties to a postnuptial agreement are more similar to the relationship of the parties to an antenuptial agreement, whereas the relationship between the parties to a reconciliation agreement is closer to the relationship of the parties to a separation agreement. This difference in the relationship of the parties is sometimes reflected in the court's requirements for enforceability of these agreements.

Traditionally, many courts would not enforce marital contracts entered into between the parties during the marriage unless they were separation agreements in contemplation of divorce because the former agreements were considered to be against public policy. Some states enforce postnuptial agreements made during a viable marriage as long as there is consideration for the agreement and the agreement is entered into freely, knowledgeably, and without duress or undue influence. Courts have noted that the circumstances of the disadvantaged party who is married and presented with a postnuptial agreement are rife with opportunity for duress, with the threat of divorce and the stigma of a failed marriage and the negative impact on the children of the marriage sometimes causing parties to feel compelled to enter into the agreement that they otherwise might not have prior to the marriage. Some states treat all postnuptial agreements the same without regard to the health of the underlying marriage. In those states, the requirements are more likely to address the substantive fairness of the agreement, for instance, enforcing the agreement only if it is equitable at the time of divorce. One state, by statute, enforces postnuptial agreements only where:

1. Both spouses possess assets amounting to at least $1.2 million;
2. Both parties are represented by independent counsel; and
3. A divorce action is not filed within two years of signing.

The Uniform Marital Property Act, § 10(f) denies enforcement to postnuptial agreements if the agreement was unconscionable when signed; the agreement was involuntarily signed; or there was inadequate disclosure.

The majority of states do enforce postmarital contracts that are not incident to divorce or separation, but they will be closely scrutinized and must evince a lack of fraud, coercion or undue influence and mutual knowledge of the property involved and the rights which would be abrogated by the signing of such an agreement.

D. Reconciliation Agreements

A reconciliation agreement is made during the marriage, generally when the parties are experiencing difficulties and may be separated or on the brink of divorce. The reconciliation agreement may be the inducement for one party to remain in the marriage.

If the parties sign a reconciliation agreement and remain married for a number of years, the court is likely to find that the agreement will govern any later divorce. On the other hand, if a divorce is filed shortly after entering into the reconciliation agreement, the court may refuse to enforce the reconciliation agreement. One court set out the criteria for evaluating a reconciliation agreement as follows:

1. Was the agreement obtained through fraud, duress or mistake, or through misrepresentation or nondisclosure of material facts?
2. Is the agreement unconscionable?
3. Have the facts and circumstances changed since the agreement was executed, so as to make its enforcement unfair and unreasonable?

A legal conundrum exists when a reconciliation agreement is silent as to its term. The purpose of the agreement is to facilitate reconciliation. The consideration that supports the agreement is the reconciliation. Some states have deemed the agreement as having been fulfilled and no longer binding on the parties if the parties remain reconciled for a substantial period of time (usually 7 or more years).

Many states review postnuptial agreements incident to divorce or reconciliation using the "second look doctrine" in which the court will review that agreement's fairness not only at the time it was signed by the parties, but also at the time a party attempts to enforce the agreement. If circumstances have changed significantly or enforcement would lead to one party becoming a public charge, the agreement may be found unenforceable as violative of public policy.

E. Settlement (Separation) Agreements

Settlement agreements are generally favored in the law, in part because the parties are presumed to know better how to resolve their divorce issues than the judge who is a stranger to the parties; in part because the overwhelming majority of cases do settle, thus preserving scarce judicial resources; and in part because a settlement between the parties is generally thought to be less costly, both financially and emotionally, for the parties and the children of the marriage. Settlement agreements generally are not subject to the public policy objection that is raised regarding other marital agreements because the marriage has already disintegrated at the time that the settlement agreement is executed. Settlement agreements are contracts between the parties, but in order to resolve the divorce litigation, the agreement must be presented to and accepted by the court in settlement of the case.

Because the parties have the option of litigation where the court will resolve their issues by applying existing law, parties to a settlement agreement are said to bargain in the shadow of the law. The clearer the law is on a given issue, the more likely the parties are to reach agreement on that issue. The more indeterminate the law is on a given issue, the more likely the parties are to engage in strategic behavior in negotiations and possibly not reach agreement, because they don't have a clear basis for comparing what is being offered in the settlement agreement against what is likely to happen in litigation.

As a general rule, the parties may contract as to all of the issues related to the divorce, including child support, custody and visitation, but the provisions related to the child will not be enforceable absent court approval. The Restatement (Second) of Contracts § 191 provides that an agreement on child custody is unenforceable on public policy grounds unless it is consistent with the child's best interests. Parties may also contract for terms beyond the court's authority to order, such as post-majority educational support, or non-modifiable spousal support.

The parties are generally given much greater flexibility for negotiating the terms regarding property division and spousal support. The requirements of disclosure are generally less than those applicable to antenuptial agreements because the parties are no longer in a confidential or fiduciary relationship. In addition, once the divorce is filed, discovery rules apply to aid each spouse in discovering the other's assets. General contract principles apply precluding enforcement upon proof of fraud, duress, unconscionability, and mistake. Some states require courts to accept settlement agreements in the absence of fraud, duress, overreaching, or unconscionability.

Some courts require that the agreement be freely and fairly entered into. If one attorney is retained by both parties that fact, alone, will generally not invalidate the agreement as long as the attorney gives the parties full disclosure and no conflicts of interest arise.

If the parties reconcile after entering into a separation agreement, courts generally find that the executed portions of the agreement remain effective, but the executory provisions are abrogated by the reconciliation of the parties, absent evidence of the parties' contrary intent.

If one party retracts or rejects the settlement agreement, courts differ on its enforceability. If the agreement has been signed, it is generally enforceable as a contract, subject to ordinary contract defenses, but the agreement is generally not binding on the court until it has been presented to and accepted by the court in settlement of the case.

Provisions in settlement agreements requiring the parties to mediate or arbitrate future disputes are generally enforceable. Any issues, including the validity of the requirement to mediate or arbitrate, related to child support, custody, or visitation are generally subject to court review and approval.

1. Undisclosed Assets

If one of the parties fails to disclose assets at the time of entering into the settlement agreement, the parties remain co-owners of any community property in community property states. In one community property state, if the nondisclosure is fraudulent, the other spouse may receive 100% of the property in question. In common law states, the approaches differ with some states allowing the affected spouse to bring a separate action to divide the undisclosed property, while other states continue to enforce the provisions of the separation agreement, finding the misconduct to be intrinsic fraud rather than extrinsic fraud.

2. Integrated Bargains

Settlement agreements which include provisions with respect to both property division and spousal support payments may be referred to as *integrated bargains*. Some states apply special rules for such agreements such as preventing modification of support payments, even upon a showing of changed circumstances, based on the rationale that any modification would change the negotiated settlement agreement and alter the *quid pro quo*.

3. Merger

State law differs widely regarding the doctrine of merger. Generally, the doctrine of merger provides that if the court incorporates by reference the settlement agreement of the parties, the agreement becomes merged into the court's decree and loses its contractual nature. It then becomes enforceable as a judgment of the court, including through application of the court's contempt powers. Some states provide that the parties may override the merger doctrine by providing that the settlement agreement will survive the court's decree. Other states take the opposite view and hold that the separation agreement merges into the court's decree, regardless of any statement to the contrary in the agreement itself. Still other courts provide that any of the contract terms that are within the power of the court to order become merged into the court's decree, but that contract terms which are beyond the court's authority to order are not merged into the court's decree and retain their contractual nature (such as post-majority support obligations). Some states differentiate between *incorporation*, which permits the agreement to be part of the judgment, but still an enforceable as a contract, and *merger*, and which causes the agreement to become a part of the judgment and no longer enforceable as a contract.

4. Modification

The general rule in states that do not recognize *integrated bargains*, discussed above, is that the property division terms are not modifiable by the courts or the parties, unless otherwise provided, but that support obligations are modifiable, to the extent that they would be modifiable if ordered by the court rather than agreed by the parties. Some courts do, however, enforce modification waiver provisions that also purport to divest the court of jurisdiction to modify, and which are approved and accepted by the court at the time of the divorce. Thus, it is the court, not the parties, that is divesting itself of jurisdiction to modify the support obligation. In some states, an agreement regarding spousal support is treated as a final judgment when presented to the court and is not modifiable thereafter. Child support, custody, and visitation are generally modifiable, based on the court's *parens patriae* power to protect the child during minority. If the separation agreement is not merged into the court's decree, it retains its contractual nature and is usually not modifiable unless permitted in the agreement or agreed to by both parties.

5. American Law Institute Principles of the Law of Family Dissolution (ALI Principles)

In almost three decades since its passage, legislators and courts alike have failed to formally adopt the ALI recommendations. The ALI, though, is still persuasive in its approach to marital agreements. The ALI Principles prohibit enforcement of agreements that substantially change the property rights or spousal support otherwise due if enforcement would substantially impair the economic well-being of a party with custody of a child or a party with substantially fewer economic resources than the other party. The court may make an exception, however, if it finds that enforcement will not work an injustice.

Subject to the limitation addressed in the preceding paragraph, separation agreements addressing property division and spousal support are enforceable and binding on the court if: (1) the agreement is in writing and signed by the parties; (2) the agreement otherwise satisfies the requirements of an enforceable contract; (3) each party had a full and fair opportunity to be informed of the other party's assets and their value, the other party's current earnings, and prospects for future earnings, and the significance of the terms of the agreement prior to accepting same; and (4) the agreement satisfies any other requirements of state law applicable to separation agreements.

Provisions regarding child support, custody, and visitation are subject to court approval as provided in the separate sections of the ALI Principles addressing those topics. If the court finds that one or more terms fail to comply with the provisions of the ALI Principles, the court is encouraged to allow the parties to renegotiate the agreement, as limited by the court.

Enforceable agreements should be incorporated into the court's decree. Unless otherwise agree, such incorporated terms become merged into the court's decree. Terms that are incorporated into a decree are enforceable by all remedies available for the enforcement of judgments generally. Incorporated terms that survive the decree as contract terms are automatically modified by modification of the decree. An exception to the foregoing is recognized in those jurisdictions that do not allow a court to enforce degree terms that the court does not have the power to order on its own. In such cases, the terms, which are otherwise enforceable as contract terms, are not incorporated in the decree and will survive the decree as enforceable contract terms (such as post-majority support obligations).

6. Uniform Marriage and Divorce Act (UMDA)

The Uniform Marriage and Divorce Act limits judicial review of settlement agreements to a finding of unconscionability as to all matters other than child support, custody, and visitation. In determining unconscionability, the court may consider the economic circumstances of the parties and any other relevant evidence. If the court finds that the separation agreement is unconscionable, it may request the parties to submit a revised separation agreement or the court may issue its own order for property division and spousal support. The terms of the agreement are presumed to be incorporated into the court's decree and are enforceable by all remedies available for enforcement of a judgment, including contempt. The terms are also enforceable as contract terms. (Contempt is not an available remedy for ordinary breach of contract.) Except for terms concerning child support, custody, and visitation, the court may expressly preclude or limit modification of the decree if a separation agreement so provides. Otherwise, terms of a separation agreement incorporated in the divorce decree are automatically modified by modification of the divorce decree.

CHECKPOINTS

- Antenuptial agreements made in contemplation of marriage generally require no other consideration but generally do fall within the Statute of Frauds and require a signed writing.
- Antenuptial agreements usually address the rights of the parties in the event of death or divorce.
- Courts typically place more stringent requirements of substantive and procedural fairness on the parties to an antenuptial agreement

because of the confidential or fiduciary relationship found between the parties.

- The scope of antenuptial agreements generally includes property division and may include spousal support, but generally does not include custody or child support that is less than the amount provided by state law.
- Postnuptial agreements are generally contracted during a viable marriage whereas reconciliation agreements are contracted after the parties have experienced marital difficulties and have determined to reconcile.
- Settlement agreements are entered into when the marriage has broken down and the parties are divorcing.
- Of all of the various types of marital contracts, the courts are most likely to enforce the settlement agreement. The requirements for enforceability of settlement agreements are usually less stringent than for the other types of marital agreements.
- As a general rule, parties may contract in a settlement agreement regarding all divorce issues, but any provisions related to a child (support, custody, visitation) will be subject to approval by the court.
- If the court modifies the terms of a separation agreement that is incorporated into the divorce decree, the underlying agreement is usually modified as well.
- Generally, unless otherwise provided, property division terms are not modifiable but spousal support terms are. In states that recognize *integrated bargains*, however, neither is modifiable if agreed to in a settlement agreement as part of the *quid pro quo*.

CHAPTER 15

Alternative Dispute Resolution

ROADMAP

After reading this chapter, you should understand:

- The differences between negotiation, arbitration, mediation, and conciliation;
- The strengths and weaknesses of each process; and
- The limitations on mediation related to domestic violence, repudiation, and confidentiality.

A. Introduction

Family law filings tend to represent the majority of filings in trial courts. The vast majority of divorce cases, however, settle prior to trial. Some estimates of the percentage of cases that settle are as high as 95%. The judicial system would be unable to handle the large numbers of divorces filed each year if settlement figures were not high. Even with the high settlement rates, many courts have long backlogs for divorce trials. Settlement is generally good for the client, as well. Litigation can be financially and emotionally devastating for the parties, particularly where there are minor children involved. The various means of reaching a settlement without going to trial are considered below.

B. Negotiation

The oldest and perhaps most frequently used technique to settle divorce cases is negotiation. The negotiations may take place between the parties, or between the attorneys, or in the presence of both parties and attorneys. Even though the court is not a party to the negotiation process, its influence is felt because the parties compare each offer against what they are likely to get if the matter goes to trial, a process that has been referred to as "bargaining within the shadow of the law." As a result, the more indeterminate the outcome at trial the less likely the parties are to reach a settlement on a given issue, and vice versa. Although courts are frequently required by statute to review and approve proposed settlement agreements, courts routinely defer to the judgment of the parties, particularly where both parties are represented by counsel.

C. Arbitration

Typically, arbitration is like a trial, without the expense, delay, and, in some instances, rules of procedure and evidence. The result is determined by one or more arbitrators (judges) and is usually binding on the parties and not subject to appeal. The parties to the arbitration usually agree on the selection of the arbitrators. Arbitration, an alternative dispute resolution process that has been used successfully in other areas of the law has found limited acceptance in family law cases. The process has been championed primarily in the area of child custody conflicts. Any result reached by arbitration is submitted to the court for approval and adoption by the court in settlement of the pending case.

Some advantages of arbitration include less expense for the parties, convenient scheduling, expertise of and ability to choose the arbitrators, and greater informality. Some disadvantages include inability to appeal in most cases (which may be considered an advantage to the "successful party"), lack of judicial oversight in most cases, lack of enforcement power in the arbitrators (although the order will be enforceable by the court if accepted in settlement of the pending litigation), and lack of discovery.

Some courts have been reluctant to accept arbitration decisions as final in custody and child support matters, two areas in which jurisdiction is typically reserved by the court, with the possibility of subsequent modification upon changed circumstances. Some courts reject arbitration clauses related to custody, visitation and child support on the ground that any agreement reached by the parties is subject to court approval, including the agreement to arbitrate and any result reached thereby.

D. Mediation

1. Mediation v. Arbitration

Mediation differs from arbitration primarily in the fact that the mediator is a neutral who facilitates the process of bargaining between the parties to reach a mutually acceptable settlement agreement, rather than a neutral who decides the matter for the parties. The process is said to be empowering to the parties when properly done and to result in less post-divorce litigation. Mediators may be, but do not have to be, attorneys. Sometimes multiple mediators will work with a divorcing couple, perhaps a financial expert trained as a mediator to assist with financial aspects; a child psychologist or other mental health professional trained as a mediator to assist with custody issues; and a lawyer trained as a mediator to assist with the other legal issues. Many states statutorily require mediation before a divorce trial will be held. Other states permit a judge to refer the matter or particularly contentious issues to mediation before trial.

2. Domestic Violence

Mediation has generally found favor in the courts and state legislatures with a number of states mandating mediation in divorce cases, particularly those cases involving custody issues. An exception to mandatory mediation is generally recognized for those cases involving domestic violence. Typically, the court can order mediation in domestic violence cases only when mediation is agreed to by the victim, the mediator is specially trained in mediation involving domestic violence, and the victim is permitted to have a supporting person in attendance during negotiations. Additional precautions may be necessary to ensure the safety of the victim, such as allowing the victim to depart the meditation session several minutes before the perpetrator, in order to avoid confrontations following the mediation session. Some critics argue that women are generally disadvantaged in mediation due to the fact that they value relationships more than men, they are more risk adverse, and they are less powerful and less sophisticated in terms of bargaining skills. Proponents of mediation argue that some studies have refuted those claims.

3. Repudiation

The mediation agreement, once reduced to writing and signed by the parties is a contract and may be enforceable as a contract, but it is not effective in settlement of the pending litigation until presented to and accepted by the court. If one of the parties repudiates the mediated settlement before it is accepted by the court in settlement of the case, most courts will not enforce the agreement as a settlement of the case. Some courts will, however, try the case and enforce the mediated settlement as a contract between the parties as it relates to the divorce issues contested at trial.

4. Confidentiality

In order to encourage settlement, nothing that is said during mediation is admissible at trial. All communications are confidential except that the mediator is usually a mandatory reporter regarding child abuse or neglect. This exception to confidentiality is addressed with the parties before mediation begins. All records, reports, and other documents developed for the mediation are generally deemed confidential and privileged. As a general rule, any other communications made during mediation may be disclosed only when all of the parties agree in writing, when there is subsequent litigation between the mediator and a party, when the tangible evidence is otherwise discoverable and not prepared specifically for the mediation, or when the parties are engaged in litigation with a third party and the court determines that fairness requires disclosure or some or all of the mediated agreement.

5. Forms of Mediation

Mediation may be conducted with or without the presence of counsel for each party. The mediation may take place with all of the participants in one room or the mediator may engage in shuttle mediation, where each side is located in a separate room and the mediator shuttles back and forth. Shuttle mediation may be most appropriate in high conflict or emotionally charged cases. Shuttle mediation also provides for easier communication between attorney and client in cases where each party's attorney is present at the mediation.

E. Collaborative Law

Collaborative law begins with an agreement between the attorneys and parties that prohibits the attorneys from ever representing the clients in contested court proceedings arising out of the divorce or family law matter that is the subject of the agreement. The parties and counsel also agree to use best efforts to resolve the dispute in good faith without resort to contested court proceedings. The agreement also typically provides for a candid exchange of information and a suspension of court proceedings while the parties are negotiating.

The agreement gives both the parties and the attorneys an extra incentive to continue negotiating when an apparent impasse arises rather than resorting to litigation. If the case cannot be settled and the parties proceed with litigation, the collaborative lawyer must withdraw from representation and be replaced by litigation counsel, unless the client decides to proceed *pro se*.

F. Cooperative/Conciliation Law

Cooperative law, also called conciliation law, is similar to collaborative law except that the parties do not sign a disqualification agreement. They do generally sign an agreement for voluntary disclosure of information and use of best efforts to work toward a settlement. They may also agree to share experts and limit use of formal discovery procedures. With cooperative/conciliation law, the threat of litigation is always an option, and the client has the option to retain the same counsel if the matter goes to trial. Some scholars and practitioners argue that cooperative/conciliation law is no different than traditional divorce practice.

G. ABA Model Rules of Professional Conduct

The Model Rules address the attorney's role as a third-party neutral in various forms of alternative dispute resolution, including the role of arbitrator, mediator, and conciliator. The Model Rules for third-party neutrals applies when the attorney assists two or more persons who are not clients of that attorney to reach agreement on a dispute between them. The attorney acting as a third-party neutral must inform that parties that the attorney is not representing either of the parties and, if it appears necessary, explain the difference between the lawyer's role as a representative of one of the parties and the lawyer's role as third-party neutral.

CHECKPOINTS

- Alternative dispute resolution plays an important role in family law because the judicial system could not handle the large volume of filings if most of the cases did not settle prior to trial.
- Negotiation is perhaps the most frequently used technique to settle cases. This form of alternative dispute resolution is said to be bargaining in the shadow of the law.
- Arbitration is similar to a trial but is conducted by one or more arbitrators. The decision is binding and final in many cases.
- Mediation is the fastest growing form of alternative dispute resolution in family law cases. In many instances it is court mandated.
- Domestic violence is a well recognized exception to court mandated mediation.
- Mediators are neutral parties who facilitate efforts by the parties to reach a settlement agreement.
- Mediation proceedings are confidential in most instances, with the notable exception of the mandatory reporting of evidence of child neglect or abuse.
- Collaborative lawyers and the parties sign a disqualification agreement. If the case proceeds to trial, the collaborative attorney must withdraw from representation.
- Conciliatory lawyers operate on the same idea of open exchange of information and best efforts to settle that governs collaborative lawyers, but conciliatory lawyers do not sign a disqualification agreement.

CHAPTER 16

Tax and Bankruptcy Issues

ROADMAP

After reading this chapter, you should understand:

- The requirements for payments to qualify as alimony and the tax consequences of such qualification;
- The tax consequences of transfers of property as part of the division of marital property;
- The tax consequences of the sale of the marital home;
- The different tax treatment of alimony, child support, and property division; and
- The different status afforded support and nonsupport debts in bankruptcy.

A. Federal Income Tax

1. Alimony

Spousal support awards ordered before December 31, 2018, were tax deductible to the payor and taxable income to the payee. Recognizing that the tax bracket of payors in most circumstances is higher than that of payees, the 2017 Tax Cuts and Jobs Act eliminated the deduction for payors and the claimed income for payees. This change eliminated the incentive to payors to pay higher support payments due to the tax deduction they would receive.

For awards issued prior to the Tax Cuts and Jobs Act, spousal support payments that qualify as alimony are deductible from the gross income of the payor spouse and are includible in the gross income of the payee spouse. Likewise, spousal payments (for spousal support, child support, property division, or otherwise) that do not qualify as alimony are not deductible from gross income by the payor or includible in gross income by the payee. Shifting income from the higher tax bracket spouse to the lower tax bracket spouse can reduce the overall taxes paid, thereby increasing the "marital pie" to be divided between the parties.

In order to qualify as alimony, the following seven criteria of the Internal Revenue Code (IRC) must be met:

1. The spouses do not file a joint return with each other;
2. The payments must be made in cash, which includes checks and money orders;
3. The payments must be made pursuant to a divorce decree or marriage settlement agreement which must be in writing;
4. The divorce decree or marriage settlement agreement must not indicate a contrary intent, *eg.*, that the alimony payment *not* be deductible by the payor and includible by the payee;
5. Spouses may not be members of the same household when the payments are made (an exception is recognized for parties not yet divorced and living separately in the same house);
6. Payments must end upon the death of the payee; and
7. The payments do not qualify as alimony if the parties file a joint return together.

Provision 4 above has the effect of allowing the parties to opt out of the IRC tax treatment of alimony payments, if they choose to do so.

2. Property Division

Property transfers incident to divorce are not taxable events. There are no tax consequences for either party at the time of the transfer. A transfer is deemed to be incident to the divorce if it occurs within one year of the date that the marriage ceases or is related to the cessation of the marriage. A transfer is presumed to be related to the cessation of the marriage if the transfer takes place within six years of the divorce and is made pursuant to a divorce or separation instrument.

Even though the transfer is not subject to gift or income taxation, the transferee will be subject to capital gains taxes upon a future sale of the property. The transferee will receive the property with the transferor's basis. The carryover basis means that the transferee will pay tax on the gain when the property is sold, based on the transferor's basis in the property rather than its value when transferred to the transferee spouse. For example, if the transferor spouse bought stock at $5 a share prior to marrying and transfers those shares to the transferee spouse at the time of the divorce when the shares are worth $10 a share, there will be no tax owed at that time. When the transferee spouse sells the shares later for $25 a share, tax will be assessed on the gain of $20 per share ($25–$5) rather than $15 ($25–$10). In considering real property, the basis would be the original cost to the transferor minus any adjustments.

Parties should also consider tax consequences when valuing property for purposes of making a property division. For instance, $1,000 in a tax deferred annuity is worth less than $1,000 in a savings account because the money in the annuity will be subject to tax upon withdrawal, whereas the funds in the savings account have already been taxed.

One tax avoidance strategy that parties have tried in the past is to disguise property division payments as alimony in order to reap the tax benefits of income shifting to reduce the overall tax liability of the parties. The IRC discourages this practice through the alimony recapture provisions. These provisions are also referred to as anti-frontloading requirements. They provide for a review of the parties' returns in the third year following the divorce for evidence of excess alimony payments. Any amount of excess payments calculated under the recapture formula will be included in the payor's income and deducted from the payee's income. The formula generally treats annual alimony payment differentials of more than $15,000 as excess payments subject to the recapture provisions. Moreover, this strategy, post-2018, is no longer an option due to the change in the way that alimony payments are taxed.

3. Sale of the Family Home

Each taxpayer, regardless of age, may now exclude up to $250,000 in gain on the sale of his or her principal residence if the home was owned and used by the taxpayer for an aggregate of two of the past five years prior to the transfer. The exclusion may be claimed every two years, but only once during the two-year period. The IRC also contains a special provision for divorcing couples that permits a displaced spouse to be treated as using the principal residence during any period that the other spouse is granted use of the residence pursuant to a divorce or separation agreement.

4. Child Support

Unlike alimony, child support payments are neither deductible by the payor nor includible by the payee. Some divorcing couples attempted to take advantage of the pre-2018 income shifting tax advantages available to alimony payments by lumping alimony and child support payments together. That strategy worked until the IRC was amended to disqualify as alimony any payment which, under the terms of the divorce or separation agreement, will be reduced, generally, on the happening of a contingency related to the child, such as the child's attaining a certain age, marrying, dying, or leaving school. For example, if the divorce agreement provides that the payor spouse will pay $5,000 per month to the payee spouse as alimony and that such payments will be reduced to zero when the parties' youngest child attains the age of eighteen, the payments will be classified as child support and not alimony. In addition, the Internal Revenue Service (IRS) has established two rebuttable presumptions that payments designated as alimony are to be treated as child support if:

1. The payments are to be reduced not more than six months before or after the date the child is to attain the age of eighteen, twenty-one, or the local age of majority; or
2. The payments are to be reduced on two or more occasions which occur not more than one year before or after a different child of the payor spouse attains a certain age between the ages of eighteen and twenty-four.

The addition of the presumptions virtually eliminates any attempt to disguise child support payments as alimony. Moreover, since the enactment of the Tax Cuts and Jobs Act, alimony is no more beneficial as a designation than child support.

5. Dependency Exemption

The primary residential parent is entitled to the dependency exemption for that child. Two exceptions to the foregoing rule apply, however. The first is when the divorce decree unconditionally allows the non-custodial parent to claim the exemption. The second is when the primary residential parent releases, by written declaration (IRS Form 8332), the dependency exemption to the other parent. The noncustodial parent must attach the declaration to the return for the year in which the dependency is claimed. If the parents have equal residential time, the parent with the higher gross income may claim the exemption.

6. Child Care Credit and Child Tax Credit

Over the years, Congress has provided childcare and child tax credits to low and mid-level earners who are the primary residential parent of a child. The age of the child for purposes of these credits has varied between thirteen and sixteen, and the credits are often phased out as income increases. During the Covid-19 pandemic, congress enacted some relief measures that were provided through the tax code, including stimulus checks to individuals and their dependents, recovery rebate credits, and expanded child tax and child dependent care credits. Many of these emergency relief efforts have expired, while others have simply been adjusted up or down in light of current economic circumstances. At present, the two main tax credits related to children are the Child Tax Credit and the Child and Dependent Care Credit.

7. Filing Status

A taxpayer's filing status is determined on the last day of the tax year for which the return is filed. For most taxpayers that date is December 31st. If a taxpayer becomes divorced on December 30, that taxpayer's filing status is single even though the taxpayer was married for most of the tax year. Married couples may choose to file a joint return or to file as married, filing separately. Couples have joint liability on joint returns unless the innocent spouse qualifies for relief under the innocent spouse doctrine.

The single taxpayer who is also the primary residential parent will usually qualify for head of household status which is a much lower tax bracket than the tax bracket for filing as single. Head of household status is available to a taxpayer who pays more than half of the costs of the household and maintains it as the principal residence of a unmarried minor child who lives with the taxpayer more than half of the year. Head of household status is not available to the noncustodial parent and cannot be transferred like the dependency exemption.

8. Attorney Fees

Prior to the 2017 Tax Cuts and Jobs Act (TCJA), attorney fees associated with divorce and paid to one's own attorney were not deductible, but any portion related to services for tax advice and planning and services provided for the production or collection of income, such as alimony, were deductible. The TCJA, however, eliminated many itemized deductions, including non-business tax advice and any services related to collection of alimony that is now no longer considered income for the payee spouse.

B. Bankruptcy

Policy provisions of bankruptcy law and family law conflict in the area of support obligations and other marital debts. The policy of bankruptcy law is to give the debtor a fresh start, even if it means discharging legitimate debts owed to creditors. The policy of family law requires a spouse to provide support for necessaries for one's child and dependent spouse. Bankruptcy law has been amended several times in the last several years in an attempt to find a proper balance between these competing interests. Before the 1994 amendments, support obligations were nondischargeable, but other marital debts were dischargeable. The 1994 amendments made both categories of debt nondischargeable but identified two defenses that the debtor could raise to make the nonsupport debts dischargeable. The most recent amendments in 2005 eliminated the defenses available to the debtor for nonsupport debts but still provided for discharge of nonsupport debts in certain types of bankruptcy filings, as discussed below.

There are basically two types of filings for most divorce debtors under the Bankruptcy Abuse Prevention and Consumer Protection Act of 2005 (BAPCPA). The first type is the Chapter 7 straight bankruptcy, which does not require a repayment plan. The other type is the Chapter 13 wage earner bankruptcy, which does require a repayment plan over a period of years. Debtors may not file for a straight bankruptcy unless they pass a means test which is designed to prevent abusive filings by above-median income debtors.

Support debts, referred to as domestic support obligations (DSO's) are nondischargeable under either Chapter 7 or Chapter 13 if they are owed to or recoverable by, generally, a former spouse, child of the debtor or a governmental unit. DSO's include child support awards and most spousal support awards. Other types of marital debt (other marital debt), such as property division obligations are also nondischargeable under a Chapter 7 straight bankruptcy but may be discharged under a Chapter 13 wage earner. Subsequent amendments to the 2005 BAPCPA have emphasized the priority of unpaid child support and alimony payments in bankruptcy proceedings. Thus, it is still important for attorneys to clarify in the settlement agreement and divorce decree whether a debt is for support of the spouse or children (nondischargeable) or is other marital debt (may be dischargeable).

Because the debtor's estate is never sufficient to pay all the debts, the priority of the nondischargeable debts is very important. BAPCPA affords first priority to DSOs. Other marital debts owed to the spouse or former spouse receive no special priority status. If these debts are determined to be non-dischargeable, however, they may be enforced post discharge. Other marital debts that are owed to a third party are not excepted from discharge and are considered general unsecured debts.

When a debtor files a bankruptcy petition an automatic stay applies to most pending and future actions against the debtor's estate during the pendency of the bankruptcy proceedings, unless the bankruptcy court lifts the stay. The automatic stay that applies when the debtor files a petition in bankruptcy does not apply, however, to DSO modification and enforcement proceedings; divorces, except to the extent of division of property that is property of the debtor's estate; actions to collect DSO's from property that is not property of the estate; and the withholding of income that is property of the debtor's estate to pay a DSO pursuant to a court order, administrative order or statute.

CHECKPOINTS

- Qualifying alimony payments that were once deductible from gross income by the payor spouse and includible in gross income by the payee spouse are, since December 31, 2018, no longer deductible or includable to either.
- Property transfers incident to divorce are not taxable events but the transferee takes the transferor's basis.
- Up to $250,000 in gain on the sale of the principal residence may be excluded per taxpayer if the home was owned and used by the taxpayer for an aggregate of two of the past five years prior to the transfer.
- Child support payments are not deductible by the payor or includible by the payee.
- The dependency exemption is claimed by the primary residential parent, but may be transferred to the other spouse by written declaration or awarded to the noncustodial spouse by the divorce decree.
- The childcare credit and the child tax credit are available to the primary residential parent.
- A taxpayer's filing status is determined on the last day of the tax year for which the return is filed.

- A single taxpayer who is also the primary residential parent will also usually qualify for head of household status. This filing status is not transferable to the noncustodial parent.
- Attorney fees related to divorce, custody, support or even tax implications related to divorce are generally not deductible.
- DSOs are generally not dischargeable in bankruptcy and are entitled to first priority status in the distribution of the debtor's estate.
- Other marital debts are nondischargeable in Chapter 7 straight bankruptcies but are dischargeable in Chapter 13 wage earner petitions. Other marital debts are not afforded priority in the distribution of the debtor's estate.

CHAPTER 17

The Role of Counsel

ROADMAP

After reading this chapter, you should understand:

- The circumstances under which an attorney may represent both parties to a divorce;
- The obligations of an attorney when the other party is not represented;
- The limitations on an attorney's entering into a sexual relationship with a client;
- The right to withdraw from representation; and
- The regulations on setting attorney fees.

A. Joint Representation

Whether joint representation in a divorce is allowed depends upon how one defines "joint representation." If taken in its traditional meaning, that one attorney is representing both spouses in a divorce that is currently filed or is contemplated to be filed, this is not permitted pursuant to the ABA Model Rules of Professional Conduct (MRPC). Such representation would constitute a conflict of interest created when one represents parties who are directly adverse and such would create a nonconsentable conflict. But the MRPC would allow an attorney to serve as an intermediary in certain circumstances and certainly as a third-party neutral, such as a mediator to both parties. Some states, in an attempt to encourage conflict resolution, have allowed one party to hire an attorney to commemorate an agreement that the spouses have reached in order to achieve an uncontested divorce. However, it is crucial for the unrepresented spouse to be informed and to understand that the attorney is working only for their client and is not looking out for the best interest of both parties. Some clients and attorneys alike mistake this arrangement for "joint representation" because the attorney may meet with both parties to ascertain the substance of their agreement. While such a meeting would impact the application of the attorney-client privilege, it does not necessarily amount to joint representation, so long as the attorney is forthright about his role to the non-client spouse.

B. Pro Se Adverse Party

The Model Rules state that a lawyer, when dealing on behalf of a client with a person who is not represented by counsel, should not state or imply that the lawyer is disinterested. The comments to the rule state that the lawyer should not give any advice to the pro se litigant, other than advice to obtain counsel. The Academy of Matrimonial Lawyers allows discussion with pro se litigants but encourages counsel to inform the pro se litigant, in writing, as soon as possible of the following:

1. I am your spouse's lawyer.
2. I do not and will not represent you.
3. I will at all times look out for your spouse's interests, not yours.
4. Any statements that I make to you about this case should be taken by you as negotiations or argument on behalf of your spouse and not as advice to you as to your best interest.
5. I urge you to obtain your own lawyer.

C. Sexual Ethics

A great deal has been written about the ethics of having a sexual relationship with one's divorce client. Most writers disapprove of the practice. In 1992, the American Bar Association Standing Committee on Ethics and Professional Responsibility opined that having a sexual relationship with a client can constitute a breach of fiduciary duty if the relationship results from the client's dependence, interferes with the attorney's professional judgment, and may otherwise impair the attorney's representation. The ABA opinion also discourages attorneys from having sexual relationships with clients and warns that disciplinary action may result if the attorney's representation is actually impaired. In 2002, the ABA House of Delegates recommended language in the Model Rules of Professional Conduct that prohibits an attorney from having sex with a client unless a consensual relationship existed prior to the beginning of the attorney's representation of that client. Such modification appears in today's Rule 1.8(j). In states that have not adopted the MRPC in toto, some have elected not to adopt a specific rule prohibiting sex with a client, but, instead, apply the general rule of current client conflicts of interest set forth in Rule 1.7, as prohibiting such conduct. The American Academy of Matrimonial Lawyers Standards of Conduct prohibits any sexual relationship with a client, opposing counsel or acting judicial officer, during the time of representation. Even though the sexual conduct may result in disciplinary action, it is unlikely, in and of itself, to affect the validity of the divorce decree in the case.

D. Withdrawing from Representation

The client may fire an attorney for any or no reason. The MRPC are liberal in the bases for which an attorney may withdraw from representation of a client:

1. withdrawal can be accomplished without material adverse effect on the interests of the client;
2. the client persists in a course of action involving the lawyer's services that the lawyer reasonably believes is criminal or fraudulent;
3. the client has used the lawyer's services to perpetrate a crime or fraud;
4. the client insists upon taking action that the lawyer considers repugnant or with which the lawyer has a fundamental disagreement;
5. the client fails substantially to fulfill an obligation to the lawyer regarding the lawyer's services and has been given reasonable warning that the lawyer will withdraw unless the obligation is fulfilled;
6. the representation will result in an unreasonable financial burden on the lawyer or has been rendered unreasonably difficult by the client; or
7. other good cause for withdrawal exists.

The MRPC list the following responsibilities when withdrawing from representation:

1. Giving reasonable notice to the client;
2. Allowing time for hiring substitute counsel;
3. Delivering to the client all relevant papers and property to which the client is entitled; and
4. Refunding any fees that have been paid but not earned.

Withdrawal is mandatory if the representation will result in violation of the rules of professional conduct or other law, the lawyer's physical or mental condition materially impairs the lawyer's ability to represent the client, the lawyer is discharged, or the client seeks to use or persists in using the lawyer's services to commit or further a crime or fraud.

E. Attorney Fees

Written fee agreements are not required by the MRPC, except in contingency fee cases, but they clearly are in everyone's best interests, both to avoid misunderstandings and to provide proof of the terms of the actual agreement. Contingent fees are generally not permissible in family law cases. An exception, however, has been carved out for enforcement actions for support and property distribution awards that have already been ordered by the court. Courts differ on whether fees computed on the results obtained are deemed contingent. Hourly fees must be reasonable. Retainers that are to be paid upfront are usually allowed but generally may not be nonrefundable. The funds must be placed in escrow until earned by the attorney's services or returned to the client.

Attorneys may not charge excessive fees. The MRPC list the following factors for determining the reasonableness of the attorney fee:

1. the time and labor required, the novelty and difficulty of the questions involved, and the skill requisite to perform the legal service properly;
2. the likelihood, if apparent to the client, that the acceptance of the particular employment will preclude other employment by the lawyer;
3. the fee customarily charged in the locality for similar legal services;
4. the amount involved and the results obtained;

5. the time limitations imposed by the client or by the circumstances;
6. the nature and length of the professional relationship with the client;
7. the experience, reputation, and ability of the lawyer or lawyers performing the services; and
8. whether the fee is fixed or contingent.

CHECKPOINTS

- The MRPC preclude joint representation of parties to a divorce, but one attorney can represent one party to draft a mutually agreed settlement summary and other documents.
- An attorney may not give any advice to a pro se adverse party other than the advice to obtain counsel.
- Restrictions vary among the states, but the ABA Model Rules prohibit an attorney from having sex with a client unless a consensual relationship existed prior to the beginning of the attorney's representation of that client.
- An attorney may withdraw from representation for a number of MRPC specified reasons and must withdraw in certain circumstances.
- Attorney fees may not be excessive.

CHAPTER 18

Constitutional Protection of Parental Rights and Children's Rights

---

ROADMAP

After reading this chapter, you should understand:

- The sources of state power to protect children;
- The bases for constitutionally protected parental rights; and
- The limited constitutional rights of the child.

A. Source of State Power

There are two sources of state power that justify state action to protect children. The broader and more general power is the general police power of the state to promote the public health, safety, and welfare of children generally, such as child labor laws and compulsory school attendance laws. The more narrowly focused power is the *parens patriae* power to protect or promote a particular child's welfare, as when the court exercises its *parens patriae* to protect the best interests of the child or children whose case is before the court.

The state's power is not unlimited, however. Parents have constitutionally protected rights that must be balanced against the state's interests. In addition, the child has state recognized or constitutionally protected rights in some cases that must also be balanced against the parents' interests and the state's interests.

B. Parental Rights Cases

In a series of cases decided by the Supreme Court beginning in 1923, the Court developed a strong constitutionally protected parental right of privacy that allows parents to make decisions concerning their children subject to limited state interference based on a balancing of interests test designed to promote and protect the child's best interests. The cases are considered below.

1. *Meyer v. Nebraska*

In *Meyer v. Nebraska*, 262 U.S. 390 (1923), a Nebraska statute made it a crime to teach any subject to any person in any language other than English, except for foreign languages after the eighth grade. The Supreme Court held that the statute was arbitrary as applied and without reasonable relation to any end within the competency of the state. Noting that it was the natural duty of the parent to give his children education suitable to their station in life, the Court held that the right of parents to permit their children to be instructed in a foreign language is within the liberty of the Fourteenth Amendment.

2. *Pierce v. Society of Sisters*

Just two years later, the Court decided *Pierce v. Society of Sisters*, 268 U.S. 510 (1925), involving the Oregon Compulsory Education Act which required children to attend public school. The statute was challenged by the Society of Sisters who ran the Catholic parochial schools in Oregon. The Court relied on the doctrine of *Meyer* to hold that the act unreasonably interfered with the liberty of parents to direct the upbringing and education of children under their control. The Court in *Pierce* stated, "The child is not the mere creature of the state; those who nurture him and direct his destiny have the right, coupled with the high duty, to recognize and prepare him for additional obligations."

3. *Prince v. Massachusetts*

Massachusetts' child labor laws were at issue in *Prince v. Massachusetts*, 321 U.S. 158 (1944). In *Prince*, an aunt/guardian was convicted of violating Massachusetts' child labor statute by allowing her nine-year-old niece to accompany her on the public sidewalks while the aunt preached and the niece sold Jehovah Witness magazines. The aunt claimed that she had a First

Amendment privilege and parental rights under the Due Process Clause based on *Meyer*.

The Court recognized the parental rights doctrine established in *Meyer* and *Pierce*, stating, "It is cardinal with us that the custody, care, and nurture of the child reside first in the parents, whose primary function and freedom include preparation for obligations the state can neither supply nor hinder." Unlike in *Meyer* and *Pierce*, however, in this case the state's interests outweighed the aunt's interests. The Court upheld the statute based on the state's interests in protecting the child's welfare which the Court said includes, to some extent, matters of conscience and religious conviction, stating, "But the family itself is not beyond regulation in the public interest, as against a claim of religious liberty."

4. *Troxel v. Granville*

Most recently, the Supreme Court reviewed the parental rights doctrine in the context of a grandparent visitation statute. In *Troxel v. Granville*, 530 U.S. 57 (2000), the Supreme Court held that a state must give some deference to the parental decision regarding whether to allow grandparent visitation, but the Court did not specify how much weight must be given because the statute at issue gave no weight or deference at all to the mother's decision regarding grandparent visitation. The Washington statute allowed any person to seek visitation at any time, subject only to a best interest determination by the court. The Court relied on the long recognized due process right of parents to make decisions regarding the nurturing, upbringing, companionship, care, and custody of their children under the Due Process Clause of the Fourteenth Amendment articulated in *Meyer, Pierce,* and their progeny. Only two of the nine justices gave any indication that they might be receptive to arguments to overrule those decisions.

C. Children's Rights

The earliest Supreme Court cases recognizing constitutionally protected parental rights, *Meyer* and *Pierce*, failed to even mention the child's rights. *Prince* did recognize the child's independent interest, separate from the aunt, to exercise one's religion and to use the highways, but the Court gave greater weight to the aunt's interests and the state's interests than to the child's interests.

1. *Brown v. Board of Education*

Ten years after *Prince*, in *Brown v. Board of Education*, 347 U.S. 483 (1954), the Supreme Court unanimously held that racial segregation in public school violated the Equal Protection Clause. The children themselves were the named plaintiffs in *Brown*.

2. *Wisconsin v. Yoder*

In *Wisconsin v. Yoder*, 406 U.S. 205 (1972), the educational rights of Amish children were indirectly before the Court when several Amish parents appealed their convictions for violating Wisconsin's compulsory education law. The parents agreed to send their children to school through the eighth grade, but refused to send them to school after that, in keeping with the Amish customs. The Court balanced only the rights of the parents and the state's interests and did not consider the children's rights. A dissent by Justice Douglas argued that the children were entitled to a hearing concerning whether they wished to continue school past the eighth grade. The majority concluded that the criminal prosecution of the parents did not implicate the children's wishes because violation of the statute did not require a showing that the children wanted to attend school.

3. *Belloti v. Baird*

In recognition of the federal abortion rights case, *Roe v. Wade*, 416 U.S. 113 (1973), in *Belloti v. Baird*, 443 U.S. 622 (1979), the Supreme Court recognized a limited right of privacy for minors regarding the right to obtain an abortion without parental consent by requiring a parental consent statute to contain a judicial bypass provision. (See further discussion of the minor's right to an abortion in the chapter on Reproductive Rights). More recently, however, in *Dobbs v. Jackson Women's Health Organization*, 597 U.S. 215 (2022), the Court eliminated the federal Constitutional right to an abortion, overturning *Roe*, and returning the authority to regulate or prohibit abortions to the states; thus, judicial bypass provisions for abortions by minors are no longer mandated, unless state law requires.

4. The Right to Divorce One's Parents

Several cases have made headlines over the years when children have attempted to bring a termination of parental rights action on their own. Courts generally find that children lack the legal capacity to bring such an action. The action must be brought by the state or by a guardian ad litem or next friend.

CHECKPOINTS

- The two sources of state power to protect children are the state's general police power and the state's *parens patriae* power.
- The Supreme Court has recognized a constitutionally protected parental right of privacy that must be balanced against the state's interest in protecting the child.
- In some instances, the child's rights are recognized and weighed against the interests of the parents and the state, but children are generally not afforded the full range of constitutional rights afforded to adults.
- Children generally do not have capacity to bring suit on their own, even if represented by counsel. Suit must be brought by the state, a guardian ad litem, or next friend.

CHAPTER 19

Definition of Parents and Family

ROADMAP

After reading this chapter, you should understand:

- The various approaches to defining mother;
- The role of the presumption of legitimacy;
- The parental rights of unwed fathers;
- The parental rights of sperm donors; and
- The difference between the traditional and functional approaches to define family.

A. Definition of Mother

Prior to the introduction of assisted reproduction techniques (ART), the definition of mother was generally limited to birth mothers and adoptive mothers. Now the courts must consider the rights of the ovum donor, who is not the intended mother or the gestational mother; the gestational surrogate (who gives birth but is not biologically related to the child); the intended mother (the party to a surrogacy contract who is neither the gestational mother or the ovum donor); the intended mother (who is either the ovum donor or gestational mother but not both); the lesbian partner who may or may not be biologically related to the child; and the traditional surrogate who is biologically related to the child. The courts have taken various approaches to these issues as technological advances have forced the courts to address a number of cases of first impression. Some states have passed statutes that address some of the above issues, but a number of states have left these issues to be determined by the courts. Prior to *Obergefell v. Hodges*, 576 U.S. 644 (2015), most states took the position that a child can have only one mother, although a few states have recognized dual motherhood in limited cases. Obviously, with the recognition of same-sex marriages, the definition of mother has expanded to potentially include more than one person.

1. Genetics

A number of courts have relied on genetics to determine the identity of the mother. The highly publicized Baby M case, *In re Baby M*, 537 A.2d 1227 (N.J. 1988), addressed the issue of the parental rights of the traditional surrogate mother. The surrogate mother contracted with a couple to be artificially inseminated with the intended father's sperm. She changed her mind, however, and sought to enforce her parental rights to the child after delivery. The court held that surrogacy contracts were unenforceable, as invalid and against public policy, and that the surrogate was the child's mother rather than the intended mother (the wife of the father and sperm donor who contracted with the surrogate mother). Following this case, a number of states enacted statutes recognizing surrogacy contracts, other states expressly outlawed them, and still other states did nothing. In 2018, New Jersey followed many other states and passed a bill that legalized gestational surrogacy, but only if certain conditions are met.

2. Parenting Intent

Other courts have relied on parenting intent rather than genetics to identify the mother. Courts that enforce surrogacy contracts may look to the surrogacy contract to identify the person intended in the contract to be the child's mother. *Johnson v. Calvert*, 851 P.2d 776 (Cal. 1993), illustrates this approach. In *Johnson*, a married couple used their sperm and ovum to create an embryo that was implanted in a gestational surrogate pursuant to a surrogacy contract. The court recognized that each woman had a claim to motherhood. The wife was the genetic mother, and the surrogate was the birth mother. The court held that the legal mother was the one who intended to procreate the child, the one who intended to bring about the birth of a child that she intended to raise as her own. The intended parent was the wife in this case. In 2012, California codified the *Johnson* rule and established specific criteria that all California surrogacy contracts must follow.

3. A Hybrid Approach

Some courts consider both parenting intent and genetics, along with other factors, such as gestation. The Tennessee Supreme Court, in *In re C.K.G.*, 173 S.W.3d 714 (Tenn. 2005), considered the case of a woman who was the birth mother to triplets after being implanted with embryos created with ova from an anonymous donor and sperm from her unmarried partner. The birth mother had no genetic link to the children but was the intended mother. The court found that she was the mother but noted that it was significant that no one else was vying for recognition as mother. The unmarried partner was contesting her status as mother. If she were not recognized as the mother, the children would have no identifiable mother.

B. Definition of Father

1. Presumption of Legitimacy

Historically, it was very important that a child be legitimated because of the stigma and lack of legal rights associated with illegitimacy. Illegitimate children were not entitled to receive support from or to inherit from their fathers. Over the years, the Supreme Court has decided a number of cases addressing the rights of illegitimate children. The Court held that illegitimate children are a quasi-suspect class under the Equal Protection Clause. Any discrimination against illegitimate children is subject to intermediate scrutiny under the equal protection doctrine. In *Lalli v. Lalli*, 439 U.S. 259 (1978), the Supreme Court held that the state must prove that the differential treatment is substantially related to the achievement of an important public interest. The result has been that illegitimate children are entitled to almost identical rights as those provided to legitimate children.

Before advancements in DNA testing, it was only possible to prove through blood tests that someone was not the father. Tests could not prove that a particular individual was the father. Consequently, the law relied heavily on legal presumptions of paternity to avoid the negative consequences associated with illegitimacy.

2. Unwed Fathers

The Supreme Court has examined the extent to which a natural father's biological relationship with his child receives protection under the Due Process Clause in four cases. The first case, *Stanley v. Illinois*, 405 U.S. 645 (1972), involved the constitutionality of an Illinois statute that conclusively presumed every unwed father to be unfit. In *Stanley*, the father had lived with the children all their lives and had lived intermittently with their mother for eighteen years. Nothing in the record indicated that the father had been neglectful, but when the mother died, the children were automatically made wards of the state based on the statutory presumption of the father's unfitness. The Court held that the Due Process Clause was violated by the automatic destruction of the custodial relationship without giving the father an opportunity to present evidence regarding his fitness as a parent.

The second case, *Quilloin v. Walcott*, 434 U.S. 246 (1978), involved the constitutionality of a Georgia statute permitting the adoption of an illegitimate child over the objection of the biological father who had never attempted to establish paternity. It was only after the mother and her new husband filed an adoption petition that the unwed father sought visitation rights and filed a petition for legitimation. The trial court found adoption by the new husband to be in the child's best interests, and the Supreme Court unanimously held that action to be consistent with the Due Process Clause.

The third case, *Caban v. Mohammed,* 441 U.S. 380, (1979), involved the conflicting claims of two natural parents who had maintained joint custody of their children from birth until they were two and four years old, respectively. The father challenged an order permitting the mother's new husband to adopt the children, relying on both the Equal Protection Clause and the Due Process Clause. The Court upheld his equal protection claim, and, therefore, did not address his due process challenge.

The Court made clear in the fourth case that the mere existence of a biological link does not merit equivalent constitutional protection for unwed fathers with that given to mothers and husbands. In *Lehr v. Robertson* 463 U.S. 248 (1983), the Court set the standard by which all unwed fathers' constitutional rights are measured. The unwed father must assume parental responsibility for the child before his parental relationship will be afforded the same constitutionally protected due process rights enjoyed by mothers and husbands. The Court in *Lehr* stated the test as follows:

> The significance of the biological connection is that it offers the natural father an opportunity that no other male possesses to develop a relationship with his offspring. If he grasps that opportunity and accepts some measure of responsibility for the child's future, he may enjoy the blessings of the parent-child relationship and make uniquely valuable contributions to the child's development. If he fails to do so, the Federal Constitution will not automatically compel a state to listen to his opinion of where the child's best interests lie.

There are numerous ways in which the unwed father can assume parental responsibilities for the child. He can offer support to the mother for medical expenses and child support before and after the birth of the child; visit the child regularly and establish a parental relationship, including assuming parenting responsibilities; sign the birth certificate as father; register with the state's putative fathers registry; or file a paternity action, to name a few.

3. Unwed Fathers v. Presumed Fathers

After *Lehr*, the Supreme Court next considered the constitutional protection of unwed fathers' rights in *Michael H. v. Gerald D.*, 491 U.S. 110 (1989), where the unwed biological father sought to establish paternity of a child presumed to be the child of the mother and her husband, based on the presumption of legitimacy of children born in wedlock. In California, where *Michael H.* arose, the legislature enacted a conclusive presumption of legitimacy in favor of the husband unless the mother joined the unwed father in the paternity petition. The unwed father challenged the conclusive presumption, relying on the constitutional protections established in *Lehr*.

While recognizing the constitutionally protected parental rights of both parties, the Supreme Court, in a 5-4 decision, held that it was not unconstitutional for California to give preference to the husband over the unwed father, stating, "Where, however, the child is born into an extant marital family, the natural father's unique opportunity conflicts with the similarly unique opportunity of the husband of a marriage; and it is not unconstitutional for the State to give categorical preference to the latter." *Id.* The Court did not say that a state *must* give preference to the husband, it just said that a state *may* do so. The case is cited for the premise that a biological father may not automatically have parental rights, particularly when a legal or presumed father has established a parental relationship with the child.

4. Sperm Donors

Most states have statutes addressing the rights of sperm donors and providing in most instances that the sperm donors have no parental rights. The statutes are not applicable, however, if the statutory prerequisites for artificial insemination are not met. For instance, some statutes apply only to married couples or to medically administered artificial inseminations. Such statutes would not be applicable to unmarried recipients, same-sex couples, or persons who perform the artificial insemination without medical assistance, giving rise to litigation over the parental rights of the sperm donor in such cases. In some cases, the sperm donor is known by the mother and is promised some involvement in the child's life, sometimes in writing. The sperm donor sues when the agreement is not honored. If the statute is found to be inapplicable, the court will apply the *Lehr* test to determine the parental rights, if any, of the sperm donor.

5. Establishing Paternity

Paternity is much easier to establish today than it was prior to the availability of DNA tests. Prior blood tests could rule someone out as a possible father if the blood types were not compatible, but they could not prove that someone was the father. States differ on the level of predictability that must be shown on genetic testing to establish paternity. The Supreme Court, in *Rivera v. Minnich*, 483 U.S. 574 (1987), held that the evidentiary standard required under the Due Process Clause of the Fourteenth Amendment in paternity cases is a preponderance of the evidence, even though the standard in termination of parental rights cases is clear and convincing. The Supreme Court also held, in *Little v. Streater*, 452 U.S. 1 (1981), that denying an indigent defendant blood grouping tests because of his inability to pay violated the due process guarantee of the Fourteenth Amendment.

6. Disestablishing Paternity

Because of fairly recent advances in DNA testing that allow proof of paternity to a virtual certainty, states have begun to wrestle with the issues of whether and under what circumstances a presumed legal father may disestablish paternity. Courts have allowed presumed fathers to prove nonpaternity with very few restrictions. Courts are much more reluctant, however, to allow a legal father to disestablish paternity once it has been legally determined, as in a paternity action or divorce decree. Yet the evidence is clear that in as many as 30% of child support cases tested, the obligor was not the biological father. Courts generally agree that disestablishment of paternity extinguishes future support obligations, but courts differ on whether the obligor continues to be liable for arrearages, if any. States are not required to provide services to noncustodial parents who seek to disestablish paternity. However, federal IV-D funding is available if the matter is now a contested paternity matter.

7. The Uniform Parentage Act (2023)

The Uniform Parentage Act, promulgated by the National Conference of Commissioners on Uniform State Laws (NCCUSL) in 1973, and amended in 2000, 2002, 2017, 2019, and 2023, has been adopted in a few states. The UPA recognizes surrogacy contracts only if the parties obtain prior judicial approval and the intended parents are screened under the same procedure applicable to adoption, including a home study. The act allows reasonable compensation to the surrogate mother.

The UPA includes a number of presumptions of paternity based on marriage and a separate presumption based on living with the mother and child for the first two years of the child's life and holding the child out as his own. Challenges to paternity based on marital presumptions must be initiated within two years of the child's birth. Paternity can also be established by a voluntary acknowledgment.

The Act provides for genetic testing, the results of which are controlling when court ordered. The court may deny a motion for genetic testing where elements of equitable estoppel are met, based on a number of factors considering the best interests of the child. The admissibility of genetic testing is limited in some circumstances including objections, filed by the opposing party within fourteen days of receipt of the results, citing specific grounds for exclusion. Further limitations apply if there is a presumed, acknowledged, or adjudicated father. The UPA also provides for a putative fathers' registry, referred to as a registry of paternity.

The 2023 revision, the most significant to date, provides a comprehensive framework for establishing parentage. The revision addresses same-sex couples, assisted reproduction and surrogacy agreements. This revision of the Act has been adopted by eight states.

C. Unrelated Gay and Lesbian Partners

Historically, gay and lesbian partners who are not genetically related to the child were the least likely to be designated parents among those seeking such status. A few states allow second-parent adoptions, but most do not. (See further discussion of second parent adoptions in the chapter on Adoption.) Some states permit limited parental rights such as visitation, but, again, most do not. Even so, the rights are generally based on the best interests of the child rather than the "detriment to the child" standard that must be met to preclude visitation rights to a legal parent. However, since the *Obergefell* decision, *supra*, all states must recognize that a child may have two mothers or two fathers, when born in wedlock. Moreover, the federal recognition of the fundamental right to marry, including same-sex marriages, was based in part on the fundamental right to procreate within the confines of marriage that, prior to *Obergefell*, could not be accomplished by same-sex partners in most states.

D. Definition of Family

1. Traditional Approach

Most courts have relied on longstanding social convention to define family, especially in the context of regulatory classification. For example, in *Moore v. City of East Cleveland*, 431 U.S. 494 (1977), the Supreme Court relied on the traditional definition of family as people related by affinity (marriage), consanguinity (blood), or adoption. In doing so the Court struck down a city ordinance defining family to prohibit a grandmother from living with her grandson.

2. Functional Approach

Occasionally, a court will use a functional approach to define family. Under this approach, the court determines whether the parties are functioning as a family traditionally does, regardless of whether they meet the traditional definition of family based on their relationship of affinity, consanguinity, or adoption. In *Braschi v. Stahl Associates Co.*, 543 N.E.2d 49 (N.Y. 1989), the New York Court of Appeals applied the functional approach to define family in interpreting a rent control law to a homosexual couple who had lived together for ten years. In determining that the two men constituted a family for purposes of applying the rent control law, the court focused on the fact that the two men operated as a family traditionally does, stating that this family included "two adult lifetime partners whose relationship is long-term and characterized by an emotional and financial commitment and interdependence." Courts have been much more reluctant to apply the functional approach to cases involving parental rights and marriage.

CHECKPOINTS

- Courts have relied on genetics, parental intention, gestation, and a combination of the foregoing to determine the legal mother.
- Historically, paternity relied strongly on the marital presumption to avoid the harsh consequences of illegitimacy.
- Unwed fathers have the same parental due process rights as mothers and husbands if they assume parental responsibilities before or shortly after the birth of the child.
- Sperm donors typically do not have parental rights.
- Courts are divided on the ability of the court to disestablish paternity once it has been adjudicated.
- If paternity is disestablished, the support obligation is generally extinguished but courts differ on whether arrearages are extinguished, as well.

CHAPTER 20

Child Neglect and Abuse

ROADMAP

After reading this chapter, you should understand:

- The various types of neglect;
- The limits of the spiritual exemption;
- The different types of abuse;
- The standard for removing a child from the home; and
- The scope of the state's duty to protect a child from abuse.

A. Neglect Defined

Parents have the initial responsibility for caring for their children. They are given a wide latitude in doing so because of (1) their constitutionally protected right to direct the upbringing of their children established in *Meyer* and its progeny (discussed in the chapter on Constitutional Protection of Parental Rights); (2) the assumption that children are better off in their family of origin under marginal conditions than in state care; and (3) the cost of caring for children in state care.

All states have statutes that define the minimum standard of care that a parent must provide, failing which, the parent may be found guilty of neglect and the state may intervene to protect the child's welfare. Neglect cases generally make up the majority of cases handled by the child welfare department in any state. Neglect may arise from failure to provide adequate food, clothing, shelter, education, or supervision, for instance. Many neglect cases arise in homes affected by poverty. States are obligated to assist the parents with state programs, where possible, to help the parents properly provide for their children so they won't have to be removed from the home and placed in state custody.

Neglect can also arise when a child is the victim of abuse. The parent who abuses the child may also be guilty of neglect of that child, but even the non-abusive parent in a family may be charged with neglect. The parent who is not the perpetrator of the abuse can be found guilty of neglect based on that parent's failure to protect the child from the abusive adult. Charges of neglect for failure to protect a child from abuse may even be based on a parent's failure to cooperate with the state in identifying the perpetrator and protecting the child from future harm. The parent may be charged with neglect for refusing to acknowledge the perpetrator's culpability or refusing to stop living with the perpetrator or allowing the perpetrator to visit the home. Allegations of neglect can be made in a civil forum—often a juvenile or family court—but they may also constitute a crime, resulting in criminal prosecution.

Total neglect occurs when a parent abandons a child. All states currently have some form of safe haven law to permit parents to abandon infants at safe locations shortly after birth, without threat of civil or criminal prosecutions.

B. Medical Neglect

1. Definition of Neglect

Failure to provide medical care can arise in three distinct ways. It may be one of several allegations in an overall situation of neglect where the parents are unable or unwilling to provide the child with basic food, clothing, shelter, and health care. With infants and very young children, neglect may be evidenced by developmental delays and malnutrition and is generally referred to as "failure to thrive."

Failure to provide medical care may also arise in cases where the parents are otherwise fully functioning parents in regard to providing their children with food, clothing, shelter, and attending to their other needs. These parents simply do not believe that medical treatment is appropriate for their child. The parental decision may be based on misinformation or a mistrust of the medical profession, but more often it is based on a spiritual belief that shuns all or certain types of traditional medicine.

The third common basis arises when the parents are the source of or contributor to the injuries or sickness of the child. Abusive and neglectful parents often avoid interaction with healthcare providers.

2. Spiritual Exemptions

A number of states have statutory exemptions for parents who choose to withhold medical treatment for religious reasons. Some of the statutes are limited to withholding vaccinations and generally contain a provision that the exemption does not apply in the event of an epidemic or an immediate threat of one. Other statutes go further and apply to medical treatments generally. The issue that arises when a child dies as a result of failure to obtain medical treatment is whether the exemption statutes are a defense to a civil or criminal action based on the failure to provide medical care. The cases generally focus on whether the statute granting the exemption is sufficiently ambiguous to result in a denial of due process in failing to give the parents notice of the point at which their reliance on spiritual treatment is no longer covered by the exemption and further withholding of medical care becomes culpably negligent or criminal conduct. The standard for interpreting the statutory language is what a person of ordinary intelligence could be expected to understand. Could a person of ordinary intelligence read the statute and be expected to understand the extent to which reliance on spiritual healing is permitted and the point at which this reliance constitutes a criminal offense under the subject statute?

3. Liability of Third Parties

A few cases have addressed the liability of third parties who assist or encourage the parents in their decision to withhold medical treatment for their children. Liability is generally based on the existence of a special relationship with the child that gives rise to a duty where the third party partakes in the spiritual treatment of the child and the withholding of medical treatment beyond the point when a reasonable person, similarly situated, would have provided traditional medical care.

C. Types of Abuse

It is difficult to understand child abuse of any kind. One generally assumes that a person would have to be mentally ill to abuse a child, especially a parent, but, in fact, many parents do abuse their children every day in this country. Oftentimes the abuse is influenced by mental illness or drug abuse, but that is not always the case.

States have the authority to define "abuse" but most similarly indicate abuse occurs when a child under age 18 is suffering from, has sustained, or may be in immediate danger of suffering from or sustaining a wound, injury, disability, or physical or mental condition caused by brutality, neglect, or other actions or inactions of a parent, relative, guardian, or caregiver.

In addition to varying types of abuse, there are levels of abuse that are used to delineate when and if states will work toward reunifying a parent with a child who has suffered abuse at the hands of their parent, with most states refusing to reunify a child with a parent whose conduct rises to the level of severe abuse. Most states similarly define "severe abuse" as exposure of a child to, or failure to protect a child from, abuse or neglect that is likely to cause serious bodily injury or death, or the knowing use of force that is likely to cause serious bodily injury. This also includes abuse or neglect that, in the opinion of qualified experts, has caused or is reasonably expected to cause severe psychological or developmental harm.

1. Physical

Cases of physical abuse are easy to decide at opposite extremes of the continuum. For instance, a swat on the seat of a two-year-old who runs into the street is not physical abuse, and deliberately burning a five-year-old with an iron is physical abuse. The cases in the middle can often be much more difficult to decide because as a nation we are quite divided on the proper role of corporal punishment, both at home and at school.

Evidence of multiple injuries may give rise to a presumption of physical abuse under the battered child syndrome. Expert evidence is relied upon to demonstrate the likelihood that the child's injuries were not accidental. Discrepancies between the parents' account of the reason for the injuries and the expert's opinion of whether the injuries are consistent with the parental explanation form the basis for the expert's opinion. Numerous prior injuries are also relevant in making a determination of abuse. Advancements in medical screening tools have allowed experts to bolster their opinions by being able to recognize injuries in varying states of healing.

2. Sexual

Child sexual abuse is generally thought to be underreported because it is a crime with few witnesses and very little in the way of physical evidence. The victim may also be too young to be a good witness. Moreover, political considerations sometimes preclude an elected prosecutor from bringing a high-profile case to trial, particularly given its evidentiary challenges.

3. Emotional

Emotional abuse may be the most difficult type of abuse to prove because it usually does not have any physical manifestations. Statutes are often written to require some physical evidence of harm associated with the emotional abuse. It is also difficult for the court to determine whether the ill effects suffered by the child are the result of the parental conduct or other factors such as heredity, temperament, or the child's environment.

D. Abuse of the Fetus

Child abuse statutes are often inadequate to sustain a petition or prosecution for abuse of a fetus because most child abuse statutes refer only to a child. But an increasing number of states include a fetus in the definition of a "child." Almost half of U.S. states and the District of Columbia consider substance use during pregnancy to either be child abuse or neglect or evidence of child abuse or neglect. Many states impose criminal penalties upon any person who negligently engages in conduct that places a child in imminent danger of death, bodily injury, or physical or mental impairment, and the child is eight years of age or less. For purposes of the statute, a person engages in conduct that places a child in imminent danger of death, bodily injury, or physical or mental impairment if the person's conduct exposes the child to a controlled substance and an analysis of a specimen of the child's blood, hair, fingernail, urine, or other bodily substance indicates the presence of any controlled substance in the child's body. Most hospitals routinely screen newborn infants for substances and report positive findings to child welfare agencies before the child is permitted to be released with the child's parent.

States have also recognized that a substance abusing mother may not be the only perpetrator of abuse. Fathers who enable their pregnant partners by procuring drugs for the mother's use during pregnancy will often be held civilly liable for abuse or neglect of the fetus and can possibly face criminal charges.

E. Standard for Removal of the Child

Because of the constitutionally protected parental rights (discussed in the chapter on Constitutional Protection of Parental Rights and Children's Rights), the state cannot remove children from parental custody without first showing that removal is necessary to protect the safety of the children. Abuse or neglect of one child generally can give rise to a presumption of abuse or neglect of other children in the same household. However, class actions against child welfare agencies, alleging violations of state and federal constitutions and federal protection statutes, have met with some success, with more than half of the states in the past two decades being forced to operate their child welfare agencies pursuant to a consent decree.

F. State's Duty to Protect

In *DeShaney v. Winnebago County Dept. of Social Svcs.*, 489 U.S. 189 (1989), the Supreme Court held that the state has no duty to protect citizens from one another. In *DeShaney*, the child, left comatose from beatings by his father, sued the state for returning the child to the custody of the father. The Court stated that the child was no worse off following state intervention by removing him from his father's care and then returning him.

G. Civil v. Criminal Liability

Perpetrators of neglect and abuse may be charged in child protective proceedings, which are civil in nature, and where the goal is protection of the child. The civil standard of proof applies. Perpetrators may also be charged in criminal proceedings where the goal is punishment of the offender. In criminal cases, the burden of proof is higher (beyond a reasonable doubt) and the defendant is entitled to the full range of constitutional protections afforded criminal defendants.

H. Termination of Parental Rights

The ultimate civil consequence for neglect and abuse of a child is termination of parental rights. Statutory grounds must be proved by clear and convincing evidence and the court must find that termination of parental rights is in the child's best interests. The state does not have to provide counsel for indigent parents in every termination of parental rights case (although many states do). *Lassiter v. Department of Social Services of Durham County*, 452 U.S. 18 (1981). The state cannot, however, condition an appeal from a trial court's termination of parental rights order on payment of the record preparation fee. *M.L.B. v. S.L.J.*, 519 U.S. 102 (1996).

The state is required under the federal Adoption and Safe Families Act of 1997 to make reasonable attempts at reunification before proceeding to terminate parental rights in most cases. An exception is recognized in aggravated circumstances including parental treatment of the child that is heinous or abhorrent to society, often described as "severe abuse." (See further discussion of termination of parental rights in the chapter on Child Support and the chapter on Adoption.)

I. Mandatory Reporting Statutes

All states have mandatory reporting statutes that require mandatory reporting of evidence of child abuse. The statutes must include as mandatory reporters those adults most likely to come in contact with evidence of abuse, such as medical personnel, teachers, and childcare providers, etc. Some statutes apply to attorneys as well. In some cases, the statutes exempt confidential communications. The ABA Model Rules of Professional Conduct do not, however, list reporting of abuse as an exception to the rules on confidentiality.

The mandatory reporting statutes also permit other parties to report suspected abuse. As long as the reports are made in good faith, which is usually presumed, the reporters are immune from civil or criminal liability.

CHECKPOINTS

- Child neglect is the most common type of child mistreatment. It includes failure to provide for the child's basic needs regarding food, clothing, shelter, education, medical care, and supervision.
- A charge of neglect may also arise from a failure to protect a child from abuse or a failure to provide medical care when necessary to protect the child from serious harm or death.
- Abuse includes physical, emotional, and sexual abuse.
- A child cannot be removed from the home absent a showing that removal is necessary to protect the child's safety.
- Abuse or neglect of one child can generally give rise to a presumption of abuse or neglect of other children in the same household.
- The state has only a limited duty to protect children who are not in state custody from harm at the hands of parents or other adults.
- A perpetrator of child neglect or abuse may be charged civilly or criminally, or both.
- Grounds for terminating parental rights must be proved by clear and convincing evidence and the court must also find that termination would be in the child's best interests.

CHAPTER 21

Medical Decision Making

ROADMAP

After reading this chapter, you should understand:

- The mature minor doctrine;
- The minor's right to an abortion;
- The minor's right to contraceptives;
- The types of other medical decisions that a minor may have statutory authority to make;
- The balance between the state and the parents in making other medical decisions for the child;
- The procedural limitations on voluntary commitments; and
- The limitations on the right to refuse medical treatment for or by a child.

A. Mature Minor Doctrine

The mature minor doctrine is a common law doctrine that permits minors to make decisions if they demonstrate that they are mature enough to make the decision on their own. The doctrine is applied to medical decision making and often acts as an exception to the common law rule that requires a physician to obtain parental consent before treating a minor. Some states have codified the mature minor doctrine, typically allowing minors to consent to treatment if they demonstrate, for instance, "sufficient intelligence to understand and appreciate the consequences of the proposed surgical or medical procedures." ARK. CODE § 20-9-602(7). Other states apply legal presumptions applicable to the Rule of Sevens—a rule that establishes a presumption that children under seven lack sufficient mental capacity to make medical decisions, that children between seven and fourteen may have sufficient capacity (no legal presumption) and that children over fourteen are presumptively competent to make medical decisions. *Cardwell v. Bechtol*, 724 S.W.2d 739 (1987).

B. Minor's Abortion Rights

A minor was once found to have a constitutionally protected right to an abortion. *Belloti v. Baird*, 443 U.S. 622 (1979). The *Belloti* Court, in compliance with *Roe v. Wade, supra*, held that if the state imposes parental notification or consent requirements, there must be an adequate judicial bypass procedure. The bypass procedure allows the minor to demonstrate to the court that she is sufficiently mature to make the abortion decision. If the court finds that the minor is not sufficiently mature, it must determine whether an abortion would be in the minor's best interests. (See further discussion of the minor's abortion rights in the chapter on Reproductive Rights.) However, in light of *Dobbs v. Jackson Women's Health Organization*, 597 U.S. 215 (2022), states are no longer obligated based upon the federal Constitution or the *Roe* decision, to allow abortions by adult women, let alone minors. While the dust has not yet settled on *Dobbs*, and many states are still adjusting their laws either in favor of retaining the right to abortions, or in further limiting access to abortions, most states allow discontinuation of a pregnancy if the mother's life is in danger or in other limited circumstances, particularly in the first trimester. In states that continue to permit abortions in limited circumstances, minors will also be permitted to have access to abortions. Whether states will continue to allow abortions by minors not only without parental consent, but in some states, without parental notice, will likely be the subject of future cases and statutes.

C. Minor's Right to Contraception

In *Carey v. Population Services International*, 431 U.S. 678 (1977), the Supreme Court struck down a New York statute that criminalized distribution of contraceptives to anyone under sixteen years of age. The opinion held only that a blanket ban on sale or distribution of contraceptives to minors was invalid. Most states allow mature minors to receive contraceptive supplies, information from physicians, and sexually transmitted disease testing and treatment without parental notice or consent.

D. Minor's Statutory Right to Make Certain Medical Decisions

A number of states have passed statutes allowing minors to seek medical treatment without parental notice or consent. The statutes generally pertain to those medical issues where the minor might be reluctant to tell the parent and, thus, forego treatment, to their detriment or that of society. Typical subjects included in such statutes include alcohol and drug therapy, access to birth control, treatment for sexually transmitted diseases, and crisis counseling.

E. Parental Decision Making

The primary medical decision makers for children are the parents. They are presumed to act in the child's best interests. Their decisions are always subject to oversight by the state, however, under its *parens patriae* power.

F. State Decision Making

When parents disagree on treatment or refuse treatment for a child, the physician or hospital will typically call the department of children's services to intervene, if the situation appears very serious or likely to be life threatening for the child. Failure to obtain medically-necessary treatment can be the basis of court intervention.

G. Voluntary Psychiatric Commitments

The Supreme Court, in *Parham v. J.R.*, 442 U.S. 584 (1979), addressed the process that is constitutionally due a minor child whose parents or guardian seek a state administered voluntary commitment for the child. Advocates for the children argued that an adversary proceeding was required, either prior to or after the commitment. The Supreme Court disagreed, however, taking into account the presumed natural affection of natural parents to act in a child's best interests as well as the statutory presumption that the state would also act in the child's best interests for those children in state custody, and held that "an independent medical judgment made from the perspective of the best interests of the child after a careful investigation is an acceptable means of justifying a voluntary commitment." *Id.*

Specifically, the court required that some kind of inquiry should be made by a neutral factfinder to determine whether the statutory requirements for admission are satisfied. That inquiry must carefully probe the child's background using all available sources, including, but not limited to, the parents, schools, other social agencies, and an interview with the child. The decision-maker must have the authority to refuse to admit any child who does not satisfy the medical standards for admission and the child's continuing need for commitment must be reviewed periodically by a similarly independent procedure. The court did not find it necessary, however, that the deciding physician conduct a formal or even a quasi-formal hearing.

H. Right to Refuse Treatment

1. Parental Refusal

Constitutionally protected parental rights to make medical decisions for the child typically include the right to decline treatment. If the child is young, the decision must be made on the basis of the child's best interests, but if the child is old enough to have qualified as a mature minor when competent, the court will usually allow the parents to use substituted judgment, to decide what the mature minor would have decided if competent to do so. In medical refusal cases likely to result in death or serious consequences for the child, the state is much more likely to intervene (often alerted by the treating hospital or doctors) with a petition alleging parental neglect or abuse by virtue of withholding medical treatment.

The court will balance the potentially competing interests: (1) the state's interest in preserving life and protecting the child; (2) the parents' interest in family integrity and their right to make medical decisions for their child; and (3) the child's right, if any, to make an independent medical decision based on statutory law or common law rights such as the mature minor doctrine, if applicable. The court will look at the benefits and risks of treatment weighed against the consequences for failing to treat. It will also consider the invasiveness of the treatment along with the pain involved and the effect of the treatments on the child.

The balancing of interests may be further complicated if the parents or the child base the right to refuse treatment on their religious beliefs. Some states have statutes that permit parents to refuse treatment for their children, including vaccinations, based on religious beliefs.

That right to refuse treatment must be balanced against the child's interests, however. As the court has said, the parents may not make a martyr of their child. Thus, the court will order insulin injections, for instance, over the religious objections of the parents where it is clear that doing so will save the child's life and failing to do so will almost certainly result in death. Parents who fail to provide medical care can face civil or criminal charges. (See further discussion of medical neglect in the chapter on Child Abuse and Neglect.)

2. Physician/Hospital Refusal

In some cases, particularly those involving infants born with multiple medical problems, the parents may insist upon state-assisted medical treatment against the advice of physicians and the hospital. Decision-making in these cases has been the subject of great controversy over the value of life, the role of the state versus the parent, medical ethics, and the allocation of scarce government resources.

In 1974, Congress enacted the Child Abuse Prevention and Treatment Act (CAPTA) which provides in part that failure to provide medical treatment to an infant may constitute child neglect. CAPTA's provisions primarily apply to states and their child protective system's response, rather than specific individuals, physicians or hospitals. CAPTA was amended to address the special needs of severely disabled infants.

CAPTA defines "withholding of medically indicated treatment" as the failure to respond to the infant's life-threatening conditions by providing treatment (including appropriate nutrition, hydration, and medication) which in the treating physician's reasonable medical judgment will be most likely to be effective in ameliorating or correcting all such conditions. CAPTA also creates the following exceptions for infants:

Withholding of medically indicated treatment does not include the failure to provide treatment (other than appropriate nutrition, hydration, or medication) to an infant when, in the treating physician's reasonable medical judgment:

1. The infant is chronically and irreversibly comatose;
2. The provision of such treatment would:
   a. Merely prolong dying;
   b. Not be effective in ameliorating or correcting all of the infant's life-threatening conditions; or
   c. Otherwise be futile in terms of the survival of the infant; or
3. The provision of such treatment would be virtually futile in terms of the survival of the infant and the treatment itself under such circumstances would be inhumane.

3. Child Refusal

We have seen that common law, constitutional law, and statutory law each allow minors, in certain circumstances, to consent to medical treatment. Does that mean that the minor can refuse medical treatment as well? Some courts answer affirmatively. Other courts answer negatively, drawing a distinction between allowing a minor to consent to medical treatment, which presumably protects and promotes the child's best interests and preserves life, and allowing a minor to refuse treatment which is not likely to protect or promote the child's best interests and may even be life threatening.

CHECKPOINTS

- Minors who demonstrate sufficient maturity may make their own medical decisions under the mature minor doctrine.
- In a state that permits abortions, a minor has a limited right to an abortion, similar to that of an adult, although the state may impose parental notice or consent requirements.
- The state may not impose a blanket ban on minors' access to contraceptives.
- Minors generally have a statutory right of access to medical care for certain medical conditions that minors might be reluctant to discuss with their parents but that are of significant consequence to the minor's best interests or that of society, such as sexually transmitted diseases, birth control, crisis counseling, and drug treatment.
- Parents have primary responsibility for medical decision making for the immature minor based on the presumption that parents will act in the child's best interests. Those parental rights can be challenged by the state under its *parens patriae* power in appropriate cases where the state asserts that the parents are not acting in the child's best interests.
- State psychiatric facilities must provide some type of inquiry by a neutral factfinder to determine whether the statutory requirements for admission are satisfied. The factfinder must have authority to refuse admission and the child's continuing need for commitment must be reviewed periodically by a similarly independent procedure.
- The right to refuse treatment requires a careful balancing of the interests of the parents, the child, and the state. The court will consider the risks and benefits of treatment weighed against the consequences for failing to treat. The court will also consider the invasiveness of the treatment, the pain involved, and the effects of the treatments on the child.
- Hospitals and physicians have a limited ability to refuse treatment in the case of severely disabled infants where the treatment would simply prolong dying.

CHAPTER 22

Sexual and Reproductive Rights

ROADMAP

After reading this chapter, you should understand:

- The parties' rights to genetic material that is not implanted;
- The limitations on parties' rights to contraception;
- The restrictions on the state's right to mandate sterilization or restricted procreation;
- The abortion rights of adult mothers, minor mothers, and fathers; and
- The sexual privacy rights.

A. Assisted Reproduction

1. Frozen Embryos

As more and more couples turn to assisted reproductive technology (ART) to help them conceive, additional legal questions arise. One question involves the ownership of the genetic material if the couple separates before the genetic material is implanted. Many couples now address these issues in a written agreement.

In *Davis v. Davis*, 842 S.W.2d 588 (Tenn. 1992), a couple divorced before the frozen embryos were implanted. The former husband later sought to prevent his former wife from using the frozen embryos to become pregnant or donating them to a childless couple. The parties did not have an agreement addressing such issues.

One of the first issues for the court was whether the frozen embryos should be treated as property or persons. The court concluded that pre-embryos were not, strictly speaking, either "persons" or "property," but occupied "an interim category that entitles them to special respect because of their potential for human life." *Id.* As such, any interest that the parties have in the pre-embryos was not a true property interest, but was "an interest in the nature of ownership, to the extent that they have decision-making authority concerning disposition of the pre-embryos, within the scope of policy set by law." *Id.*

To determine the extent of decision-making authority each possessed, the court adopted a balancing of interests approach that included a presumption against allowing one party to force the other into parenthood as follows:

> If no prior agreement exists, then the relative interests of the parties in using or not using the pre-embryos must be weighed. Ordinarily, the party wishing to avoid procreation should prevail, assuming that the other party has a reasonable possibility of achieving parenthood by means other than use of the pre-embryos in question. If no other reasonable alternatives exist, then the argument in favor of using the pre-embryos to achieve pregnancy should be considered. However, if the party seeking control of the pre-embryos intends merely to donate them to another couple, the objecting party obviously has the greater interest and should prevail. *Id.*

The court stressed that its rule did not contemplate the creation of an automatic veto and should not be construed to create one. In a subsequent case, *Szafranski v. Dunston*, 993 N.E.2d 502 (Ill. App. 2013), the court set forth three options for deciding a parental dispute related to embryos, one of which was the balancing test announced in *Davis*. The court prioritized the agreement of the parties in a case wherein any agreement, even an oral one, exists.

2. Frozen Sperm

In a California case, the issue was whether the decedent's children could block his bequest of frozen sperm to his girlfriend. The court treated the frozen sperm as property and held that it was not against public policy for the unmarried girlfriend to be artificially inseminated posthumously.

3. The Uniform Parentage Act (UPA)

The Uniform Parentage Act (UPA), promulgated in 1973, and amended in 2000, 2002, 2017, 2019 and 2023, by the National Conference of Commissioners on Uniform State Laws (NCCUSL), has been adopted in a few states. The UPA states that if the couple divorces before the placement of the genetic material, the former spouse is not a parent unless he or she consented in writing. The UPA further provides that consent may be withdrawn at any time prior to placement of the genetic material, and the revoking spouse will not be considered a parent of the resulting child, but only as a "donor" under the Act.

B. Contraception

Virtually free access to contraceptives may be taken for granted today, but that right of access was not always automatic or free. It is the result of three cases that had to be taken to the Supreme Court. These cases are reviewed below.

1. Married Persons

The first of these cases, *Griswold v. Connecticut*, 381 U.S. 479 (1965), addressed the constitutionality of Connecticut's statutes restricting the right of married couples to use contraceptives by criminalizing their use. The Court found the statute unconstitutional based on a married couple's right to privacy, with Justice Douglas stating that "one aspect of the 'liberty' protected by the Due Process Clause of the Fourteenth Amendment is 'a right of personal privacy, or a guarantee of certain areas or zones of privacy.'" *Id. Griswold's* holding was reaffirmed the Court in *Dobbs v. Jackson Women's Health Org.*, 597 U.S. 215 (2022), specifically noted its implications for *Roe v. Wade, supra,* did not impact *Griswold.*

2. Unmarried Persons

In *Eisenstadt v. Baird*, 405 U.S. 438 (1972), the constitutional right of privacy to use contraceptives recognized in *Griswold* was extended to unmarried persons. The court found unconstitutional a Massachusetts statute prohibiting distribution of contraceptives except upon a physician's prescription to a married person. The Court held that the statute violated the equal protection rights of unmarried persons, stating, "If the right of privacy means anything, it is the right of the individual, married or single, to be free from unwarranted governmental intrusion into matters so fundamentally affecting a person as the decision whether to bear or beget a child." *Id.* The court found no rational basis for treating married and unmarried persons differently. Like *Griswold*, the *Dobbs* Court noted its decision does not overturn *Eisenstadt*.

The Supreme Court next addressed the issue of state regulation of the distribution of contraceptives only through pharmacists. In *Carey v. Population Services International*, 431 U.S. 678 (1977), the statute before the court made it a crime for anyone other than a pharmacist to sell nonmedical contraceptive devices to persons over sixteen years of age. The court did not prohibit all regulation of the manufacture and sale of contraceptives but, instead, held that the state was unable to demonstrate a compelling interest in limiting distribution to pharmacists that would justify the burden that the statute placed on an adult's freedom of choice.

3. Minors

Carey v. Population Services International, 431 U.S. 678 (1977), discussed above, also addressed the right of minors to have access to contraceptives. The statute before the court contained a blanket prohibition on the sale of contraceptives to persons under sixteen. The restriction on the sale of contraceptives to children was struck but with only a plurality opinion written by Justice Brennan in which he implied that even minors have some rights to freedom of choice in the use of contraceptives.

C. Sterilization and Restricted Procreation

Involuntary sterilization in this country has an appalling history with the Eugenics movement, which aimed to "improve" the population by eliminating "undesirable" medical traits. The Supreme Court, in *Buck v. Bell*, 274 U.S. 200 (1927), upheld a Virginia statute which permitted sterilization of insane or retarded persons with the infamous statement in Justice Holmes' opinion that "three generations of imbeciles are enough." *Id.* The Court required notice and a hearing and held that the decision to sterilize could not be arbitrary or punishment for a crime.

The Supreme Court, in *Skinner v. Oklahoma*, 316 U.S. 535 (1942), struck down, on equal protection grounds, an Oklahoma statute that allowed the state to order sterilization of certain habitual, hereditary criminals. The Court found that the statute was both under-inclusive in that it failed to include all offenders of intrinsically the same quality, and over-inclusive in that all habitual criminals are not hereditary criminals.

Some states continue to have laws that allow for forced sterilization of individuals with disabilities under certain circumstances, particularly if the court finds it to be in the individual's best interest.

At least one state, in a legally suspect, 4–3 decision, upheld a restriction on procreation as a valid condition of probation for a father of nine children who was convicted of intentional nonpayment of child support. Noting that the father would have had no procreative rights while serving six years, the court held that conditioning the obligor's procreative rights upon proof that he could support that child and his current children was not unreasonable under the facts of the case. *State v. Oakley*, 629 N.W. 2d 200 (Wis. 2001). A strong dissent argued that the probation condition was unconstitutional because the "right to have children is a basic human right and an aspect of the fundamental liberty which the Constitution jealously guards for all Americans."

D. Abortion

1. The Adult Mother's Rights

In *Roe v. Wade*, 410 U.S. 113 (1973), the Supreme Court declared unconstitutional the Texas statute that criminalized abortion except when necessary to save the mother's life. The Court relied on privacy rights that the Court traced to an 1891 case, *Union Pacific Ry. Co. v. Botsford*, 141 U.S. 141 (1891), which recognized "the right of every individual to the possession and control of his own person, free from all restraint or interference by others." *Id.* The Court concluded that this right of privacy was "broad enough to encompass a woman's decision whether or not to terminate her pregnancy" and held that the statute unnecessarily infringed on the woman's right to privacy in violation of the Due Process Clause of the Fourteenth Amendment.

Even though the Court concluded that the right of personal privacy includes the abortion decision, it also held that this right is not unqualified and must be considered against important state interests such as safeguarding the mother's health, maintaining medical standards, and protecting potential life. The Court applied a strict scrutiny analysis requiring the state to show (1) a compelling state interest; and (2) that the statute is narrowly drawn to express only the compelling state interests at stake.

In applying strict scrutiny to the claimed governmental interests, the court devised a three-part test tied to the trimesters of a woman's pregnancy and the fetus's point of viability:

1. For the stage prior to approximately the end of the first trimester, the abortion decision and its effectuation must be left to the medical judgment of the pregnant woman's attending physician;
2. For the stage subsequent to approximately the end of the first trimester, the state, in promoting its interest in the health of the mother, may, if it chooses, regulate the abortion procedure in ways that are reasonably related to maternal health; and
3. For the stage subsequent to viability the State, in promoting its interest in the potentiality of human life, the state may, if it chooses, regulate, and even proscribe, abortion except where necessary, in appropriate medical judgment, for the preservation of the life or health of the mother.

For nearly five decades, statutes were enacted and repealed by states attempting to either comply with or avoid *Roe*'s application. In 2022, *Roe* was overturned by *Dobbs, supra*, to the extent that the decision found a constitutional right to an abortion. The *Dobbs* decision allows individual states to authorize, prohibit or limit abortion access. In the relatively few years since the *Dobbs* opinion, many laws have changed, with states often split by political divisions.

2. The Minor Mother's Rights

Following *Roe v. Wade, supra*, the Supreme Court first addressed a minor's right to obtain an abortion in *Planned Parenthood of Central Missouri v. Danforth*, 428 U.S. 52 (1976), when the Court struck down a Missouri statute that required written parental consent for unmarried minors. In *Belloti v. Baird*, 443 U.S. 622 (1979), the Supreme Court recognized a limited right of privacy for minors regarding the right to obtain an abortion without parental consent by requiring a parental consent statute to contain a judicial bypass provision. (See further discussion of the judicial bypass provision in the chapter on Medical Decision-Making.)

States modified their laws to create judicial approval of abortions for minors who chose not to obtain or could not obtain parental consent for an abortion. But, as discussed above, with *Roe*'s overturning, a litany of laws, including judicial bypass for minors, are now up to individual states, with those favoring abortion allowing minors to either consent without parental consent or, at least, to avail themselves of judicial bypass procedures. Other states, however, have precluded or significantly limited abortions by all, including minors.

3. The Father's Rights

In *Planned Parenthood of Central Missouri v. Danforth*, 428 U.S. 52 (1976), the Supreme Court considered the constitutionality of a Missouri statute which required the prior written consent of the husband for a wife to obtain an abortion during the first trimester of pregnancy, unless the abortion was necessary to save the mother's life. The court was cognizant of the father's interest in the mother's abortion decision, stating:

> We are not unaware of the deep and proper concern and interest that a devoted and protective husband has in his wife's pregnancy and in the growth and development of the fetus she is carrying. Neither has this Court failed to appreciate the importance of the marital relationship in our society. Moreover, we recognize that the decision whether to undergo or to forego an abortion may have profound effects on the future of any marriage, effects that are both physical and mental, and possibly deleterious. *Id.*

Nonetheless, the court held that as between the father's interests and the mother's privacy rights, the mother's rights must prevail, "since it is the woman who physically bears the child and who is the more directly and immediately affected by the pregnancy, as between the two, the balance weighs in her favor." *Id.* The Court reasoned that it could not find that the state had the constitutional authority to grant the husband a unilateral veto on the wife's abortion decision when the state itself did not have that right.

While *Danforth* was not overturned by *Dobbs, supra*, the broader context of abortion rights has been significantly altered. It is still unlikely today that a woman's right to an abortion under state law could be legally thwarted by the child's father's veto.

4. Partial-Birth Abortions

The Supreme Court first considered the validity of a state ban on partial birth abortions in *Stenberg v. Carhart,* 530 U.S. 914 (2000) and found the state statutory ban to be unconstitutional. In response, Congress passed the Partial-Birth Abortion Ban Act of 2003 which imposed a national ban on the practice of partial-birth abortions, a procedure that involves partially removing the fetus intact from the woman's uterus and then crushing or cutting the skull to complete the abortion. The Partial-Birth Abortion Ban Act of 2003 was challenged in *Gonzales v. Carhart,* 550 U.S. 124 (2007), and found constitutional. Justice Kennedy, who dissented in *Stenberg,* wrote the majority opinion in *Gonzales,* stating that as compared with the state statute at issue in *Stenberg,* the federal Act was more specific concerning the instances to which it applied and in this respect was more precise in its coverage. These cases differ from previous abortion cases in that they attempt to regulate the procedure for performing the abortion rather than the right to obtain an abortion.

E. Sodomy

The Supreme Court reversed itself on the issue of the constitutional right of privacy as applied to homosexual couples. In *Bowers v. Hardwick,* 478 U.S. 186 (1986), the Supreme Court upheld a Georgia statute that criminalized consensual homosexual sexual conduct.

The Court revisited the issue, however, seventeen years later, in *Lawrence v. Texas,* 539 U.S. 558 (2003). In *Lawrence,* the Court overruled *Bowers* and struck down a Texas statute that criminalized consensual homosexual sodomy between two adults in the privacy of their home. *Lawrence* held that the statute violated a liberty interest guaranteed by the Due Process Clause of the Fourteenth Amendment because the statute interfered with one's fundamental right to have intimate personal relationships that involve sexual activity which extend to married and unmarried couples and to homosexual and heterosexual couples, as well.

Despite the invalidation of sodomy statutes by the *Lawrence* decision and the recognition of the fundamental right to marry in a same-sex relationship in *Obergefell v. Hodges,* 576 U.S. 644 (2015), several states continue to ban sodomy, some in same-sex relationships and others in both same-sex and opposite-sex relationships.

CHECKPOINTS

- Rights to genetic material that is not implanted may be governed by agreement or by a balancing of interests of the parties with a presumption against forced parenthood.
- Adults, married or unmarried, have a constitutional right of privacy that extends to contraceptives. Minors have a limited right of access to contraceptives.
- States have limited rights to mandate sterilizations if due process requirements are met, and the decision is not arbitrary or imposed as a criminal punishment.
- Abortion rights are no longer determined at the federal level. Each state is free to prohibit, authorize or limit abortions, with those laws often based upon the political leanings of each state.
- A minor has a limited right to abortion that may be subject to parental notification or consent requirements. Some states who favor abortion may require a judicial bypass option for minors who do not obtain parental consent.
- A father does not have a right to limit the mother's right to an abortion.
- Consensual sexual activity is a protected liberty interest.

CHAPTER 23

Adoption

ROADMAP

After reading this chapter, you should understand:

- The legal consequences of adoption;
- The general prerequisites for adoption;
- The various types of adoption; and
- The limitations on selection of adoptive parents.

A. Background

Adoption was unknown at common law. It was created by statute. Being in derogation of common law, adoption statutes are strictly construed. Sometimes, however, courts will look to implementing language setting out the purpose of the statute, which is usually to promote the best interests of the child, as a basis for a broader interpretation of statutory language.

B. Legal Effect of Adoption

1. Generally

The legal consequence of a traditional adoption is that the legal relationship of parent and child is terminated as between the biological parent and the child, and a new legal relationship of parent and child is created as between the adoptive parent and the child.

2. Grandparent Visitation

As a general rule, adoption terminates the relationship between the child and the parents of the biological parents. This general rule applies even in cases where the court has previously ordered grandparent visitation, as in the case of divorce or the death of one parent. The underlying rationale is that the visitation rights of the grandparents are derivative. When the parents' rights are terminated, so are any grandparent visitation rights. Some statutory exceptions are recognized, however, in cases of stepparent adoptions or relative adoptions, in some states.

C. Jurisdiction

1. Interstate Adoptions

The 1960 Interstate Compact on the Placement of Children (ICPC) has been adopted by fifty states and applies to interstate placements and adoptions. The ICPC addresses procedural requirements for transferring a child from one state to adoptive parents in another state, but the act does not establish jurisdiction. Noncompliance may result in dismissal of the adoption petition, but other courts are reluctant to impose such harsh sanctions if the adoption is in the child's best interest.

The Uniform Child Custody Jurisdiction and Enforcement Act (UCCJEA), which governs jurisdiction in multistate child custody cases, expressly states that it does not apply to adoptions. The UCCJEA does apply, however, to termination of parental rights hearings, which may precede the adoption hearing. Further, the adoption statutes in some states provide that the UCCJEA will apply to adoptions.

2. Indian Child Welfare Act (ICWA)

Following allegations of the discriminate removal of Indian children from their homes in the 1970s, including allegations that approximately 90% of the Indian placements were in non-Indian homes, Congress, in 1978, enacted a restorative law, the Indian Child Welfare Act (ICWA), 25 U.S.C. §§ 1901–1963. The ICWA requires state welfare agencies to make active efforts to prevent removal of an Indian child, and, when necessary, requires placement of the child with extended family, members of the child's tribe or other Native

American families. ICWA requires that grounds for an involuntary termination of parental rights be proved beyond a reasonable doubt. The child's tribe must receive notice of any proceeding involving the child and is permitted to intervene in the matter.

ICWA grants exclusive tribal jurisdiction over child custody proceedings involving Indian children domiciled on the tribe's reservation. The ICWA does not define domicile. The meaning of that term was at issue in *Mississippi Band of Choctaw Indians v. Holyfield*, 490 U.S. 30 (1989), in which the Supreme Court held that the act did not intend the definition of domicile to be a matter of state law but instead intended a uniform federal law of domicile under the ICWA. The Supreme Court applied the general definition of domicile applicable to illegitimate children: "In the case of an illegitimate child, that has traditionally meant the domicile of its mother."

The ICWA provides that an adoption decree entered in violation of the provisions of the act can be invalidated by the tribe or custodian at any time after the decree is entered. The Act applies to any child who is either a member of an Indian tribe, or eligible for membership and the biological child of a member of an Indian tribe. Some states interpret the ICWA to apply only when the state is attempting to remove a child from an "existing Indian family." The "existing Indian family" doctrine has been criticized by some as being inconsistent with the underlying purposes of the ICWA. Although the Court did not specifically address the "existing Indian family" exception that has been carved out by many state courts, the Supreme Court has held that ICWA does not apply to noncustodial biological fathers of a Native American child. The Court reasoned that all of the preservation efforts for an Indian child are not applicable when the child has never lived with the parent with the tribal connection. *Adoptive Couple v. Baby Girl*, 570 U.S. 637 (2013). Although ICWA's constitutionality has been questioned on multiple grounds, it has been upheld. *Haaland v. Brackeen*, 599 U.S. 255 (2023).

3. International Adoptions

The United States signed the Hague Convention on Intercountry Adoption in 1994, and Congress enacted implementing legislation in 2000. The Intercountry Adoption Act of 2000, 42 U.S.C. § 14901 *et seq*. The Act was amended in 2012 by the Universal Accreditation Act, which mandated that most intercountry adoption follow Hague Convention requirements. The convention preferences in-country adoption over intercountry adoption and focuses on the best interests of the child. The child's country is responsible for determining that the child is eligible for adoption, that the adoption is in the child's best interests, and that necessary consents are obtained. The adoptive parents' country is responsible for approving the adoptive parents and ensuring that immigration requirements are satisfied to allow the child to enter the country and reside there permanently. Congress also passed the Child Citizenship Act of 2000 which permits children adopted by U.S. citizens to acquire U.S. citizenship automatically upon entry into the U.S. as legal permanent residents. At present, there are multiple proposals to amend the Immigration and Nationality Act in ways that could impact the application of the CCA.

Typically, three different sets of laws are involved in international adoptions. The child will need to be adopted in the birth country. Federal immigration laws will have to be satisfied. Finally, the child will probably have to be adopted in the U.S., as well.

D. Termination of Parental Rights

Most states limit the number of parents that a child may have at any one time to one mother and one father, although same-sex marriages have caused modern adoption courts to recognize that a child may have two mothers or fathers. Moreover, some states recognize that a child could have a legal father and a putative father, both of whom may have standing to contest an adoption. Thus, the parental rights of one or more parents must be terminated before an adoption can take place. The termination of parental rights can occur though a voluntary surrender or through an involuntary termination of parental rights.

1. Voluntary

The biological parent may decide to make the child eligible for adoption by voluntarily surrendering his or her parental rights. Voluntary surrenders are effective even when made by underage parties. Typically, an adoption statute will contain several safeguards to protect the parent's rights and to make the adoption less vulnerable to attack. Those safeguards may include requiring that the surrender be made after the birth of the child, in court, and in writing; and providing for a short retraction period. Some states, however, extend the retraction period until the adoption or termination of parental rights is final. Other states do not have any retraction period. Once the surrender is final, however, courts are very reluctant to set it aside, except upon a showing of fraud or duress.

2. Involuntary

Parental rights can also be terminated through an involuntary procedure upon a showing of parental unfitness. Typically, a termination of parental rights is a two-step process. First, the statutory grounds for termination must be proved by clear and convincing evidence. Second, the court must determine, again by clear and convincing evidence, that termination of parental rights would be in the child's best interests. Statutory grounds usually include such things as willful abandonment, willful nonsupport, or abuse. (See further discussion of termination of parental rights in the chapter on Child Support and the chapter on Child Neglect and Abuse.)

3. Rights of Unwed Fathers

Historically, unwed fathers played no role in adoptions. They were not entitled to notice and could not veto an adoption. Through a series of cases dealing with the rights of unwed fathers, the Supreme Court set forth the rule in *Lehr v. Robertson*, 463 U.S. 248 (1983), that biology offers the unwed father an opportunity to assume the emotional and financial obligations of parenthood. If the unwed father seizes that parental responsibility before or shortly after the child's birth, the unwed father will be entitled to the same constitutional protections as the mother, meaning that his parental rights must either be voluntarily surrendered or involuntarily terminated for cause. The unwed father can assume parental responsibility by offering support for the child or by offering to pay the mother's birthing expenses. The time limit on assuming parental responsibility is tolled if the mother, or someone involved in the adoption, lies to or deceives the father regarding the existence of the child or otherwise thwarts his efforts to assume parental responsibilities.

Many states rely on putative father registries to eliminate the need to recognize the rights of unwed fathers who fail to register within the statutory period, usually within thirty days after the birth of the child.

E. Types of Adoption

1. Agency Adoption

Traditionally, adoptions took place through state-operated child welfare agencies or private adoption agencies licensed by the state. Some of the state-licensed private adoption agencies have religious affiliations. Both state-operated agencies and state-licensed private adoption agencies interview and counsel prospective birth parents. They also interview and screen prospective adoptive parents. The agencies handle the transfer of the child from the birth parents to the home of the prospective adoptive parents. Agencies do home inspections and usually report to the court with a recommendation for or against adoption.

Agencies also impose limitations on prospective adoptive parents regarding age, health, income, criminal history, and religious affiliation (for those private adoption agencies that are religiously affiliated).

2. Independent Adoption

Some states allow independent or private adoptions, meaning adoptions not handled through a state or private agency licensed by the state. These adoptions may be negotiated directly between the birth parents and the adoptive parents, or they may include an intermediary, generally a lawyer. Some states require the intermediary to be licensed. Statutes generally preclude charging a fee for facilitating a private adoption, but the lawyer is nonetheless able to charge for their professional services associated with the adoption process. Independent adoptions often avoid the long waiting lists, delays, home inspections, and limiting criteria applicable to prospective adoptive parents that are associated with adoption agencies. The adoption must still be approved by the court, however, as being in the child's best interests and for the court's assurance that the child has not been purchased.

3. Stepparent Adoption

The statutory requirements for adoptions involving stepparents are generally more relaxed than other adoptions because the child will be remaining in the home with a birth parent. Some exceptions are recognized for relative adoptions as well. The exceptions typically waive the requirement of a home inspection, for instance.

4. Open Adoption

The term open adoption has more than one meaning. Generally, in an open adoption, the birth parent(s) is(are) permitted to choose the adoptive family. An open adoption may also indicate some form of contact between the parties. The parties may agree to an exchange of information about or contact with the child after the adoption. Ongoing contact with the child is more likely to occur in relative adoptions, and in adoptions of older children who have established relationships with birth parents and in cases where continued contact is the carrot that induces the birth parent to consent to the adoption. Most states do not recognize such agreements and even those states that do recognize such agreements impose an ongoing best interests of the child limitation on their enforcement.

5. Adult Adoptions

Some states permit the adoption of adults. Many states also require the consent of older children who are adopted.

6. Foster Parent Adoptions

Historically, foster parents were discouraged from adopting children in their care. Paid foster parents were considered contract employees of the state, who acquired no constitutionally protected rights to a relationship with the child. *Smith v. Organization of Foster Families for Equality and Reform*, *431 U.S. 816 (1977)*. More recently, however, some states have begun to take a child centered approach and even create a statutory preference for foster parents who have fostered a child or some period of time, usually a year, if that child later becomes eligible for adoption. While a child's best interest is usually facilitated by the continuity of remaining with the foster parents, sometimes foster parents who wish to adopt are disincentivized from facilitating a reunification with the child's parents.

F. Limitations on Adoption

1. Baby Selling

Most state statutes prohibit baby selling, defined as taking or receiving money or other valuable consideration associated with an adoption. An exception is generally recognized for the birth parent's prenatal and birth medical expenses as well as any professional fees to adoption agencies, lawyers, and doctors associated with the adoption process. Some states also recognize an exception in the case of indigent mothers who are permitted to accept sufficient income during a pregnancy to promote the child's health and well-being.

2. Special Needs Children

Children with special needs or hard-to-place children are more difficult to place in adoptive homes. A child might be considered a special needs child because of one or more of the following factors: "ethnic background, age, or membership in a minority or sibling group, or the presence of factors such as medical conditions or physical, mental or emotional handicaps." Adoption Assistance and Child Welfare Act of 1980, 42 U.S.C. §§ 673–74. Financial assistance is available to encourage the adoption of special needs children. Persons who adopt special needs children may also take advantage of several tax incentives.

G. Selection of Adoptive Parents

1. Single Adoptive Parents

Historically, single parents were often discouraged from fostering or adopting, oftentimes limited to adopting only special needs children. But many states have recognized the value of even a single loving parent and the growing needs of the child welfare system, thus eliminating some of the prior barriers to single parent placements.

2. Homosexual Adoptive Parents

Prior to *Obergefell v. Hodges*, 576 U.S. 644 (2015), many states, either formally, or in practice, prohibited homosexual parties from adopting. Other states expressly allow second-parent adoptions, usually by analogy to stepparent adoptions, or based on fulfilling the overarching purpose of the adoption statute to promote the child's best interests. Oftentimes, the second parent who seeks to adopt will be the monied partner. Adoption in such cases protects the child's financial interests by making the child eligible for insurance benefits, child support, and inheritance rights.

3. Race Matching

Race matching was the norm in adoptions prior to the late 1950s and early 1960s. There was greater acceptance of transracial adoption influenced by the civil rights movement and the increase in international adoption after the Korean War. Transracial adoption became controversial, however, in the 1970s, with regard to placement of African American children, when the National Association of Black Social Workers adopted a resolution opposing transracial placement of African American children. The Multiethnic Placement Act (MEPA), amended in 1996, makes it illegal for a state to delay or deny an adoptive or foster placement solely on the basis of race. The act provides that a person or a government that is involved in an adoption or foster placement may not:

1. Deny the right to adopt or foster on the basis of race, color, or national origin; or
2. Delay or deny the placement of a child on the basis of race, color, or national origin of the parents or the child.

4. Religious Matching

Historically, religious matching was mandated. Following a number of challenges, the practice is no longer mandated but the religious preference, if any, of the birth parents may be a consideration in the selection of the adoptive parents. Some states also give a preference for placing children with adoptive parents of the same religion.

5. Age

The age of the adoptive parents may be a factor that the agency or court takes into consideration. Age may cause one set of parents to be selected over another but will generally not preclude someone from being able to adopt, unless it is clear that age-related health issues of the parent could impact the best interest of the child.

6. Role of the Attorney

Some states allow an attorney to represent both the birth parents and the adoptive parents, provided there is informed consent as to potential conflicts of interest. If a conflict arises, the attorney must withdraw from representation. The ABA opposes joint representation claiming that inherent conflicts exist in such cases.

H. Adoption Records

In the early 1900's adoption records were routinely sealed, in part to remove the stigma of illegitimacy from adopted children and to facilitate their integration into their adoptive families. Exceptions were recognized for "good cause" such as the need for medical histories. Currently, a few states allow access to the adoption records when the child becomes an adult, although contact with the birth parents may be prohibited if the birth parent signs a contact veto. Other states allow information to be exchanged if both the adult child and birth parent register to allow contact.

I. Adoption Revocation

The general rule is that adoptions are not revocable. Some exceptions have been recognized where the adoption jeopardizes the health of another child, such as in cases of sexual abuse of one child in a family by an adopted child in the same family. Some states address the issue in the adoption statute, setting specific grounds for revocation or annulment. Exceptions are also recognized in some cases where a stepparent adoption has been filed but not finalized when the parents file for divorce or separation. Since adoptive parents have the same legal status as birth parents, adoptive parents have the option to surrender their parental rights, with the same considerations and limitations as would ordinarily be found for a birth parent.

J. Agency Liability

A number of states recognize the tort of wrongful adoption when the adoption agency intentionally or negligently misrepresents information concerning the child's mental, emotional, or physical health. Liability can also arise from withholding such information. States generally have not imposed a duty to investigate such issues and report to prospective adoptive parents.

K. Equitable Adoption

Equitable adoption does not result in an adoption, but it does permit the child who was treated as a natural or adopted child to share in the estate of the "adoptive parent" or to receive other financial benefits available to an adopted child, such as insurance proceeds. Courts generally require some direct expression of an intent to adopt along with some objective conduct indicating mutual recognition of an adoptive parent-child relationship such that in equity and good conscience an adoption should be deemed to have taken place. Courts generally apply a clear and convincing standard of proof.

L. Uniform Laws

1. Uniform Adoption Act (UAA)

The Uniform Adoption Act (UAA), promulgated in 1994 by the National Conference of Commissioners on Uniform State Laws (NCCUSL), has been adopted, at least in part, by only a few states. Under the Act, a parent may make a voluntary surrender to the court or to an adoption agency, attorney, or other public official. A minor mother must have access to counseling, and the advice of a lawyer who is not also representing the adoptive parents or agency. The consent may not be executed prior to birth of the child, and it may be revoked for eight days after the child's birth. The UAA also allows the termination of rights of a biological father who has not demonstrated an interest in the child unless he demonstrates a compelling reason for his conduct. The UAA lists in order of preference the following factors for an agency to consider in selecting adoptive parents:

1. Previous adoption of a sibling;
2. Characteristics requested by the birth parents;
3. Custody of the child for six of the preceding twenty-four months or half of the child's life; and
4. Relative who has a positive emotional relationship with the child.

After considering the above factors, the agency can consider other prospective adoptive parents. The Act also allows the birth parents to select the adoptive parents and proceed with an independent placement.

Stepparent adoptions have no effect on:

1. The relationship between the child and the parent who is the stepparent's spouse or deceased spouse;
2. An existing order for visitation or contact between the child and a relative of the stepparent's spouse or deceased spouse;
3. The child's inheritance rights through or from the former parent; and
4. A court order for visitation or contact with the child, if approved by the court.

2. Uniform Parentage Act

The Uniform Parentage Act (UPA), promulgated in 1973, and amended in 2000, 2002, 2017, 2019 and 2023 by the National Conference of Commissioners on Uniform State Laws (NCCUSL), has been adopted by many states, albeit not all its different amendments. The UPA sets out different notice requirements for putative fathers based on the age of the child involved.

The 2017 amendment to the UPA attempted to move away from the earlier versions that favored married fathers, and recognizes the importance of the biological parent-child relationship, regardless of marital status. However, an unmarried father does not have legal rights until paternity is established through one of the ways delineated in the Act. The 2017 amendment also eliminated gender-based distinctions.

M. Adoption and Safe Families Act 1997 (ASFA)

The Adoption and Safe Families Act 1997 (ASFA) requires states, in most circumstances, to initiate termination of parental rights when children have been in foster care for fifteen of the previous twenty-two months. The ASFA also provides financial incentives for states that increase adoptions of children in foster care. Special needs children are guaranteed health insurance under the act. The 2008 amendment of the Act increased federal funding to facilitate permanent placements for children in foster care. One notable change required states to make reasonable efforts to keep siblings together in foster placements. Planning requirements are illustrated in the Permanency Planning documents that child welfare agencies must use to create a comprehensive plan for foster children and their families to work promptly toward reunification or other permanency goals.

CHECKPOINTS

- Adoption is a creature of statute.
- Adoption statutes are strictly construed.
- The legal effect of an adoption is to terminate the biological parent -child relationship and to create a parent-child relationship between the child and the adoptive parents.
- Generally, adoption terminates the rights and responsibilities of the biological parents, and other relatives as well.
- Parental rights must be terminated either voluntarily or involuntarily before an adoption can take place.
- Voluntary surrenders of parental rights generally cannot take place prior to the birth of the child, and once finalized, generally cannot be set aside absent a showing of fraud or duress.
- An involuntary termination of parental rights requires a showing of statutory grounds by clear and convincing evidence as well as a finding by the court that termination of parental rights is in the child's best interests.
- Unwed fathers are entitled to the same constitutional protections of parental rights as mothers and married fathers if they have assumed or attempted to assume parental responsibilities for the child before or shortly after the child's birth.
- Equitable adoption, where recognized, does not result in an adoption but does permit the child to receive some of the financial benefits otherwise available to an adopted child.

MASTERING FAMILY LAW CHECKLIST

The following reflects the topics covered in each chapter. A good understanding of the overall material would require a detailed knowledge of each of these topics.

CHAPTER 1 • INTRODUCTION

- ☐ Scope of Family Law
- ☐ Sources of Family Law

CHAPTER 2 • MARRIAGE AND MARRIAGE REGULATIONS

- ☐ Marriage Regulations
- ☐ Void and Voidable Marriages
- ☐ Common Law Marriage
- ☐ Breach of the Promise to Marry

CHAPTER 3 • MARRIAGE ALTERNATIVES

- ☐ Putative Spouse Doctrine
- ☐ Contractual Cohabitation
- ☐ Implied Partnership
- ☐ Reciprocal Beneficiaries
- ☐ Civil Unions

CHAPTER 4 • MARITAL RIGHTS AND OBLIGATIONS

☐ Doctrine of Necessaries

☐ Property Management During Marriage

☐ Interspousal Tort Liability

☐ Loss of Consortium

☐ Heartbalm Claims

☐ Marital Communications Privilege

CHAPTER 5 • DOMESTIC VIOLENCE

☐ Orders of Protection

☐ Federal Laws

☐ Civil Remedies

☐ Effect of Domestic Violence in Divorce Actions

☐ Marital Rape Exception

CHAPTER 6 • DIVORCE

☐ Jurisdictional Issues

☐ Venue

☐ Divorce Grounds and Defenses

☐ Alternatives to Divorce

CHAPTER 7 • JURISDICTION TO DIVIDE PROPERTY AND ORDER SUPPORT

☐ Jurisdiction to Divide Property

☐ Jurisdiction to Order Support

☐ Interstate Support Jurisdiction

CHAPTER 8 • PROPERTY DIVISION

☐ The Common Law System

☐ The Community Property System

- ☐ Three Step Analysis for Dividing Property at Divorce
- ☐ Special Classification Issues
- ☐ Debt Allocation

CHAPTER 9 • SPOUSAL SUPPORT

- ☐ Types of Alimony
- ☐ Standard for Modification
- ☐ Termination
- ☐ Reinstatement
- ☐ Enforcement

CHAPTER 10 • CHILD CUSTODY JURISDICTION AND ENFORCEMENT

- ☐ Jurisdiction to Make an Initial Child Custody Determination
- ☐ Jurisdiction to Modify an Existing Child Custody Determination
- ☐ Enforcement Provisions
- ☐ International Custody Disputes

CHAPTER 11 • DIVORCE CUSTODY DETERMINATIONS

- ☐ Types of Custody
- ☐ Standards for Determining Custody
- ☐ Modification Standards
- ☐ Parenting Plans
- ☐ Enforcement of Custodial Rights

CHAPTER 12 • VISITATION

- ☐ Standards for Determining Visitation
- ☐ Relocation
- ☐ Enforcement
- ☐ Third Party Visitation

CHAPTER 13 • CHILD SUPPORT

- ☐ Obligation of Support
- ☐ Duration of Support
- ☐ Establishment of the Support Obligation
- ☐ Modification of the Child Support Obligation
- ☐ Enforcement Provisions
- ☐ Defenses to Child Support Enforcement
- ☐ Interstate Enforcement of Support

CHAPTER 14 • MARRIAGE CONTRACTS

- ☐ Antenuptial Contracts
- ☐ Postnuptial Agreements
- ☐ Reconciliation Agreements
- ☐ Settlement Agreements

CHAPTER 15 • ALTERNATIVE DISPUTE RESOLUTION

- ☐ Negotiation
- ☐ Arbitration
- ☐ Mediation
- ☐ Collaborative Law
- ☐ Cooperative/Conciliation Law

CHAPTER 16 • TAX AND BANKRUPTCY ISSUES

- ☐ Alimony
- ☐ Property Division
- ☐ Child Support
- ☐ Dependency Exemption
- ☐ Filing status
- ☐ Bankruptcy Treatment of DSO's and Other Marital Debt

CHAPTER 17 • THE ROLE OF COUNSEL

- ☐ Joint Representation
- ☐ Pro Se Adverse Party
- ☐ Sexual Ethics

CHAPTER 18 • CONSTITUTIONAL PROTECTION OF PARENTAL RIGHTS AND CHILDREN'S RIGHTS

- ☐ Source of State Power
- ☐ Parental Rights Cases
- ☐ Children's Rights

CHAPTER 19 • DEFINITION OF PARENTS AND FAMILY

- ☐ Definition of Mother
- ☐ Definition of Father
- ☐ Unrelated Gay and Lesbian Partners
- ☐ Definition of Family

CHAPTER 20 • CHILD NEGLECT AND ABUSE

- ☐ Neglect
- ☐ Medical Neglect
- ☐ Types of Abuse
- ☐ Abuse of the Fetus
- ☐ Standard for Removal of the Child
- ☐ State's Duty to Protect
- ☐ Termination of Parental Rights

CHAPTER 21 • MEDICAL DECISION MAKING

- ☐ Mature Minor's Decision Making Authority
- ☐ Parental Decision Making
- ☐ State Decision Making
- ☐ Voluntary Psychiatric Commitments
- ☐ Right to Refuse Treatment

CHAPTER 22 • SEXUAL AND REPRODUCTIVE RIGHTS

- ☐ Assisted Reproduction
- ☐ Contraception
- ☐ Sterilization and Restricted Procreation
- ☐ Abortion
- ☐ Sodomy

CHAPTER 23 • ADOPTION

- ☐ Legal Effect of Adoption
- ☐ Termination of Parental Rights
- ☐ Types of Adoption
- ☐ Adoption Records
- ☐ Adoption Revocation
- ☐ Equitable Adoption

ABOUT THE AUTHOR

April Carroll Meldrum, Lincoln Memorial University Professor of Law, has been teaching at LMU since 2009. In addition to her juris doctorate degree, she has doctorate degrees in both Higher Education and Executive Leadership. She has co-authored a textbook on Tennessee family law and co-authored two law review articles urging reform to Tennessee family and juvenile laws. She completed her dissertation by publishing *A Practitioner's Guide to Tennessee Dependency and Neglect Law*. Prior to entering academia, she was elected and served as the Anderson County, Tennessee, Juvenile Court Judge. Her prior law practice focused on family law, juvenile law, social security disability, and personal injury.

INDEX